EXPLORING BIG HISTORICAL DATA

HISTORICAL DATA

The Historian's Macroscope

EXPLORING BIG HISTORICAL DATA

The Historian's Macroscope

Shawn Graham *(Carleton University, Canada)*

Ian Milligan *(University of Waterloo, Canada)*

Scott Weingart *(Indiana University, USA)*

Imperial College Press

ICP

Published by

Imperial College Press
57 Shelton Street
Covent Garden
London WC2H 9HE

Distributed by

World Scientific Publishing Co. Pte. Ltd.
5 Toh Tuck Link, Singapore 596224
USA office: 27 Warren Street, Suite 401-402, Hackensack, NJ 07601
UK office: 57 Shelton Street, Covent Garden, London WC2H 9HE

Library of Congress Cataloging-in-Publication Data
Graham, Shawn.
  Exploring big historical data : the historian's macroscope / Shawn Graham, Carleton University,
Canada, Ian Milligan, University of Waterloo, Canada, Scott Weingart, Indiana University, USA.
    pages cm
  Includes bibliographical references and index.
    ISBN 978-1-78326-608-1 (hardcover : alk. paper) -- ISBN 978-1-78326-637-1 (pbk. : alk. paper)
1. History--Computer network resources. 2. Big data. 3. Historiography--Methodology. 4. History--
Research. I. Milligan, Ian, 1983–   II. Weingart, Scott (Scott B.) III. Title.
    D16.117.G73 2015
    902.85'57--dc23

                                                                    2015021509

British Library Cataloguing-in-Publication Data
A catalogue record for this book is available from the British Library.

Typeset by Stallion Press
Email: enquiries@stallionpress.com

Printed in Singapore

Contents

Acknowledgments

This book has been an enormous experiment and learning experience for us. We would like to thank and acknowledge our students and the readers of the online versions for discussing and working through with us in public the potentials and perils of big digital history. The peer reviewers made extremely useful suggestions that significantly enhanced the final draft of this book. Alice Oven, Catharina Weijman, Jane Sayers, and the rest of the editorial staff at Imperial College Press also deserve a big round of thanks for helping us conceive of the project, as well as finessing our prose and content throughout.

Ben Marwick has commented on our code and often rewritten it to be cleaner and better. We strongly recommend that folks check out Ben's own GitHub repository at https://github.com/benmarwick for more ideas of ways to deal with big data! David Hussey, Kim Martin and Kaitlin Wainwright read over and improved the next-to-last draft of this work, casting critical and thoughtful eyes. Jo Van Every's writing workshop and its participants helped keep Shawn on track. Michelle Moravec discussed what worked and what didn't on Twitter and shared her own research process, which taught us much. Elijah Meeks, Andrew Goldstone, Ted Underwood, Ben Schmidt and Michael Widner, inspired us. Tim Evans and Alice Oven got the ball rolling in the first place. The Massachusetts Historical Society graciously allowed us to scrape and data mine John Adams' diaries. The initial anonymous reviewers of our proposal pushed us to work more productive veins, and we thank them for their time and thoughtful consideration.

Amanda Seligman assigned parts of the work-in-progress site to her students as part of a graduate course in digital history; their comments were most helpful.

On the macroscope site the following folks made numerous comments, queries, and provided feedback on whether or not our tutorials were working; we could not have completed this work without their input: Angela Zoss; David Baglien; Dan Shore; Nieya Dudley; James Waller; Amanda Workman; Jessica Daase; Marcus Van Grinsven; Jasmine; Isaura Leon; Arlardy; Christian Wilhelm; Charles Mehlberg; Andrew Heding; Zakea Jones; Benjamin Gautsch; Beth Mudlaff; Elizabeth Young; Danielle Alvaro; Tony Hugill; Karlie; Nicole Spangler; Ashley Carlson; Bricelyn; Will Tchakirides; Ruth Jones; Eric Gajdostik; Cassidy; Johanna; Michael Kramer; Rebecca Greer; Joyce Zhou; Christi Bose; Diana Moreno; Caleb McDaniel; Marten Duering; John Laudun; Zack Batist; Jonathan McQuarrie; Arianna Ciula; Peter Holdsworth; Clement Levallois; Jim Clifford; José Igartua; Rob Blades; Hollis Peirce; and William Denton.

And finally, Shawn would like to thank Tamara, Carys and Conall for their patience with him as he was chained to the computer; Ian would like to thank Jennifer Bleakney for her extensive editing and review of this book, as well as his colleagues at the University of Waterloo for letting him test out these ideas on students; and Scott would like to thank his family and his co-authors for their incredible patience at every step of the process.

Figures, URLs, and Code: themacroscope.org

Digital copies of all figures may be found on our supporting website, http://themacroscope.org. All URLs provided in the text are also listed on the website for easy click-throughs. Code snippets, supporting data files, and further essays and pointers may also be found on the website.

Chapter 1

Chapter 3

Chapter 4

Chapter 5

Chapter 6

Chapter 7

Preface

The historian sits down at her desk, flicking on the lamp. She begins to pore over a stack of badly photocopied court proceedings from late 18th century London, transcribing the text. As she works, she begins to notice interesting patterns in the language used to describe young female prisoners. "I wonder...." She turns to the Old Bailey Online and begins to search. Soon, she has a corpus of a thousand court proceedings featuring women prisoners. She downloads the complete transcriptions and loads them into Voyant Tools. Moments later, she has a graph of key words, their collocations, and their frequencies over time. A suspicion grows. She turns to MALLET and begins to look for the underlying semantic structure in the records. The algorithm, after much exploration, seems to suggest that 23 topics account for the majority of the words in each text.

But what do these topics, these lists of words, mean? She begins to explore the relationship between the topics and the texts, uncovering a web of discourse, seemingly surrounding the moral duty of the state towards women prisoners. She takes this web and begins to explore its formal characteristics as a network — what words, what ideas, are doing the heavy semantic lifting? — while at the same time, she runs the RezoViz tool on the corpus (part of Voyant Tools) to extract the named individuals and organizations in the document. She begins to query the social network that she has extracted and is able to identify sub-communities of women and warders, children and men, zeroing in on a smaller set of key individuals who tied the prison community together. Soon, she has a powerful, macroscopic sense of not just the discourses surrounding a century of women's trials, but also of the key individuals, organizations, their connections. She looks at the clock; two hours have passed. Satisfied, she turns off her historical macroscope, her computer, and turns once again to the transcription at hand.

We live in an era where humanities scholars need to understand what digital media, their algorithms, assumptions, usage, and agency, are doing to the traditional projects of humanistic scholarship. The humanities and digital media — new media — go back decades and have often informed each other's development. Taking a more broad view of what "new media" can mean, we note that the introduction of previous revolutions in communication technology *and the ways they represent/construct human knowledge* have similarly required new perspectives and new methods in response. Our scholar above describes one way historians might engage with so-called "big data" in history. There are others. Between the three authors of this work, we have explored many different tools and perspectives in big data for historical and humanistic scholarship. This volume represents our view of what some of the most useful of these developing approaches are, how to use them, what to be wary of, and the kinds of questions and new perspectives our macroscope opens up.

We call this book the *Historian's Macroscope* to suggest both a *tool* and a *perspective*. We are not implying that this is *the* way historians will "do" history when it comes to big data; rather, it is but one piece of the toolkit, one more way of dealing with the "big" amounts of data that historians now have to grapple with. What is more, a "macroscope" — a tool for looking at the very big — deliberately suggests a scientist's workbench, where the investigator moves between different tools for exploring different scales, keeping notes in a lab notebook. Similarly, an approach to big data for the historian (we argue) needs to be a *public* approach, with the historian keeping an open notebook so that others may explore the same paths through the information, while possibly reaching very different conclusions. This is a *generative* approach: big data for the humanities is not only about *justifying* a story about the past, but *generating* new stories, new perspectives, given our new vantage points and tools.

Structure of the Book

The book is structured in three broad sections. In the first two chapters, we provide a general overview of the field. Chapter 1 introduces you to the era of big data and why we believe that it matters for historians. We begin by discussing what big data means for humanities researchers, surveying the current state of the field by pointing towards a few major projects, and then providing a brief history of our own field from its unlikely origins with a priest at the Pontifical Gregorian University of Rome. This first chapter then concludes with a discussion of big data and the academy, as well as how we believe that historians are now embarking upon a "third wave" of computational engagement. Chapter 2 continues this general introduction by focusing in on the more particular question of what the digital humanities, or DH, moment is. We provide an overview to several key terms, including open access, copyright, and data mining, argue that all historians are already digital even if they do not self-identify as digital historians, and begin to gently show you how to build your own historian's toolkit. The section ends with a treatment on how to get your own historical data, gearing you up for the section that follows.

The second section of our book, an emphasis on hands-on textual analysis tools, kicks off with Chapter 3 and our explanation of several data mining tools that can access the data that you began to grab at the end of Chapter 2. We start gently: word clouds and other off-the-shelf software that can help you quickly make sense of large amounts of text. Things then begin to ramp up with an exploration of regular expressions. We warn you here that they are challenging to learn, but think of it as both an introduction to what they are *and* a reference manual. You can do amazingly powerful things with them, and regular expressions are a useful thing to have for any historian who works with text to have in their back pocket.

One catch with many of the tools in Chapter 3 is that you have to know what you are looking for. Accordingly, in Chapter 4, we provide an in-depth exploration of various ways to "topic model" your sources. This is one of the most exciting new tools in the digital humanities, and in short, reconstructs the various "topics" that make up the body of data, or corpus, that you are exploring. It can be a bit complicated, so we open with a "topic modeling by hand" exercise to help explain things. This is definitely a hands-on chapter, with some great rewards and payoff by the end.

Chapters 5, 6, and 7 kick off the third section of our book, which provides a strong emphasis on networks; as networks are both a kind of analysis *and* a powerful form of visualization, we spend some time discussing the basics of visualizations. We address one of the key fears that scholars have with big data: that it could mean losing the trees for the forest. We argue that network analysis allows historians to connect the micro and macro, situating individual actors within a complex interconnected economy. Network analysis has been one of the most fruitful ways that topic models, discussed in the previous chapter, have been visualized. For historians, network analysis fruitfully explores concepts of space and time. Chapter 5 provides a basic breakdown of the concept and vocabulary of network analysis, which is a unique and transformative modeling technique. All of these can be performed with a spreadsheet program or other rudimentary software. Chapter 7 then explores more detailed topics and the opportunities offered by them, as well as several more hands-on tools to get right into network analysis.

In the conclusion, we point to a few more things that you might be interested in learning, notably around how to disseminate all the fantastic work that you have been able to do as a result of progressing through this book. We will also check on our good friend from the opening preface, to see how her work is going after a while experimenting with her own *Macroscope*.

This book is not an exhaustive introduction to the entire field of digital history, nor could any work be. We are three scholars based within North America — two in Canada and one in the United States — and our examples are often drawn from the scholarly milieu with which we are most comfortable. This book mostly concerns itself with text. We make an effort to draw on diverse examples, but we want to recognize where we are writing from and our bias towards English-language sources. Furthermore, the book has a particular interest in textual analysis, manipulation, and networks: we do not, for example, deal with historical Geographical Information Systems (GIS) or database theory. Quite a bit of work has been done on GIS, including the recent open-access publication, *Historical GIS Research in Canada*, released by the University of Calgary Press and available for download at http://uofcpress.com/books/9781552387085.

The Backstory to this Volume

Shawn was approached in March of 2013 by Imperial College Press (ICP) with the idea of writing some sort of volume exploring "big data" and history. Big history is almost by definition something that cannot be done by one scholar in isolation, and Shawn turned quickly to Ian Milligan and Scott Weingart. Together, the three of us wrote a proposal over a shared Google doc and submitted it to one of ICP's commissioning editors, Alice Oven. ICP sent the proposal out to four anonymous peer reviewers, whose quick and constructive feedback allowed us to develop a much better proposal. That proposal was accepted by ICP's board in the summer of 2013.

One key element in our discussion with ICP was the idea that we wanted to do this work in public, that we wanted to live-write, test-drive, and bounce our work off the wider digital history community. There was a very understandable concern that this approach might cannibalize sales. After much discussion, we all agreed to a clause that we would clearly state that the final published product would be different in structure and coherence than what might appear online, and that we would provide a link to the purchase site for the physical and digital versions of the final product. If it can be demonstrated that sales are harmed by the web version being available, we have agreed that the web version will be shuttered. This seems reasonable. Good editorial guidance has already made this project better than it might otherwise have been, and neither we nor you would want you citing and building an argument on our work if that version contains flaws. Indeed, we think it a good thing to make our mistakes in public, so as to rapidly iterate to a better version (a key point in open source software development, as it happens). We are inspired by the success of projects like Dougherty and Nazrawtoski's *Writing History in the Digital Age*, which have opened up the writing process — Shawn certainly feels that his work was manifestly improved by participating in that experiment — and we are excited to see what will happen next.[1] The website continues to grow and respond to its users. We are delighted to see that it has already, before the draft is even complete, appeared on graduate level syllabi in digital history courses in the United States. We encourage feedback at our site, http://www.themacroscope.org/2.0/answers/, and we promise to respond to questions, new developments, queries, and comments! And, if the unthinkable happens and the website disappears, we will make sure that it is preserved with the Internet Archive at archive.org.

It came together very quickly. The question of how fast to work was always at the forefront of our minds but, in this ever-changing research field, one does need to move relatively quickly. We have tried to stick to general principles as much as possible but even these are often situated within particular software environments or tools that humanities scholars use. One cannot write a book like this over a five-year period. We had to make speed, but not haste.

---

[1] Jack Dougherty and Kristen Nawrotzki (2013). *Writing History in the Digital Age*, University of Michigan Press, Ann Arbor, MI. It is available at http://www.press.umich.edu/6589653/writing_history_in_the_digital_age.

Who is this Volume for?

Our ideal reader is an advanced undergraduate looking for guidance as they encounter big data for the first time. For use in undergraduate digital history classes, we would suggest instructors use this present text in conjunction with *The Programming Historian* at http://programming historian.org and Daniel Cohen and Roy Rosenzweig's *Digital History: A Guide to Gathering, Preserving, and Presenting the Past on the Web*.[2] Students and instructors should also keep a keen eye on http://digitalhumanitiesnow.org. We imagine this volume as a handbook also for the graduate student confronted by a vast corpus of material, for the researcher encountering these methods for the first time, and for the interested individual who has stumbled across a trove of genealogical data or digitized newspapers, or the local historical society who are trying to see the value in digitizing their holdings in the first place. We have kept the jargon to a minimum, and at all times we have tried not to make assumptions about levels of digital proficiency that are unwarranted. We do assume that, if you are holding this volume, you are interested in using your computer's power for more than simply consuming media online or typing a Word document; that you wish to actively create and interrogate digital data.

And, finally, we assume that you're willing to get your hands dirty.

There will be times, however, where perhaps there is something missing, something not quite as clear as it could be. Please do leave us a comment on the book's website, and we will try to provide clarification. Also, you should be aware of sites like:

Digital Humanities Questions and Answers: http://digitalhumanities.org/answers/

Stack Overflow: http://stackoverflow.com/

Digital Humanities Questions and Answers and Stack Overflow are websites designed to help people who need information connect with those who have it handy! If you have a question, the first step should be to simply plug it into your search engine of choice. If the answer does not appear, create an account on either of these two websites and ask away. Try to be as specific as possible: make sure to mention what program you're using, what operating

---

[2]Daniel J. Cohen and Roy Rosenzweig (2005). *Digital History: A Guide to Gathering, Preserving, and Presenting the Past on the Web*, University of Pennsylvania Press, Philadelphia, PA, http://chnm.gmu.edu/digitalhistory/.

system, and provide an example of what you have been doing to answer the question.

The best part is that, when you ask your question, you're also helping other people who might have the question in the future! There are some other sites to keep your eyes open for as well:

Digital Humanities Now: http://digitalhumanitiesnow.org

The Journal of Digital Humanities: http://journalofdigitalhumanities. org/

These are two of the leading online publications for what's going on *right now* in the digital humanities, circa 2015. The former curates and collects the blogs of active researchers and contributors, of which selected pieces are then put into the more formal *Journal of Digital Humanities*. They are well worth bookmarking to see how the field evolves!

And follow the Twitter accounts of figures in the field. Daniel Cohen maintains a good list at https://twitter.com/dancohen/digitalhumanities.

Shawn is on Twitter https://twitter.com/electricarchaeo

Ian is on Twitter at https://twitter.com/ianmilligan1

Scott is on Twitter at https://twitter.com/scott_bot

Come say hi!

Who Are We and How Did We Get Into Digital History?

Ian Milligan, like many historians, got into digital history in a roundabout fashion. As a child, he was a computer geek: programming in BASIC, finagling to get computer games to run, and hitting up garage sales for hardware to take apart. In this, he was part of a cohort of largely "middle-class white men" who had access to this as a child, and so is conscious of this (as Miriam Posner has helpfully cautioned) when thinking about whether coding is necessary or not to be part of the digital humanities.[3] A disastrous semester or two with higher-level calculus and a detour with

---

[3]Miriam Posner, "Some things to think about before you exhort everyone to code," *MiriamPosner.com*, 29 February 2012, http://miriamposner.com/blog/some-things-to-think-about-before-you-exhort-everyone-to-code/.

the Canadian Forces took him away from computational work and eventually towards his love of history, to be rediscovered a few years later during the waning years of his doctoral degree.

In his PhD, Milligan studied youth culture, which involved studying large amounts of people. Unsure of where to go next in a second project, a serendipitous conversation with digital historian William Turkel and a visit to a humanities and technology un-conference — a THATCamp — led him down the digital humanities rabbit hole. He learned his text analysis and data mining skills first through the *Programming Historian* and then months upon months of trial and error. It all worked out, as today he works as an assistant professor of digital history at the University of Waterloo, a school intensively focused on science and engineering. His advice to his students is that *anybody* can do computational work, provided an ability to fail.

Shawn's background is similar to Ian's: his first computer was a Commodore Vic-20 that his older brother had saved up to purchase. Games were hard to come by, so he and his brothers developed a workflow for reading out the code published in magazines like *Compute!*, typing it in, and error checking. If they were lucky, two weeks later there'd be a space-invaders clone to play. In junior college and then university, Shawn successfully internalized the idea that "scholarship" could only mean essay writing; asked to go on this new "World Wide Web" in 1995 to find out about the Etruscans, Shawn was dismayed at the dreck he encountered and dutifully wrote a paper whose first line read, "The World Wide Web will never be of use to academics."

Eating his words some years later, Shawn's doctoral thesis on the epigraphy and archaeology of the Roman brick industry necessitated a re-engagement with digital tools for network analysis as it was the only method that could help sort out the tangled relationships. Returning to video games provided the motivation to reanimate these networks (readings in artificial intelligence showed Shawn the potential of agent-based modeling for dealing with contingency in the past), Shawn won a postdoctoral fellowship at the University of Manitoba where Lea Stirling took a chance on this admittedly odd idea. This work was recognized at the first University of Nebraska, Lincoln, Digital Humanities Workshop where Alan Liu and William G. Thomas III suggested that he should blog about his work; thus http://electricarchaeology.ca/ was born. Shawn's exploration of new tools for teaching and research in archaeology via his blog (including chronicling his failures as much as his successes) became a cornerstone of his research and pedagogy as he worked in the online education world. Eight years after his PhD, he won a position as assistant professor of digital humanities at Carleton University in the history department.

Scott grew up with a passion for history but a dedication to computers, believing they would lead to his eventual career. Three and a half years through a computer engineering degree, however, Scott grew disenchanted with the engineering aspect and vowed never to touch a computer again. Having taken just as many history courses as engineering, he easily finished off his degree as a historian of science, happy in the knowledge that he would spend much of the rest of his life in a dusty old archive. When he applied to Indiana University and got accepted in both the history of science and information science graduate programs, Scott figured the information science could help fund the history, so he pursued a dual degree. In very short order, he learned of the existence of digital humanities and that computers were much more fun when applied to one's passions.

As a historian of science, Scott became interested in modeling and mapping the large-scale growth of science. He became interested in those punctuation periods where science seems to lurch forward and those lacunae where research is all but stalled. These periods tend to be described in very broad terms but without much depth; Scott's research imagines combining those macroscopic broad strokes with individual datum, seeing the big and the small at once. As such computational approaches were still rare, he began to develop software techniques and packages to aid his goals. His forward-thinking mentors, particularly the historian Robert A. Hatch and the information scientist Katy Börner, have been instrumental in helping him achieve these goals.

Scott's journey into history, data, and the digital humanities is chronicled on his blog, the scottbot irregular. He currently holds the position of Digital Humanities Specialist at Carnegie Mellon University, while still finishing his PhD at Indiana University.

The key element that ties our biographies together is that, despite some false starts, we were willing to look under the hood. If you are too, then let's start with Chapter 1.

Chapter 1

The Joys of Big Data
for Historians

In this chapter, we look at the emergence of the idea of "big data" for historians, examining some case studies in the broader field of the digital humanities. We discuss the limits of big data in terms of historical practice, and make an argument for why all of us — whether we employ the methods discussed in this book or not — need to be aware of why this matters.

A macroscope is a bit like a microscope or a telescope, but instead of allowing you to see things that are small or far away, the macroscope makes it easier to grasp the incredibly large. It does so through a process of compression, by selectively reducing complexity until once-obscure patterns and relationships become clear. Often, macroscopes produce textual abstractions or data visualizations *in lieu* of direct images.[1]

Pointed at human history, the macroscope offers a stark contrast to what has become standard historical practice. Rather than through compression, good historians, like good detectives, test their merit through expansion: the ability to extract complex knowledge from the smallest crumbs of evidence that history has left behind. By tracing the trail of these breadcrumbs, a historian might weave together a narrative of the past. A historian's macroscope offers a complementary, but very different, path to knowledge. It

---

[1] On visualizations and abstractions, Lorraine Daston has written "these techniques aim at more than making the invisible visible. They aspire to all-at-once-ness, the condensation of laborious, step-by-step procedures into an immediate *coup d'oeil,*... What was a painstaking process of calculation and correlation — for example, in the construction of a table of variables — becomes a flash of intuition." See Lorraine Daston, "On Scientific Observation," *Isis* 99.1, March 2008, 97–110. This is the goal of the macroscope: to highlight immediately what often requires careful thought and calculation, sometimes more than is possible for a single person.

allows you to begin with the complex and winnow it down until a narrative emerges from the cacophony of evidence.[2]

In this, an important distinction needs to be made between our understanding of the micro- and macroscope versus micro- and macro-history; the two do not dovetail perfectly together. Microhistory involves the rigorous and in-depth study of a single story or moment in history, whereas macrohistory susses out long-term trends and eddies, such as Fernand Braudel's longue durée. A macroscope, by studying large quantities of data, could fit into microhistory; imagine the parsing of hundreds of thousands of tweets around a single American trial, for example. Yet it also helps us understand macrohistory: tracing fluctuating word and topic frequency over decades, or even centuries. Macroscopes are not bound by time, but rather quantity. They also draw upon a rich heritage of computational history, stretching back to early cutting-edge work done with censuses in the 1960s.

As history becomes digitized in ever-increasing scales, historians without the ability to research both micro- and macroscopically may be in danger of becoming mired in evidence or lost in the noise. This book is aimed at those historians who aspire to turn the macroscope on their own research, an increasingly important skill in our historical moment.[3] It is neither exhaustive in scope nor terribly deep in any one methodology; instead, we have filled this book with the first stepping-stones for many different roads. We hope interested readers will follow those paths into areas yet unexplored.

---

[2] We are neither the first to coin the term macroscope, nor the first to point its gaze toward human history. It was originally used by Joël de Rosnay (1979), *The Macroscope: A New World Scientific System* (Harper & Row, New York, NY) to discuss complex societies and has most recently been popularized by Kay Börner (March 1, 2011) "Plug-and-Play Macroscopes." *Communications of the ACM*, **54**(3), 60, in the context of tools that allow one to see human activities at a distance. Macroscopes have been brought up in the humanities as well, such as by Tim Tangherlini (see his "Tracking Trolls: New Challenges from the Folklore Macroscope," eHg Annual Lecture, Royal Netherlands Academy of Arts and Sciences, December 12, 2013, http://www.ehumanities.nl/ehg-annual-lecture-tim-tangherlini-ucla/) to similar effect. In literary criticism and history, similar concepts have been called "distant reading," as articulated by Franco Moretti (2005), *Graphs, Maps, Trees: Abstract Models for Literary History* (London, New York, NY: Verso,) or "macroanalysis" in Matthew L. Jockers (2013), *Macroanalysis: Digital Methods & Literary History* (Urbana-Champaign, IL: University of Illinois Press). In their recent *Uncharted: Big Data as a Lens on Human Culture* (2013, New York, NY: Riverhead,) on culturomics, Erez Aiden and Jean-Baptiste Michel wrote of their intent "to build a scope to study human history."

[3] Jo Guldi and David Armitage effectively argue the importance of macroscopic thinking in their monograph *The History Manifesto* (2014, Cambridge: Cambridge University Press).

Big Data

"How big is big?" we rhetorically ask: big data for literature scholars might mean a hundred novels ("the great unread"),[4] for historians it might mean an entire array of 19th century shipping rosters,[5] and for archaeologists it might mean every bit of data generated by several seasons of field survey and several seasons of excavation and study. For computer scientists, they are often focused not just on materials of a scope that can't be read but on volumes of information that elude processing by conventional computer systems, such as Google's collection or the shocking amount of information generated by experiments such as CERN's Large Hadron Collider.

For us, as humanists, *big is in the eye of the beholder*. If there are more data than you could conceivably read yourself in a reasonable amount of time, or that require computational intervention to make new sense of them, it's big enough! These are all valid answers. Indeed, there is some valid hesitancy around the use of the term "data" itself, as it has a faint whiff of quantifying and reducing the meaningful life experiences of the past to numbers. We believe that this book outlines various methods to computationally explore historical data in a way that would previously seem resistant to quantification. With that proviso in mind, of course, we do take "big data" to be a central concept in this book.

As scholars, we have all used varying degrees of datasets and considered them "big." On one extreme lie the datasets that stretch the constraints of individual researchers and personal computing, such as the monumental 80-terabyte sweep of much of the publicly-accessible World Wide Web in 2011, made available by the Internet Archive.[6] Such projects may require high performance computing and specialized software. But others work with more manageable sets of data: popular music lyrics, proposals or papers submitted to conferences, databases of dissertations, and historiographical inquiries.

Historians must be open to the digital turn, thanks to the astounding growth of digital sources and an increasing technical ability to process them

---

[4]See Franco Moretti (2005), *Graphs, Maps, Trees*, London; New York, NY: Verso, and Margaret Cohen (1999), *The Sentimental Education of the Novel*, Princeton, NJ: Princeton University Press.

[5]See Trading Consequences (2014), "Trading Consequences | Exploring the Trading of Commodities in the 19th Century," http://tradingconsequences.blogs.edina.ac.uk/.

[6]Internet Archive (October 26, 2012), "80 Terabytes of Archived Web Crawl Data Available for Research," *Internet Archive Blog*, http://blog.archive.org/2012/10/26/80-terabytes-of-archived-web-crawl-data-available-for-research/.

on a mass scale.[7] Both trends are discussed in this book. Historians are collectively witnessing a profound transformation in how they research, write, disseminate, and interact with their work. As datasets expand into the realm of the big, computational analysis ceases to be "nice to have" and becomes a simple requirement. While not all historians will have to become fluent with data (just as not all historians are oral historians, or use GIS, or work within communities), digital historians will become part of the disciplinary mosaic. Computational skills may be increasingly viewed as akin to language requirements: in some cases, a nice to have and in other programs, a rote requirement.

In this chapter, we introduce you to what big data means, what opportunities it affords, where it came from, and the broader implications of this "era of big data." New and emerging research tools are driving cutting-edge humanities research, often funded by transnational funding networks. Historians are asking new questions of old datasets with new tools, as well as finding new avenues on previously inaccessible terrain. After this survey of the current state of affairs, we then turn our eyes to the historical context of this current scholarly moment. These projects must be situated in the context of an original big data scholar, Father Busa and his *Index Thomisticus*, as well as the more recent shift from "humanities computing" to the "digital humanities." Finally, we discuss the broader implications of an "era of big data." Here we see the joys of abundance but also the dangers of information overload.[8] The contours of this challenge and opportunity are fascinating, and help anchor the discussion that follows. While there will certainly be bumps on the road ahead to come, we generally see a promising future for an era of big data.

Putting Big Data to Good Use: Historical Case Studies

For 239 years, accused criminals (initially Londoners, subsequently all Britons accused of major crimes) stood for justice before judges at the

---

[7]The foundational text in this field is Daniel J. Cohen and Roy Rosenzweig (2005). *Digital History: A Guide to Gathering, Preserving, and Presenting the Past on the Web*. This work primarily focuses on putting information on the web, whereas we explore various ways to improve your research with that information.

[8]Roy Rosenzweig (2003), "Scarcity or Abundance? Preserving the Past in a Digital Era," *American Historical Review*, **108**(3), 735–762, available online at http://chnm.gmu.edu/digitalhistory/links/pdf/introduction/0.6b.pdf.

Old Bailey. Thanks to a popular fascination with crime amongst Londoners, the events were recorded in the *Proceedings*: initially as pamphlets, later as bound books and journals replete with advertisement, and subsequently becoming official publications. These sources provide an unparalleled look into the administration of justice and the lives of ordinary people in 17th, 18th, and 19th century England (their publication ceased in 1913).[9] While there are gaps, this is an exhaustively large source for historians using customary methods who seek to answer questions of social and legal history in the 20th and 21st centuries.

The Old Bailey records are, by the standards of historians and most humanists, *big data*. They comprise 127 million words, cover 197,000 trials, and have been transcribed to a high standard by two typists working simultaneously to reduce error rates. Computers can read this amount of information quickly, but it would take years for a single scholar to read this (and then they probably would have forgotten half of what they had read). As the research team put it: "it is one of the largest bodies of accurately transcribed historical text currently available online. It is also the most comprehensive thin slice view of eighteenth and nineteenth-century London available online." [10] Tackling a dataset of this size, however, requires specialized tools. Once digitized, it was made available to the public through keyword searches. Big data methodologies, however, offered new opportunities to make sense of this very old historical material.[11]

The *Data Mining with Criminal Intent* project sought to do that.[12] A multinational project team, including scholars from the United States, Canada, and the United Kingdom, sought to create "a seamlessly linked digital research environment" for working with these court records. Pulling their gaze back from individual trials and records, the team made new and relevant discoveries. Using a plugin, a little program or component

---

[9] "The Proceedings - Publishing History of the Proceedings - Central Criminal Court," April 2013, available online at http://www.oldbaileyonline.org/static/Publishinghistory.jsp.

[10] Dan Cohen *et al.* (August 31, 2011), *Data Mining with Criminal Intent: Final White Paper*, http://criminalintent.org/wp-content/uploads/2011/09/Data-Mining-with-Criminal-Intent-Final1.pdf.

[11] The best explanation of this is probably the Piled Higher and Deeper (PhD Comics) video explaining British historian Adam Crymble's work. See "Big Data + Old History," YouTube video, 6 September 2013, http://www.youtube.com/watch?v=tp4y-_VoXdA.

[12] For an incredible overview of this, see Tim Hitchcock (9 December 2013), "Big Data for Dead People: Digital Readings and the Conundrums of Postivism," *Historyonics Blog*, http://historyonics.blogspot.ca/2013/12/big-data-for-dead-people-digital.html.

that adds something to a software program, for the open source reference and research management software *Zotero* (http://www.zotero.org/), Fred Gibbs at George Mason University developed a means to look at specific cases (e.g. those pertaining to "poison") and look for commonalities. For example, "drank" was a common word; closer to that, the word "coffee"; conversely, the word "ate" was conspicuously absent. In another development, closely related trials could be brought up. Through comparing differences in documents (using Normalized Compression Distance, or the standard tools that compress files on your computer) one can get the database to suggest trials that are structurally similar to the one a user is currently viewing. And, most importantly, taking this material and visualizing it allowed the research team to discover new findings, such as a "significant rise in women taking on other spouses when their husbands had left them," or the rise of plea bargaining around 1825, based on the figure below (Fig. 1.1) showing a dramatic shift in the length of trials in that time period.[13]

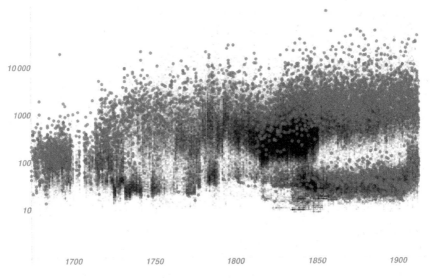

Fig. 1.1   The length of trials, in words, in Old Bailey Proceedings. Copyright Tim Hitchcock and William J. Turkel, 2011. Used with permission.

---

[13]Dan Cohen *et al.* (August 31, 2011), *Data Mining with Criminal Intent: Final White Paper*, http://criminalintent.org/wp-content/uploads/2011/09/Data-Mining-with-Criminal-Intent-Final1.pdf.

All of these tools were put online, and researchers can now access the *Old Bailey* both through the traditional portal as before and through a dedicated Application Programming Interface or API. APIs are a set of rules or specifications that let different software programs talk to each other. In the case of the *Old Bailey*, the API allows researchers to use programs like Zotero, or their programming language of choice, or visualization tools such as the freely accessible Voyant Tools, to access the database. The project thus leaves a legacy to future researchers, to enable them to point their macroscope toward the trials, to make sense of that exhaustive dataset of 127 million words.

Findings are sure to emerge over the next few years, but one eye-opening study — "The Civilizing Process in London's Old Bailey" by Sara Klingenstein, Tim Hitchcock, and Simon DeDeo — has already made a provocative argument that required computational intervention. Drawing on the massive *Old Bailey* dataset, the researchers used an innovative method of creating "bags of words" out of related words from *Roget's Thesaurus* and were able to convincingly demonstrate a major shift that occurred in the early 19th century: violent crimes began to be both discussed and treated differently. Before that time, while the crime itself was mentioned, the violence within it was not a discrete category. The work helps confirm the hypothesis of others, which sees a "civilizing process" as a:

> Deep-rooted and multivalent phenomenon that accompanied the growing monopoly of violence by the state, and the decreasing acceptability of interpersonal violence as part of normal social relations. Our work [in this article] is able to track an essential correlate of this long-term process, most visibly in the separation of assault and violent theft from nonviolent crimes involving theft and deception.[14]

As the *New York Times* explained in their coverage of the study, the routine nature of violence in the 1700s gave way by the 1820s to an emphasis on "containing violence, a development reflected not just in language but also in the professionalization of the justice system."[15] Distant reading enabled historians to pull their gaze back from the individual trials and to consider

---

[14]Sara Klingenstein, Tim Hitchcock, and Simon DeDeo (2014), "The Civilizing Process in London's Old Bailey," *Proceedings of the National Academy of Sciences U. S. A.*, **111**(26), 9419–9424. Available online at http://www.pnas.org/content/111/26/9419.full.
[15]Sandra Blakeslee (June 16, 2014), "Computing Crime and Punishment," *The New York Times*, June 16, 2014, http://www.nytimes.com/2014/06/17/science/computing-crime-and-punishment.html.

the 197,000 trials as a whole. The "civilizing process" study will probably, in our view, emerge as one of the defining stories of how big data can reveal new things that were not possible without it.

The high quality of the *Old Bailey* dataset is, however, an outlier: most researchers will not have ready access to nearly perfectly transcribed databases like these criminal records. Even digitized newspapers, which on the face of it would seem to be excellent resources, are not without serious issues at the level of the optical character recognition (OCR).[16] There is still joy to be found, however, in the less-than-perfect records. The *Trading Consequences* project is one example of this. Bringing together leading experts in natural language processing (NLP) and innovative historians in Canada and the United Kingdom, this project confirmed and enhanced existing understandings of trade by tracing the relationships between commodities and global locations. They adapted the Edinburgh Geoparser (which is publicly forthcoming) to find and locate place names in text files, and then identified commodities that were mentioned in relationship with these place names. One useful example the project gave us was that of cinchona bark, a raw material used to make quinine (an anti-malaria drug) — it was interesting because it allowed them to confirm the secondary literature on the research question. They confirmed via computational analysis that until the 1850s it was closely related to Peruvian forests as well as markets and factories in London, England; by the 1860s, it had shifted towards locations in India, Sri Lanka, Indonesia, and Jamaica. By drawing on thousands of documents, changes can be quickly spotted. Even more promisingly, it can be put online in database fashion, enabling historians to test out their own hypotheses and findings. There are several ways to access their database, including searches on specific commodities and locations, and it can all be found at http://tradingconsequences.blogs.edina.ac.uk/access-the-data/. For historians interested in this form of work, their project white paper is extremely useful.[17]

Moving beyond anecdotes and case studies, *Trading Consequences* drew on over six million British parliamentary paper pages, almost four million documents from Early Canadiana Online, and a smaller series of letters, British documents ("only" 140,010 images, for example), and other

---

[16]Ian Milligan (2013), "Illusionary Order: Online Databases, Optical Character Recognition, and Canadian History, 1997-2010," *Canadian Historical Review*, **94**(4), 540–569.
[17]Ewan Klein *et al.* (March 2014), *Trading Consequences: Final White Paper*, http://tradingconsequences.blogs.edina.ac.uk/files/2014/03/DiggingintoDataWhitePaper-final.pdf.

correspondences. This sort of work presages the growing importance of linked open data, which points towards the increasing trend in putting information online in a format that other computer programs can read. In this way, Early Canadiana Online can speak to files held in another repository, allowing us to harness the combined potential of many numerous silos of knowledge.

An automated process would take a document, turn the image into accessible text, and then "mark it up:" London, for example, would be marked as a "location," grain would be marked as a "commodity," and so forth. The interplay between trained programmers, linguists, and historians was especially fruitful for this: for example, the database kept picking up the location "Markham" (a suburb north of Toronto, Canada) and the historians were able to point out that the entries actually referred to a British official, culpable in smuggling, Clements Robert Markham. As historians develop technical skills and computer scientists develop humanistic skills, fruitful collaborative undertakings can develop. Soon, historians of this period will be able to contextualize their studies with an interactive, visualized database of global trade in the 19th century. Yet, while collaborative outcomes are laudable when dealing with *big* questions, we still believe that there is a role for the sole or small group undertaking. We personally find that exploratory research can be fruitfully carried out by a sole researcher, or in our cases, three of us working on a problem together. There's no one size of a team that will fit all questions.

Beyond court and trading records, census records have long been a staple of computational inquiry. In Canada, for example, there are two major and ambitious projects underway that use computers to read large arrays of census information. The Canadian Century Research Infrastructure project, funded by federal government infrastructure funding, draws on five censuses of the entire country in an attempt to provide a "new foundation for the study of social, economic, cultural, and political change."[18] Simultaneously, researchers at the Université de Montréal are reconstructing the European population of Quebec in the 17th and 18th centuries, drawing heavily on parish registers.[19] This form of history harkens back to the first wave of computational research, discussed later in this chapter, and shows some of the potential available to historians computationally querying large datasets.

---

[18]For more information, see the Canadian Century Research Infrastructure Project website at http://www.ccri.uottawa.ca/CCRI/Home.html.
[19]See the Programme de recherche en démographie historique at http://www.genealogy.umontreal.ca/fr/LePrdh.

The Google Ngram Viewer — https://books.google.com/ ngrams

Throughout the book you'll see boxes like this, introducing you to some of the major issues surrounding a tool!

General Principles

The Google Ngram Viewer allows users to see the *relative frequency* of a given term within a corpus of some five million books digitized by the Google Books project. This lets you see what percentage of all words your search term made up and to compare them to each other. We can learn, for example, when the *Great War* gave way to *World War I* in common usage.

Description

It is a simple viewer, run in your web browser. You type in your terms, separated by commas, and a line chart appears below.

Critique

It is limited to only the books that are digitized. It suffers from some issues of poor optical character recognition, which means a computer program has tried to turn the letter shapes into plain text files. It may only capture elite culture before the advent of accessible popular publishing.

How to Use It

It is very easy to use! Simply navigate to http://books.google.com/ ngrams and enter your terms. More advanced options can be found in the "help" page.

How to Analyze the Results

Remember that they're presenting normalized frequency! Run your mouse over each year to see a pop-up window with data.

Any look at textual digital history would be incomplete without a reference to the Culturomics Project and Google Ngrams.[20] Originally co-released as an article and an online tool, a team from Harvard University

---

[20]Michel *et al.* (2011), "Quantitative Analysis of Culture Using Millions of Digitized Books," *Science*, **331**, 6014, and http://books.google.com/ngrams.

(the composition of which is discussed shortly) collaborated to develop a process for analyzing the millions of books that Google has scanned and applied OCR to as part of its Google Books project. This project indexed word and phrase frequency across over five million books, enabling researchers to trace the rise and fall of cultural ideas and phenomena through targeted keyword and phrase searches and their frequency over time.[21] The result is a powerful look at a few hundred years of book history. One often unspoken tenet of digital history is that simple methods can produce incredibly compelling results, and the Google Ngrams tool exemplifies this idea.[22] In terms of sheer data, this is the most ambitious and certainly the most widely accessible (and publicized) big history project in existence. Ben Zimmer used this free online tool to show when the United States began being discussed as a singular entity rather than as a plurality of many states by charting when people stopped saying "The United States are" in favor of "The United States is" (Fig. 1.2).[23]

This is a powerful finding, both confirmatory of some research and suggestive of future paths that could be pursued. There are limitations, of course, with such a relatively simple methodology: words change in meaning and typographical characteristics over time (compare the frequency of *beft* with the frequency of *best* to see the impact of the "medial s"), there are OCR errors, and searching only on words or search phrases can occlude

Fig. 1.2 "The United States are" versus "The United States is".

---

[21] Remember, to do a phrase search, use quotation marks around your phrase. Otherwise, the search will return results where the words are in close proximity, which can skew your results. See http://books.google.com/ngrams/info.

[22] Aptly put in Ted Underwood (20 February 2013), "Wordcounts are Amazing," *The Stone and the Shell Research Blog*, http://tedunderwood.com/2013/02/20/wordcounts-are-amazing/.

[23] Ben Zimmer (18 October 2012), "Bigger, Better Google Ngrams: Brace Yourself for the Power of Grammar," *The Atlantic.com*, http://www.theatlantic.com/technology/archive/2012/10/bigger-better-google-ngrams-brace-yourself-for-the-power-of-grammar/263487/.

the surrounding context of a word. Some of the hubris around culturomics may rankle some historians, but taken on its own merits, the Culturomics Project and the Ngram viewer have done wonders for popularizing this model of big digital history and have become recurrent features in the popular press, academic presentations, and lectures.

Culturomics also presents historians with some professional cautionary notes, as Ian Milligan brought up in a *Journal of the Canadian Historical Association* article.[24] The authorship list of the paper and the tool was extensive: 13 individuals and the Google Books team. There were mathematicians, computer scientists, scholars from English literature, and psychologists. However, there were no historians present on the list. This is suggestive of the degree to which historians had not then yet fully embraced digital methodologies, an important issue given the growing significance of digital repositories, archives, and tools. Given the significance of culturomics and its historical claims, this omission did not go unnoticed. Writing in the American Historical Association's professional newspaper, *Perspectives*, then-AHA President Anthony Grafton tackled this issue. Where were the historians, he asked in his column, when this was a historical project conducted by a team of doctoral holders from across numerous disciplines?[25] To this, project leaders Erez Lieberman Aiden and Jean-Baptiste Michel responded in a comment, noting that while they had approached historians and used some in an advisory role, no historians met the "bar" for meriting inclusion in the author list: every one of the project participants had "directly contributed to either the creation or the collection of written texts (the 'corpus'), or to the design and execution of the specific analyses we performed." As for why, they were clear:

> The historians who came to the [project] meeting were intelligent, kind, and encouraging. But they didn't seem to have a good sense of how to yield quantitative data to answer questions, didn't have relevant computational skills, and didn't seem to have the time to dedicate to a big multi-author collaboration. It's not their fault: *these things don't appear to be taught or encouraged in history departments right now.*[26] [Emphasis added.]

---

[24]Ian Milligan (2012), "Mining the 'Internet Graveyard': Rethinking the Historians' Toolkit," *Journal of the Canadian Historical Association*, **23**(2), 21–64.

[25]Anthony Grafton (March 2011), "Loneliness and Freedom," *AHA Perspectives*, http://www.historians.org/perspectives/issues/2011/1103/1103pre1.cfm.

[26]Comment by Jean-Baptiste Michel and Erez Lieberman Aiden on Anthony Grafton, "Loneliness and Freedom."

To some degree it is an overstatement, as the previous examples in this chapter illustrate. Historians are doing amazing things with data. Yet there is a kernel of truth to this (still, as of 2015), in that the teaching of digital history perspectives and methods are not yet in the mainstream of the profession, though this is certainly changing: witness American Historical Association panels on both teaching and doing digital history, as well as the emergence of exciting and well-received books such as *History in the Digital Age*.[27]

While the Ngram database is a good way to begin to understand and think about textual analysis, other important resources exist for humanities scholars: the refined version of the Ngram database, *Bookworm*, as well as the JSTOR (Journal STORage) text mining database, *Data for Research*. To use their database, visit their website at http://bookworm. culturomics.org/. In *Bookworm*, we see that size is not everything. Its "open library" search functionality "only" searches a little over a million books (the http://openlibrary.org/collection), but it draws those books from the pre-1923 corpus; this means that it has functionality not available to a tool that incorporates copyrighted works. Consider the following search depicted in Fig. 1.3.

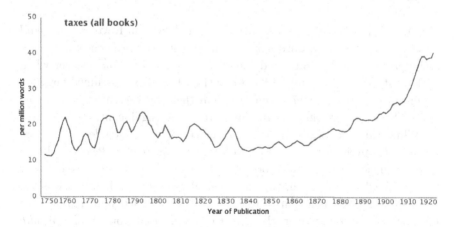

Fig. 1.3   Bookworm search of "taxes", all books. Courtesy Ben Schmidt.

[27]Toni Weller (ed) (2013), *History in the Digital Age*, Routledge, Abingdon, UK. See also increasingly prominent venues such as *Global Perspectives on Digital History*, http://gpdh.org/.

The frequency of taxes is increasing, with initial valleys and peaks from 1750 through 1830, and then a steady ascendency up to and continuing into the end of the database in 1923. In the former Ngram database, this would be all we could see. But, due to the granularity of the database, we can see where discussion of taxes has been increasing. If we focus our search so it simply considers books published in the United States, we see this (Fig. 1.4):

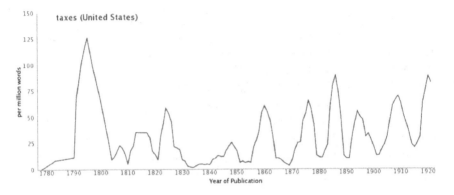

Fig. 1.4   Bookworm search of "taxes" for books published in the United States.

The peak here occurs much earlier — the American Revolution — and only begins to trend upwards into much later in the 19th century. We are seeing more refined results, and the overall contours become clearer when we look at taxes in the United Kingdom (Fig. 1.5). Taxes assumed far more significance in the late 17th century than they did thereafter, unlike the United States where they became more relatively significant.

While this occludes context at a glance, because included books are not under copyright, we can move from the distant reading level of relative word frequency to individual books by clicking on a given year. We discover that the peak year is 1776, the American Revolution, and that it was the discussion of taxes as a central role. By clicking on each year, readers can be taken to the texts themselves: in this case, discussions of the *Wealth of Nations*, political pamphlets published in England concerning taxation, speeches published, and government reports. There are other options: users can discover the percentage of books that a word features in, for example, or in the American context go down to the level of the author's state. It thus serves the distant reading purpose of looking at overall trends, but also the close reading perspective of finding individual works. *Bookworm*

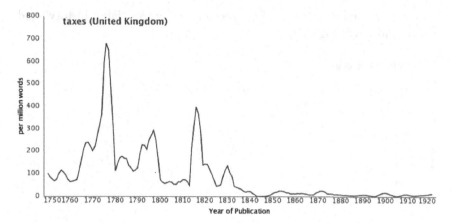

Fig. 1.5 Bookworm search of "taxes" for books published in the United Kingdom. Courtesy Ben Schmidt.

is even more versatile than we have the space to do it justice here: as of writing (2015) it has similar features for scientific literature (*ArXIV*), bills passed in the United States Congress, the American *Chronicling America* newspaper database, and the Social Science Research Network.

As the datasets made available in *Bookworm* indicate, there is much value in extracting word and phrase frequency from the body of academic literature. As historians, we often find ourselves writing historiographies — a process which involves, in part, understanding the trends in the literature that has come before. One of the major repositories that we use as researchers is JSTOR. Recognizing the value of distant reading and textual analysis to researchers, JSTOR has made it so that anybody — even members of the general public who would not normally have access to the collections — can carry out queries.

An example can help show the usefulness of this. Visit http://dfr. jstor.org/. You do not even need to have a subscription to JSTOR to use this tool! Let's take two subdisciplines of history that have seen relative waning and booming of fortunes, in terms of scholarly interest, over the last few decades. In the search engine, we search first for "labor history". Now, knowing that there is an alternative English-language spelling, "labour history", we do a second search for that. Searches stack on top of each other, so we are seeing the combined results. The default results are a list of citations, so to generate visualizations we click on the "graph" icon. You can see that between 1960 (where the first mentions occur) and the present, the combined relative frequency of the phrases "labor history" and "labour history" (Fig. 1.6):

Publication Year

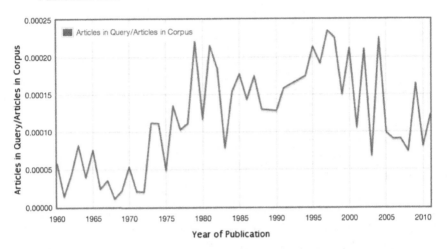

Fig. 1.6   "labor history" and "labour history" search results in articles in JSTOR, via dfr.jstor.org.

Remember that JSTOR is not a perfectly comprehensive database — many journals are not included in it — but, even so, this is a useful starting point. We see labour history rising to peak in the late 1970s, early 1980s, with another surprising late 1990s bump. It then declines throughout the 2000s. If we want to generate a list of citations, we can download them all by clicking "submit a dataset request" in the upper menu bar.

Let's return to our search, however, and look for "environmental history". We do our search, we click the graph button, and see a sharp rise in mentions (Fig. 1.7).

Interesting — a subdiscipline ascendant! But, what if this reflects the use of "environmental history" in other disciplines: environmental history not as a historical subdiscipline but as literature reviews in scientific or technical papers? We can continually refine our data, however. On the left column, we see a list of search criteria. We click on "discipline," then select "history," and look at the results (Fig. 1.8).

Aha! The results are seeing a decline in history, from the mid-2000s onwards. Anecdotally, this can be borne out by the North American job market as well. These data must be used with caution but are an additional

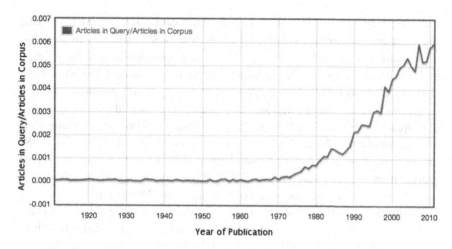

Fig. 1.7 "environmental history" search results in articles in JSTOR, via dfr.jstor.org.

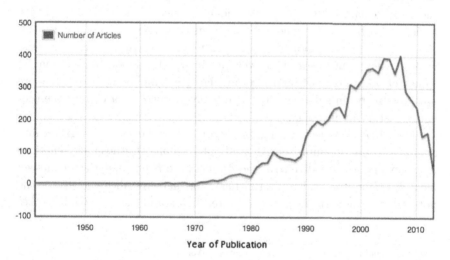

Fig. 1.8 "environmental history" search results, filtered by "discipline," in JSTOR, via dfr.jstor.org.

resource to add to your digital humanities toolkit. They can be a useful contextualizing tool for those historiographical papers.

Textual analysis is not the be all and end all of digital history work, as a project like *ORBIS: The Stanford Geospatial Network Model of the Roman World* vividly demonstrates. *ORBIS*, developed by Walter Scheidel and Elijah Meeks at Stanford University, allows users to explore Roman understandings of space as temporal distances and linkages, dependent on stitching together roads, vehicles, animals, rivers, and the sea.[28] Taking the Empire, mostly circa AD 200, *ORBIS* allows visitors to understand that world as a geographic totality: it is a comprehensive model. As Scheidel and Meeks explained in a white paper, the model consists of 751 sites, most of them urban settlements but also including important promontories and mountain passes, and covers close to 10 million square kilometers (~4 million square miles) of terrestrial and maritime space. There are 268 sites that serve as seaports. The road network encompasses 84,631 kilometers (52,587 miles) of road or desert tracks, complemented by 28,272 kilometers (17,567 miles) of navigable rivers and canals.[29] Wind and weather are calculated, and the variability and uncertainty of certain travel routes and options are well provided. 363,000 "discrete cost outcomes" are made available. A comprehensive, "top down" vision of the Roman Empire is provided (given how we are used to understanding space), drawing upon conventional historical research. Through an interactive graphical user interface, a user — be they a historian, a lay person, or student — can decide their start, destination, month of travel, whether they want their journey to be the fastest, cheapest, or shortest, how they want to travel, and then specifics around whether they want to travel on rivers or by road (from foot, to rapid march, to horseback, to ox cart, and beyond). For academic researchers, they are now able to begin substantially more finely-grained research into the economic history of antiquity.

The *ORBIS* project has moved beyond the scholarly monograph into an accessible and comprehensive study of antiquity. Enthusiastic reactions from media outlets as diverse as the *Atlantic*, the *Economist*, the technology blog *Ars Technica*, and the ABC television network all demonstrate the potential for this sort of scholarship to reach new audiences.[30]. *ORBIS* takes

---

[28] Walter Scheidel, Elijah Meeks, and Jonathan Weiland (2012), "ORBIS: The Stanford Geospatial Network Model of the Roman World," http://orbis.stanford.edu/#.

[29] Walter Scheidel, Elijah Meeks, and Jonathan Weiland (May 2012), "ORBIS: The Stanford Geospatial Network Model of the Roman World," http://orbis.stanford.edu/orbis 2012/ORBIS_v1paper_20120501.pdf.

[30] "Travel Across the Roman Empire in Real Time with ORBIS," *Ars Technica*, accessed 25 June 2013, http://arstechnica.com/business/2012/05/how-across-the-roman-empire-in-real-time-with-orbis/; "London to Rome, on Horseback," *The Economist*, accessed 25 June 2013, http://www.economist.com/blogs/gulliver/2012/05/business-travel-romans; Rebecca J. Rosen (23 May 2012), "Plan a Trip Through History With ORBIS, a Google Maps for Ancient Rome," *The Atlantic*, http://www.theatlantic.com/technology/archive/2012/05/plan-a-trip-through-history-with-orbis-a-google-maps-for-ancient-rome/257554/

big data, in this case an entire repository of information about how long it would take to travel from point A to point B (remember, 363,000 cost outcomes), and turns it into a modern day Google Maps for antiquity.

From textual analysis explorations in the Old Bailey, to the global network of 19th century commodities, to large collections of Victorian novels or even millions of books within the Google Books database, or to the travel networks that made up the Roman Empire, thoughtful and careful employment of big data has much to benefit historians today. Each of these projects, representative samples of a much larger body of digital humanities work, demonstrate the potential that new computational methods can offer to scholars and the public.[31] None of them would be possible, of course, if information professionals had not done such a fantastic job of collecting all this material — in a theme that we will return to, librarians and archivists often do yeoman's work in curating, collecting, and preserving these traces of the past in aggregate form for us. Now that we have seen some examples of the current state of the field, let us briefly travel back to 1946 and the first emergences of the digital humanities. Compared to the data centers of the Old Bailey online or the scholars of Stanford University, the field had unlikely beginnings.

Early Emergences: Father Busa, Humanities Computing, and the Digital Humanities

To know where we are today, and indeed where we are going, we need to understand where we as a discipline came from. In this section, we provide a brief overview of the evolution of the digital humanities and digital history: the intellectual tradition that has led to the projects discussed earlier in this chapter. This is not an exhaustive history, but provides a basic sense of where our discipline has emerged in part; it does not capture the many national and linguistic traditions that underlie the very diverse field of the broader digital humanities today.[32] While today the digital humanities

---

[31] The interested reader should follow http://www.digitalhumanitiesnow.org and @dh now on Twitter to be kept abreast of current developments and projects in digital history. The resource is a machine–human collaboration meant to surface the best recent digital humanities work, which is itself a leveraging of big data that has only recently become possible.

[32] The annual digital humanities conference is testament to the diversity of the field; the DH 2014 Conference Call for Proposals was translated into more than 20 languages alone. As historians, we acknowledge that "digital history" can be viewed as having a rather

seems centered within universities, dominated by academics in one form or another, the field often traces its unlikely beginnings to the hopes and dreams of a Roman Catholic priest. Writing a history of such a diverse field is difficult — one that draws from so many different origin stories, from corpus linguistics, computer science, English literature, historical studies, archaeology, and so forth — but we anchor our work within the twin fields of digital humanities and quantitative history.

In 1946, Father Roberto Busa had a problem.[33] He had just defended his doctoral dissertation at the Pontifical Gregorian University of Rome, in which he called for a comprehensive concordance of the works of St. Thomas Aquinas. A concordance provides a list of where a given word appears, in its context, everywhere in a given work: for example, if one took the *Old Bailey* sessions above and wanted to see the immediate context in which every incidence of the word "poison" appeared, one would use a concordance. This is relatively simple to do with the computer programs of today — we will discuss one easy way, *AntConc*, in Chapter 3 — but in 1946, it was a tall order. Busa conceived of a series of cards, which would — he estimated — number 13 million in total.[34] It would be his *Index Thomisticus*, a new way to understand the works of St. Thomas Aquinas. Recognizing the tall order, at a 1948 conference in Barcelona, Spain, Busa appealed "[for] any information [fellow scholars could] supply about such mechanical devices as would serve to achieve the greatest possible accuracy, with a maximum economy of human labor."[35]

Busa's subsequent search would bring him to the United States and into contact with International Business Machines Corporation, or IBM. Fortuitously for Busa, IBM had some machine-time to spare. Its long-time president, Thomas J. Watson, met with Busa and, despite staff reservations that what Busa wanted was impossible, he agreed to help. Using mechanical

---

different foundational narrative, emerging out of work in oral and public history (though our own personal trajectories are more from the digital humanities side of things than from those subfields of history). See for instance the post by Stephen Robertson, where he draws out the differences between "digital humanities" and "digital history." http://drstephenrobertson.com/2014/05/23/the-differences-between-digital-history-and-digital-humanities/.

[33] See Susan Hockey (2004), "The History of Humanities Computing," in *A Companion to Digital Humanities*, Susan Schreibman, Ray Siemens and John Unsworth (eds), Oxford: Blackwell, http://www.digitalhumanities.org/companion/view?docId=blackwell/9781405103213/9781405103213.xml&chunk.id=ss1-2-1.

[34] Thomas Nelson Winter (1999), "Roberta Busa, S.J., and the Invention of the Machine-Generated Concordance," *Classical Bulletin*, **75**(1), 6.

[35] *Ibid.*

punchcard readers, Busa set out to produce a concordance. As the cards were limited to 80 characters each, this called for short lines. A test case of St. Thomas Aquinas' poetry was carried out. This 1951 test represented a groundbreaking moment in the development of humanities computing. As recounted by Thomas N. Winter, the mechanical (not computational, yet) construction of a codex would require five steps: the transcription of phrases found in the text; multiplying cards by the number of words on each; breaking words down into entries (lemmas, or the roots of words, so that various forms of the same word would appear as one i.e. "go" and "goes" represent the same concept); selecting and alphabetizing cards; and then publishing the final product in print. Importantly, the final product offered the following outcomes:

1. Words and their frequency, forwards.
2. Words and their frequency, written backwards.
3. Words set out under their lemmata (e.g. *aemulis* under *aemulus aemula aemulum*), with frequency.
4. The Lemmata.
5. Index of the words.
6. Keyword-in-context concordance.

Busa's high standards and unwillingness to compromise with a lesser version meant that the *Index* was many years in the making, but it eventually appeared in printed form in 1974 and online in 2005.[36] Busa had lofty dreams, which became reality. As IBM employee Paul Tasman, assigned to Busa, prophesied in 1957, "[t]he use of the latest data-processing tools developed primarily for science and commerce may provide a significant factor in facilitating future literary and scholarly studies."[37] This is now a reality.

As Susan Hockey recounts in her history of humanities computing, the 1960s saw the rise of scholars interested in the opportunities offered by large-scale concordances. Scholars began with collections of texts and subsequently moved into areas such as authorship attribution and quantitative approaches to literary style; notably, in 1964, statisticians

---

[36] Susan Hockey (2004), "The History of Humanities Computing," in *A Companion to Digital Humanities*, Susan Schreibman, Ray Siemens and John Unsworth (eds), Oxford: Blackwell.

[37] Thomas Nelson Winter (1999), "Roberta Busa, S.J., and the Invention of the Machine-Generated Concordance," *Classical Bulletin*, **75**(1), 6.

Frederick Mosteller and David Wallace used computers to attempt to identify the authors of a dozen disputed *Federalist Papers*; an attempt generally
deemed successful.[38] Conferences and journals emerged, such as the *Computers and the Humanities*, accompanied by the establishment of research
centers.

Historians would seem initially well positioned, by the 1950s and 1960s,
to become involved with large-scale computational inquiries. The *Annales*
school, today an inspiration of literary scholars such as the aforementioned Franco Moretti, aimed to dramatically expand the scope of historical inquiry. In particular, the work of Fernand Braudel is worth briefly
discussing. Braudel, amongst the most instrumental historians of the 20th
century, pioneered a distant approach to history: his inquiries spanned large
expanses of time and space, that of civilizations, the Mediterranean world,
as well as smaller (only by comparison) regional histories of Italy and
France. His approach to history did not necessitate disengagement with
the human actors on the ground, seeing instead that beyond the narrow
focus of individual events lay the constant ebb and flow of poverty and
other endemic structural features.[39] While his methodology does not apply
itself well to rapidly changing societies (his focus was on the long-term slow
change), his points around distant reading and the need for collaborative
interdisciplinary research are a useful antecedent for today's researchers.

Quantitative and computational history was on the rise by the late
1960s. Articles and special issues on the subject littered several contemporary journals, including *The American Historical Review*, *The Journal
of American History*, *The Journal of Contemporary History*, and *History
and Theory*. In 1965, 35 historians attended a three-week seminar on computing in history at the University of Michigan; by 1967, over 800 scholars
were receiving a newsletter aimed at computing for history.[40] Two AHA

---

[38]Susan Hockey (2004), "The History of Humanities Computing," in *A Companion to
Digital Humanities*, Susan Schreibman, Ray Siemens and John Unsworth (eds), Oxford:
Blackwell.

[39]The *longue durée* stands opposite the history of events, of instances, covering instead
a very long time span in an interdisciplinary social science framework. In a long essay,
Braudel noted that one can then see both structural crises of economies, and structures that constrain human society and development. For more, see Fernand Braudel,
"History and the Social Sciences: The Longue Durée" in Fernand Braudel, *On History*,
trans. Sarah Matthews (Chicago: University of Chicago Press, 1980), 27. The essay was
originally printed in the *Annales E.S.C.*, no. 4 (October–December 1958).

[40]Charles M. Dollar (1969), "Innovation in Historical Research: A Computer Approach,"
Computers and the Humanities, **3**(3).

conferences on quantification in history were held in 1967, and many of the earliest issues of *Computers and the Humanities* featured the work of historians.

For historians, however, computational history became associated with demographic, population, and economic histories. For a time in the 1970s, it looked like history might move wholesale into quantitative histories, with the widespread application of math and statistics to the understanding of the past. By 1972, at least half a dozen new journals and magazines were devoted to some aspect of computing and history.[41] Literature scholars pursued textual analysis; historians, to generalize a bit, preferred to count. A book like Michael Katz's *The People of Hamilton, Canada West*, which traced economic mobility over decades using manuscript censuses, was a North American emblem of this form of work. These were fruitful undertakings, providing invaluable context to the more focused social history studies that fleshed out periods under study.[42] A potential downside, however, was that computational history became associated with quantitative studies. This was not aided by some of the hyperbole that saw computational history as making more substantial "truth" claims, or the invocation of a "scientific method" of history.[43] As mainstream historians increasingly questioned this strand of "objectivism," itself a trend dating back to the 1930s, cliometrics became estranged from the mainstream of the profession.[44] This stigma would persist early into the 21st century, even while

---

[41] Joel H. Silbey (1972), "Clio and Computers: Moving into Phase II, 1970–1972," *Computers and the Humanities*, **7**(2).

[42] Michael Katz (1975), *The People of Hamilton, Canada West: Family and Class in a Mid-Nineteenth-Century City*, Cambridge, MA: Harvard University Press. See also A. Gordon Darroch and Michael D. Ornstein (1980), "Ethnicity and Occupational Structure in Canada in 1871: The Vertical Mosaic in Historical Perspective," *Canadian Historical Review*, **61**(3), 305–333.

[43] Computational historians in 1967 were already arguing against the common notion that quantitative history needed to be positivist history. Vern L. Bullough (1967), "The Computer and the Historian–Some Tentative Beginnings," *Computers and the Humanities*, **1**(3).

[44] Witness the debate over Robert William Fogel and Stanley L. Engerman (1974), *Time on the Cross: The Economics of American Negro Slavery*, New York, NY: W.W. Norton and Company, which was condemned for reducing the human condition of slavery to numbers. On the flip side, it also provided context in which to situate individual stories. The debate continues in countless historical methods classes today. For the general estrangement between the historical profession and cliometrics, see Ian Anderson (2008), "History and Computing," *Making History: The Changing Face of the Profession in Britain*, http://www.history.ac.uk/makinghistory/resources/articles/history_and_computing.html, (accessed 20 December 2012).

literary scholars pursued increasingly sophisticated forms of textual analysis, social networking, and online exploratory portals. This 1960s and 1970s explosion of digital work represented the first "wave" of computational history.

Yet, in part due to hubris, debates over seminal works such as *Time on the Cross*, and a more general move towards social history within some elements of the historical profession, computational history retreated in the 1970s. The first wave had come to an end. Yet it would re-emerge in the 1990s with the advent of personal computing, easy-to-use graphical user interfaces, and improvements in overall accessibility. This represented a second "wave" of computational history. Painstaking punchcards and opaque input syntax gave way to relatively easy to use databases, GIS, and even early online networks such as H-Net and USENET. Early conferences, like Hypertext and the Future of the Humanities, held at Yale in 1994, included some of the founders of modern digital history.[45] The *Journal of the Association for History and Computing* (*JAHC*) was published between 1998 and 2010, growing out of annual meetings of the American Association for History and Computing, itself founded in Cincinnati in January 1996. Seeing digital methods as transforming *both* the creation and dissemination of history, *JAHC* published forward-thinking articles on hypertext, digital teaching methods, barriers to adoption, and new means of representing the past (whether through sound, graphics, maps, or the Web). The back issues represent a snapshot of the cutting-edge work going on.[46] Crunching away at census manuscripts, or attempting to identify authorship, or counting words, the broad interdisciplinary scholarly field known as humanities computing emerged, bringing together historians, philosophers, literary scholars, and others under a broad computational tent.[47]

One could spend pages defining humanities computing, and its eventual successor the digital humanities. Indeed, several other authors have. In a provocative essay, "What is Humanities Computing and What it is Not," John Unsworth defined the field as "a practice of representation, a form of modeling or [...] mimicry. It is [...] a way of reasoning and a set of ontological commitments, and its representational practice is shaped

---

[45] Attendees included Gregory Crane and Roy Rosenzweig. Program at http://www.cis.yale.edu/htxt-conf/.
[46] Available at http://quod.lib.umich.edu/j/jahc/browse.html.
[47] Willard McCarty (2005), *Humanities Computing*, Basingstoke, England; New York, NY: Palgrave Macmillan.

by the need for efficient computation on the one hand, and for human communication on the other."[48] Simply using word processors, email, or communicating by list-servs did not a humanities computationist make. To be "DH," required a new method of thinking. The shift towards the digital humanities was not simply a shift in nomenclature, although there are elements of that as well. Patrik Svensson has traced the shift from humanities computing to the digital humanities, showing how the nomenclature change staked a new definition that was even more inclusive, and broad: inclusive of questions of design, the born-digital, new media studies, and more emphasis on tools with less emphasis on more straightforward methodological discussions.[49]

As recounted in Matthew Kirschenbaum's take on the history of the digital humanities, the term also places a different emphasis on different parts of the phrase. As the National Endowment for the Humanities Chief Information Officer put it to him, he "appreciated the fact that it seemed to cast a wider net than 'humanities computing' which seemed to imply a form of computing, whereas 'digital humanities' implied a form of human-ism."[50]

This expanded definition seemed to extend to digital history as well. As previously discussed, digital history has an uneasy relationship to digital humanities; some see the former as a subset of the latter, while others see them as overlapping but not hierarchically connected communities. Digital history, for one, sits closer to the public humanities than many of its counterparts. The group is also much less well represented at digital humanities conferences than those coming from literature and modern language backgrounds,[51] leading some recent popular accounts of the digital humanities to ignore digital history entirely.[52] Conversely, digital historians often do not trace their roots back to Father Busa. We do not plan on resolving those

---

[48] John Unsworth (November 8, 2002), "Unsworth: What Is Humanities Computing and What Is Not?," http://computerphilologie.uni-muenchen.de/jg02/unsworth.html.

[49] Patrik Svensson (2009), "Humanities Computing as Digital Humanities," *Digital Humanities Quarterly* **3**(3), http://www.digitalhumanities.org/dhq/vol/3/3/000065/000065.html.

[50] Matthew G. Kirschenbaum (2010), "What Is Digital Humanities and What's It Doing in English Departments?," *ADE Bulletin*, no. 150, 55–61.

[51] See Weingart's blog series on digital humanities conferences, http://www.scottbot.net/HIAL/?tag=dhconf.

[52] Stephen Richardson (23 May 2014), "The Differences between Digital History and Digital Humanities," *drstephenrobertsom.com*, http://drstephenrobertson.com/blog-post/the-differences-between-digital-history-and-digital-humanities/.

differences here, but instead will draw from every corner of the big tent of digital humanities in order to facilitate training new digital historians.

In short, the term "digital humanities" is difficult to define. A fun way to open a digital humanities or history course is to visit Jason Heppler's succinctly-named website, "What is Digital Humanities?"[53] Participants in the annual Day of DH, which began with the University of Alberta but now rotates between universities every two years based on an open call for proposals, are annually asked to provide their own definitions. Between 2009 and 2012, Heppler has compiled 511 entries, all made available in raw data format. A visitor to his website can refresh it for a new definition: ranging from the short and whimsical ("[a]s a social construct," "[t]aking people to bits"), to the long and comprehensive ("Digital Humanities is the critical study of how the technologies and techniques associated with the digital medium intersect with and alter humanities scholarship and scholarly communication") to more specific definitions focused on making or digital preservation. Amongst such crowded and thoughtful conversation, we hesitate to add our own definition. A definition, however, is in order for the purposes of this book. We believe that the digital humanities are partly about understanding what digital tools have to offer, but also — and perhaps more importantly — about understanding what the digital understanding what the digital does and has done to our understanding of the past and ourselves. In this book, with this in mind, we peel back the layers of a particular approach to big data using specific tools such as topic modeling and network analysis. Yet we realize that they need to be critically studied, as they have come from divergent disciplines and domains. With an understanding of how the digital humanities have evolved, from Father Busa through to humanities computing, we seek to explore the implications of a new era: the challenge and opportunity of big data.

Why this All Matters Now: The Third Wave of Computational History

We have entered an era of big data. Big data emerges from the context of constant, always-on, notificated, checked-ins, National Security Agency (NSA)-metadata-gleaned, pervasive computing world. Even our

---

[53] Jason Heppler (2013), "What Is Digital Humanities?," http://whatisdigitalhumanities. com/.

thermostats, as we write this on a chilly January morning, are watching what we do to generate insights from our big data lives.[54] This makes decisive movement towards digital methods, over the next ten or 20 years, imperative for the profession. As IBM noted in 2012, "90% of the data in the world today has been created in the last two years alone."[55] Yet while big data is often explicitly framed as a problem for the future, it has already presented fruitful opportunities for the past. The most obvious place where this is true is archived copies of the publicly accessible Internet. The advent of the World Wide Web in 1991 has had revolutionary effects on human communication and organization, and its archiving presents a tremendous body of non-commercialized public speech. There is a *lot* of it, however, and large methodologies will be needed to explore it. It is this problem that we believe makes the adoption of digital methodologies for history especially important.

As we saw above, historians have been through these questions before. In the 1960s, large censuses met punchcard computing to result in significant scholarly contributions that continue to contextualize more focused studies today. Now, as the digital humanities flourish, we can see the current historical interest in them as owing its roots to that initial flurry of interest. Putting this into historical context, if the first wave of computational history emerged out of humanities computing, and the second wave developed around textual analysis (and H-Net, Usenet, and GIS), we believe that we are now on the cusp of a third revolution in computational history. There are three main factors that make this instrumental: decreasing storage costs, with particular implication for historians; the power of the Internet and cloud computing; and the rise of open source tools.[56] We are asking similar questions, in many cases, to the 1960s pioneers: just with more powerful and even more accessible tools (for all the frustrations that the tools discussed in this book can occasionally produce, they luckily are not punchcard based).

Significant technological advances in how much information can be stored herald a new era of historical research and computing that we need

---

[54] A great overview of big data can be found in Viktor Mayer-Schönberger and Kenneth Cukier (2013), *Big Data: A Revolution that Will Transform How We Live, Work, and Think*, Boston, MA: Eamon Dolan Book.

[55] See, for example, http://www-01.ibm.com/software/data/bigdata/.

[56] Presaged in the aforementioned Roy Rosenzweig (2003), "Scarcity or Abundance? Preserving the Past in a Digital Era," *American Historical Review*, **108**(3), 735–762, available online at http://chnm.gmu.edu/digitalhistory/links/pdf/introduction/0.6b.pdf.

to prepare for *now*. Historical methods need to develop in order to keep up with where our profession might go in the next ten or 20 years. In short, we can retain more of the information produced every day, and the ability to retain information has been keeping up with the growing amount of generated data. As author James Gleick argued:

> The information produced and consumed by humankind used to vanish — that was the norm, the default. The sights, the sounds, the songs, the spoken word just melted away. Marks on stone, parchment, and paper were the special case. It did not occur to Sophocles' audiences that it would be sad for his plays to be lost; they enjoyed the show. Now expectations have inverted. Everything may be recorded and preserved, at least potentially.[57]

This has been made possible by the corollary to Moore's Law (which held that the number of transistors on a microchip would double every two years), Kryder's Law.[58] He argues, based on past practice, that storage density will double approximately every 11 months. While this law may be more descriptive than predictive, the fact remains that storage has been getting cheaper over the last ten years and has enabled the storage and, hopefully, the long-term digital preservation of invaluable historical resources.

We store more than we ever did before, and increasingly have an eye on this digital material to make sure that future generations will be able to fruitfully explore it. The creation or generation of data and information do not, obviously, in and of themselves guarantee that they will be kept — for that we have the field of digital preservation. In 2011, humanity created 1.8 zettabytes of information. This is not an outlier: from 2006 until 2011, the amount of data expanded by a factor of nine.[59]

These data take a variety of forms, some accessible and some inaccessible to historians. In the latter camp, we have walled gardens and proprietary networks such as Facebook, corporate databases, server logs, security data, and so forth. Save a leak or forward-thinking individuals, historians may never be able to access those data. Yet in the former camp, even if smaller than the latter one, we have a lot of information: YouTube (seeing 72 hours of video uploaded every single minute); the hundreds of millions

---

[57] James Gleick (2011), *The Information: A History, A Theory, A Flood*, New York: Pantheon.

[58] Chip Walter (25 July 2005), "Kryder's Law," *Scientific American*, http://www.scientificamerican.com/article.cfm?id=kryders-law.

[59] John Gantz and David Reinsel (June 2011), "Extracting Value from Chaos," IDC iView, http://www.emc.com/collateral/analyst-reports/idc-extracting-value-from-chaos-ar.pdf.

of tweets sent every day over Twitter; the blogs, ruminations, comments, and thoughts that make up the publicly-facing and potentially archivable World Wide Web.[60] Beyond the potentialities of the future, however, we are already in an era of archives that dwarf previously conceivable troves of material. While this book is not about accessing these archives in particular, it does concern itself with the methods necessary to access these sorts of datasets. Historians need to begin to think computationally *now*, so that our profession is ready to access these data in the next generation.

The shift towards widespread digital storage, preserving information longer and conceivably storing the records of everyday people on an ever more frequent basis, represents a challenge to accepted standards of inquiry, ethics, and the role of archivists. How should historians respond to the transitory nature of historical sources, be it the hastily deleted personal blogs held by MySpace, the destroyed websites of GeoCities? How can we even use large repositories such as the over two million messages sent over USENET in the 1980s alone? Do we have ethical responsibilities to website creators who may have had an expectation of privacy, or in the last had no sense that they were formally publishing their webpage in 1996? These are all questions that we, as professionals, need to tackle. They are, in a word, disruptive.

It is important to pause briefly, however, and situate this claim of a revolutionary shift due to ever-bigger datasets into its own historic context. Humanists have long grappled with medium shifts and earlier iterations of this big data moment, which we can perhaps stretch back to the objections of Socrates to the written word itself.[61] As the printing press and bound books replaced earlier forms of scribed scholarly transmission, a similar medium shift threatened existing standards of communication. Martin Luther, the German priest and pivotal figure in the Protestant Reformation, argued that "the multitude of books [were] a great evil;" this 16th century sentiment was echoed as well by Edgar Allen Poe in the 19th century and Lewis Mumford as recently as 1970.[62] Bigger is certainly not better, at least not inherently, but it should equally not be dismissed out of hand.

---

[60]Twitter (November 2012), "Total Tweets Per Minute | Twitter Developers," Twitter.com, https://dev.twitter.com/discussions/3914; YouTube (May, 29, 2013), "Statistics – YouTube," YouTube, http://www.youtube.com/yt/press/statistics.html.

[61]See the *Phaedrus* dialogue by Plato, available in English translation at http://classics.mit.edu/Plato/phaedrus.html.

[62]James Gleick (2012), *The Information: A History, A Theory, A Flood*, New York: Pantheon.

Accessing the Third Wave Today

This big data, however, is only as useful as the tools that we have to interpret it. Luckily, two interrelated trends make interpretation possible: more powerful personal computers, and, accessible open source software to make sense of all these data. Prices continue to fall, and computers continue to get more powerful: significantly for research involving large datasets, the amount of Random Access Memory, or RAM, that computers have continues to increase. Information loaded into RAM can be manipulated and analyzed very quickly. Even humanities researchers with limited research budgets can now use computers that would have been prohibitively expensive only a few years ago.

It is, however, the ethos and successes of the open source movement that have given digital historians and the broader field of the digital humanities wind in their sails. Open source software is a transformative concept that moves beyond simply "free" software: an open source license means that the code that drives the software is freely accessible, and users are welcome to delve through it, make changes, and distribute the original or their altered version as they see fit. Notable open source projects include the Mozilla Firefox browser, the Linux operating system, the Zotero reference-management software system developed by George Mason University's Centre for History and New Media (CHNM), the WordPress and Drupal website Content Management System (CMS) platforms, and the freely-accessible OpenOffice productivity suite.

For humanists, then, carrying out large-scale data analysis no longer requires a generous salary or expense account. Increasingly, it does not even require potentially expensive training. Take, by way of preface, the *Programming Historian*, an open source textbook dedicated to introducing computational methods to humanities researchers. It is a useful introduction, as well, to the potential offered by these programs, which include several that we saw in our preface:

- **Python**: An open source programming language, freely downloadable, that allows you to do very powerful textual analysis and manipulation. It can help download files, turn text into easily-digestible pieces, and then provide some basic visualizations.
- **Komodo Edit**: An open source editing environment, allowing you to write your own code, edit it, and quickly pinpoint where errors might have crept in.

- **Wget**: A program, run on the command line, that lets you download entire repositories of information. Instead of right-clicking on link after link, wget can quickly download an entire directory or website to your own computer.
- **MALLET**: The MAchine Learning for LanguagE Toolkit provides an entire package of open source tools — notably topic modeling, which takes large quantities of information and finds the 'topics' that appear in them.

These four tools are just the tip of the iceberg and represent a significant change. Free tools, with open source documentation written for and by humanists, allow us to unlock the potential inherent in big data.

Big data represents a key component of this third wave of computational history. By this point, you should have an understanding of what we mean by big data and some of the technical opportunities we have to explore it. The question remains, however: what can this do for humanities researchers? What challenges and opportunities does it present, beyond the short examples provided at the beginning of the chapter?

The Limits of Big Data, or Big Data and the Practice of History

A quick proviso is in order here. Will big data have a revolutionary impact on the epistemological foundation of history? As historians work with ever-increasing arrays of information, we need to consider the intersection of this trend with broader discussions around the nature of history and the past itself. At first glance, larger amounts of data would seem to offer the potential of empirical advances in 'knowing' history: the utopian promises of a record of all digital communications (turned into a dystopian reality by the NSA, unfortunately), for example, or the ability to process the entirety of a national census over several years. In some ways, it is evocative of the modernist excitement around "scientific" history.[63] Big data has substantial implications for historians, as we again move from studies based on positive examples to the findings of overall trends from extensive computational databases. This is similar to debates from the 1970s and 1980s,

---

[63] Robert William Fogel (1983), "'Scientific History' and Traditional History," in Robert William Fogel and G.R. Elton (eds), *Which Road to the Past? Two Views of History*, New Haven, NJ and London: Yale University Press.

where quantitative historians faced criticisms around the reproducibility of their results that were derived from early computer databases and often presented only in tables. Yet we believe that, for all the importance of big data, it does not offer any change to the fundamental questions of historical knowing facing historians.

For all the excitement around the potential offered by digital methods, it is important to keep in mind that it does not herald a transformation in the epistemological foundation of history. We are still working with traces of the past. The past did happen, of course. Events happened during the time before now: lives lived, political dynasties rose and fell, working people made do with the limited resources that they had before them. Most of the data about these experiences and events, however, have disappeared: the digital revolution may make it possible to consider more than before, perhaps even on an order of magnitude.[64] Yet even with terabytes upon terabytes of archival documents, we are still only seeing traces of the past today. While there is a larger debate to be had about the degree of historical knowing possible, we believe that, amidst the excitement of big data, this is a point that needs to be considered.

History, then, as a professional practice, involves the crafting of this available information and transforming it into scholarly narratives.[65] Even with massive arrays of data, historians do not simply cut and paste findings from computer databases; such an approach would be evocative of the "scissors and paste" model noted by historian R.G. Collingwood.[66] Having more data is not a bad thing. With more data, in practical terms, there is arguably a higher likelihood that historical narratives will be closer in accordance with past events, as we have more traces to base them on. But this is not a certainty. History is not merely a reconstructive exercise, but also a practice of narrative writing and creation.[67]

---

[64] See, for a brief introduction, Keith Jenkins (1991), *Rethinking History*, London: Routledge and Alun Munslow (2010), *The Future of History*, New York, NY: Palgrave Macmillan.

[65] In the years ahead, it is possible the digital turn will render the word "narrative" too confining for describing what historians produce. We continue to use the word in this book, however projects like *SCALAR* and *ORBIS* (available at http://scalar.usc.edu/ and http://orbis.stanford.edu/respectively) are making the term increasingly inaccurate. A more encompassing term may be "historiographies."

[66] R.G. Collingwood (1965), *The Idea of History*, London: Oxford University Press.

[67] A point made by a good number of historians, but see Keith Jenkins (1991), *Rethinking History*, London: Routledge and Alun Munslow (2010), *The Future of History*, New York, NY: Palgrave Macmillan for concise introductions to this line of reasoning.

Throughout the methodological chapters that follow, the "subjective" appears throughout: decisions about how many topics to search for as we generate a topic model, for example; what words to exclude from computations; what words to look for; what categories of analysis to assume. Underlying this too are fundamental assumptions made by computational linguists, such as the statistical models employed or even premises around the nature of language itself.[68] At a more obvious and apparent level, much of what we do also involves transforming data, or altering these traces of the past into new and in many cases — for the purpose of our narrative construction — more fruitful forms. Many of the techniques discussed in this book involve text, yet many sources are more than just texts: they have images, texture, smell, or are located in specific areas. Even if attuned to issues of historical context, these can and often will be lost.

On a philosophical level, however, the digital transformation of sources does not represent a significant challenge to historical practices. Historians are always changing their sources and are always engaged in choices and decisions. What notes to take? What digital photograph to snap? Who to interview? What sources will lead to a better publication? What will my dean/manager/partner think? What will help build my career? To this litany of issues, digital techniques add new questions that we will discuss in this book: how to break up texts (should you separate "tokens" on word breaks, punctuation, or so forth, as discussed in Chapter 2), what topic modeling algorithm to use, or whether to ignore non-textual information, or is a network a useful visualization of the results, or not.

If we do not believe that big data is here to correct what other historians are doing in their subdisciplines, however, this also means that we do not believe that the issues briefly outlined above are fundamental shortcomings in our methodologies. Yes, mediums will be transformed, decisions will be made, but this is within the historical tradition. Digital history does not offer direct truths, but only new ways of interpreting and understanding traces of the past. More traces, yes, but still traces: brief shadows of things that were.

But to what end? Trevor Owens draws attention to the purpose behind one's use of computational power — generative discovery versus justification

---

[68] A point discussed at the Stanford Digital Humanities Reading Group, as recounted by Mike Widner, "Debating the Methods in Matt Jockers's Macroanalysis," *Stanford Digital Humanities Blog*, https://digitalhumanities.stanford.edu/debating-methods-matt-jockerss-macroanalysis, accessed 6 September 2013.

of an hypothesis. For Owens, if we are using computational power to deform our texts, we are trying to see things in a new light, new juxtapositions, to spark new insight.[69] Ramsay talks about this too in *Reading Machines*, discussing the work of Jerome McGann and Lisa Samuels. "Reading a poem backward is like viewing the face of a watch sideways — a way of unleashing the potentialities that altered perspectives may reveal."[70] Owen's purpose in highlighting "justification" against "discovery" though is not to condemn one approach over another, but rather to draw attention to the fact that:

> When we separate out the context of discovery and exploration from the context of justification we end up clarifying the terms of our conversation. There is a huge difference between "here is an interesting way of thinking about this" and "This evidence supports this claim."[71]

This then is the nub of big data for digital history. Archaeologists have used computers for decades to try to justify or otherwise span the gap between our data and the stories we would like to tell. A digital archaeology that sat within the digital humanities would worry less about that and concentrate more on discovery and generation of "interesting way[s] of thinking about this." So too with digital history. Digital approaches to the past that sit within the digital humanities use our computational power to force us to look at the materials differently, to think about them playfully, and to explore what these sometimes jarring deformations could mean.

Conclusion

This chapter has provided a basic introduction to the joys and pitfalls of abundance in this new era of big data. Certainly, the authors of this book are all hopeful about the potential of digital history and big datasets. This potentially has already been fruitfully realized in several successful projects: from the criminal trials of the *Old Bailey Online*, the Roman travel patterns of *ORBIS*, or the global commodities of the *Trading Consequences* project. We, however, do believe that this all needs to be both contextualized in

---

[69]Trevor Owens (February 3, 2012), "Deforming Reality with Word Lens," *Trevor Owens*, http://www.trevorowens.org/2012/02/deforming-reality-with-word-lens/.

[70]Stephen Ramsay (2011), *Reading Machines: Toward an Algorithmic Criticism*, Urbana, IL: University of Illinois Press, p. 33.

[71]Trevor Owens (February 3, 2012), "Deforming Reality with Word Lens," *Trevor Owens*, http://www.trevorowens.org/2012/02/deforming-reality-with-word-lens/.

terms of the field's historical development, and nuanced with respect to the knowledge claims that can be made.

As the next chapter notes, we believe that we are in a transitory moment within both the historical field and the digital humanities more broadly: the "DH" moment is upon us. Considered engagement with this field, however, requires an understanding of where we have come from and where we are at this present moment in time. Much of what you will encounter and read over the next five chapters will seem new, just as the methods pioneered by Father Busa in the wake of the Second World War were novel. We are straddling a line between revolution and continuity; resolving this tension is going to be a central part of historians' tasks over the coming years. In the chapters that follow, we draw on elements of both perspectives, fully understanding that this book itself is as much a historical artefact of this particular moment as are the tools themselves that we study.

The point of this chapter, however, is to stress that, for all the novelty, there are still points of continuity. Debates over historical knowing have continued into the digital era, but still remain much as they have been over the last hundreds of years: digital history is no more objective, nor no more subjective, than what has come before. The fundamental questions remain the same around humanistic inquiry. What can we know of the past? What voices can we try to remediate from the past? How can we use historical knowledge in the present day, from informing policy decisions, to inspiring marginalized communities, or simply telling entertaining stories?

Digital history has come a long way since Father Busa searched for a technological solution for a concordance of the works of St. Thomas Aquinas. As the next chapter shows, a new moment is upon us and a familiarity with macroscopic knowledge is becoming ever-important. As our world is profoundly reshaped by the digital revolution, as historians increasingly engage with digitized sources, and as we begin to reflect on how to study the 1990s, Busa's questions become even more pressing.

Chapter 2

The DH Moment

In this chapter, we examine how we are all digital now, and we introduce several key digital history and humanities terms and ideas. With inspiration from Stephen King, we build the historian's digital toolkit, exploring basic scraping and data operations, and explain why you might wish to become a "programming historian." We begin by laying out some of the foundational issues that we must grapple with before we can begin scraping and manipulating the data we find: issues of copyright, ethics, and how digital resources affect our work as historians.

What is the digital humanities, or DH, moment? In short, it is the necessity for historians and other humanities scholars to begin to grapple and engage with the implications of the widespread accessibility of digital information. As Hal Abelson, Ken Ledeen, and Harry Lewis have provocatively argued, our world has been *Blown to Bits*.[1] They argue that we need to rethink nearly countless social aspects: what bits mean and represent (from perfect copies through to the philosophical issues around transmitting binary code into various representations of image, voice, and text), privacy, the differences between analog and digital documents, search engines, encryption, speech, and even whether old metaphors can still hold true. While it all seems sudden, scholars have been grappling with these issues for decades. The sheer acceleration of the retention of digital information and the growing capability to deal with it thanks to more powerful computers, cheaper storage, and open source software, all combine to help make this the DH moment. The third computational wave, discussed in the last chapter, just got supercharged.

---

[1] Hal Abelson, Ken Ledeen and Harry Lewis (2008), *Blown to Bits: Your Life, Liberty, and Happiness after the Digital Explosion*, Boston, MA: Pearson, http://www.bitsbook. com/wp-content/uploads/2008/12/B2B_3.pdf

The DH moment is upon us, but how can you seize it? We deliberately do not unpack DH into either "digital history" or "digital humanities" in the chapter's title as we believe it is applicable, in varying degrees, to both fields. In the previous chapter, we laid out and established the "big picture" of big digital history, and we now turn to a general discussion of what this moment can specifically offer you as a researcher or student in this field. To do so, we use the metaphor of a "toolkit": the various pieces of software and knowledge of algorithms that you can carry from one "job" to the next.[2] There is no one-size-fits-all approach to any research question, of course, and the humanist needs to know what tool might fit best, what kind of results they are curious to uncover, and what specific cautionary notes they need to have first-and-foremost in their minds.

In this chapter, we will give you the foundational knowledge of key terms, concepts, and issues for subsequent development in the four increasingly applied chapters that follow. Beginning with the basic terms that we feel define this wave of computational history (open source, copyright, and textual analysis), we then continue to discuss why we think that we are *already* all digital scholars. As Google searches, primary source databases, and digitized primary sources become increasingly common, we believe that scholars need to be more self-reflective in their use of these everyday tools. Finally, we conclude with some reflections around the unplumbed depths that await humanities scholars.

Intro to Several Key Digital History Terms

There are three issues of critical importance to understanding big data as a historian: the open access and open source movements, copyright, and what we mean by textual analysis. As discussed in the previous chapter, open source software lies at the heart of the third computational wave of history. Issues of copyright loom large for historians working on 20th century topics. When accumulating large troves of data, researchers will almost certainly bump against these questions. Finally, textual analysis and basic visualizations provide the heart of the lessons provided in this book. Yet, as we argue, odds are that you are already using textual analysis. You may

---

[2] We are not the first to use such a metaphor, of course. Elaine G. Toms and Heather L. Obrien (2008), "Understanding the Information and Communication Technology Needs of the E-Humanist," *Journal of Documentation*, **64**(1), 102–130 use the similar metaphor of the "e-humanist's workbench."

just not be completely cognizant of it yet. While these are not completely comprehensive or exhaustive terms — as we noted in our introduction, GIS is another area of research — we believe that these three areas help move you towards a broader understanding of the field.

Many, although not all, of the tools discussed in this book are free software, or of the closely related yet distinct **open source** philosophy.[3] While free software has been around since the 1980s, epitomized by movements such as GNU (a free operating system with a name stemming from "GNU's Not Unix", complete with manifesto in 1985), 1998 saw it rise to the level of a movement.[4] Christopher Kelty's *Two Bits* carries out an indispensable anthropological and historical study of the movement, tracing its origins to the 1998 decision of Netscape to freely distribute the source code of its Netscape Communicator software (which would lead to today's Mozilla Firefox browser).[5] Netscape had been charging for its full-suite product, as opposed to Microsoft's bundled browser, and the decision to release the source code was a path-breaking one.[6] Defining open source can be tricky, as there are competing interests, but essentially to speak of "open source software" means adhering to the definition laid out by the "Open Source Definition."[7] In short, open source software requires free redistribution, the source code, allowing derived works (modifications to the program), keeping the integrity of the authors' source code, no discrimination, and general licenses with a few other restrictions.

Open source software has tremendous, mostly positive, implications for digital historians, but there are some cautionary notes to make as well. The programs discussed in this book can largely be used for free, with a few exceptions for full features in a handful of programs. This has obvious benefits in an era of diminishing government budgets and austerity. More

---

[3]The differences largely have to do with philosophy; free software has a much more significant political point, as opposed to the license-focused open source approach. For more on what these differences may imply in your own research, see Richard Stallman, "Why Open Source misses the point of Free Software," https://www.gnu.org/ philosophy/open-source-misses-the-point.html.

[4]Richard Stallman (1985, revisions 1993), "The GNU Manifesto," http://www.gnu.org/gnu/manifesto.html, accessed 29 July 2013.

[5]Christopher M. Kelty (2008), *Two Bits: The Cultural Significance of Free Software*, Durham, NC: Duke University Press, pp. 99–100.

[6]The processes leading to this are discussed in Christopher M. Kelty (2008), *Two Bits: The Cultural Significance of Free Software*, Durham, NC: Duke University Press, p. 108.

[7]See "The Open Source Definition," *OpenSource.Org*, http://opensource.org/osd, accessed 29 July 2013.

importantly, the open nature of them means that they are often modular and can be continually improved: one scholar may note an issue with a certain algorithm and suggest or implement a suggestion herself. This lends itself well to experimentation. For publicly-supported scholars, whether by virtue of being in a public university or from a granting council, it also allows scholars to give something back to a community of practice or even the general public.

This ethos also informs other aspects of digital history. Digital history largely, but not completely, grew out of public history. Websites and portals are created that allow the public to interact with and engage with the past, and other scholars are beginning to call for the open source ethos to be applied to more scholarly practices: witness the rise of open access publishing. While open access may take an author-pays model (where the author pays the associated charges for his or her article) or be provided on a free or supported basis, it tries to take the ethos of free access to the public. This book, for example, was inspired by this ethos in our decision to live write it using the *CommentPress* platform — itself an open access WordPress theme and plugin.[8]

As with many movements, there is a darker side to some of this. Author pay models can discriminate against junior scholars, those at non-research-intensive universities, and graduate students who may not have funds to support their research. Similarly, releasing free software is advantageous in many ways and perhaps even morally right for tenure- and tenure-track faculty members who have generous salaries; it may be more of an imposition to ask of untenured and contingent researchers who have monetary need. Furthermore, the demands on researcher time are substantial. Scholars may not have the necessary "start-up" funds to get into this world, and to this we add that they may not have the requisite "start-up" *time* either. The learning curve can be steep, and above all, digital tools and rhetoric require an investment in time. These are all questions that digital historians, alongside the more specific research considerations discussed in this book, will have to consider.

An essential addition to a digital historian's toolkit is an understanding of the issues surrounding **copyright**. This book does not purport to be a comprehensive guide to copyright law in your jurisdiction: it varies dramatically from country to country and we are not lawyers. As historians,

---

[8] "Welcome to CommentPress," *FutureoftheBook.org*, http://www.futureofthebook.org/commentpress/, accessed 29 July 2013.

however, we want to provide context to the copyright wars and provide a call for our readers to pay considerable attention to this pressing issue. We do so by using the more focused example of Google Books and the ensuing legal imbroglio.

Google emerged from the search engine battles of the early 2000s as the victor, controlling a dominant share of the user base for those who wanted to find information on the World Wide Web. Ironically, Tim Wu has suggested that copyright infringement may have been key to their success: its search index, first created in 1996, required a comprehensive copy of the World Wide Web. While it was an unsettled legal question at the time, nobody filed suit so under legal norms this sort of mass copying for indexing is probably okay.[9] In any case, Google would not be out of the copyright weeds as they moved forward with their search empire.

Following their dominance of the World Wide Web search engine market, Google then decided to turn their attention to another large repository of knowledge: books. As early as late 2003, Google was approaching university librarians, beginning to scan the first chapters of books, and began to quietly thread search results into the queries of users under the moniker *Google Print*. A year later, in December 2004, Google announced that they would enter into a partnership to digitize books held by Harvard University, Oxford University, the University of Michigan, Stanford University, and the New York Public Library.[10] *Google Print*, as it was called, would achieve several objectives: they would democratize knowledge locked away in often-inaccessible elite institutions, they would facilitate keyword searching throughout books as one could throughout the World Wide Web, and Google would also gain users who could then be exposed to their advertisements. Institutions joined by varying degrees: Michigan wanted their entire 7.4 million volume collection digitized, the NYPL digitized only out-of-copyright materials, and Harvard went forward with a 40,000 book trial. Books under copyright would only be available via a "snippet search."[11]

This was a controversial project. France's National Library raised concerns that this would give "prominence to Anglophone texts above those written in other languages," due to the Anglophilic nature of the five

[9]Tim Wu (2010), *The Master Switch: The Rise and Fall of Information Empires*, New York, NY: Knopf, p. 287.
[10]David Vise (14 December 2004), "Google to Digitize Some Library Collections; Harvard, Stanford, New York Public Library Among Project Participants," *Washington Post*, E05. Accessed via Lexis|Nexis. See also http://www.bio-diglib.com/content/2/1/2.
[11]Ibid.

institutions.[12] More importantly, many authors and publishers became agitated. Questions were asked by worried organizations, such as the Association of American University Presses: how long and frequent were the snippets of copyrighted books, and would this have an effect on sales?[13] As industry groups raised their voices in protest, including the large and powerful American Association of Publishers, Google suspended its project in August 2005, announcing a pause until at least November.[14] The debate, playing out across the World Wide Web and in leading news organizations, was a fascinating one: the rights of authors and publishers, who produced knowledge; but also the desires of readers, who wanted a quick and easy way to find relevant information. Google's idea was to slow things down so publishers could opt out of the system, whereas the publishers wanted an opt-in system.

The lawsuit came quickly. On 20 September 2005, three representative authors filed suit in Manhattan's United States District Court on behalf of their peers and alleged "massive copyright infringement."[15] Google claimed "fair use," while the authors claimed that their copyright-protected work was being used for commercial purposes by the search engine giant. A month later, McGraw-Hill, Pearson Education, Penguin Group, Simon & Schuster and John Wiley & Sons filed a joint lawsuit. Google then resumed its digitization process.[16] In October 2008, a sweeping settlement was reached that would facilitate the digitization of out-of-print books, purchase options, and crucially, allow up to 20% of a book to be displayed as a free snippet and to let universities subscribe to a service to view them all.[17] Authors' groups not part of the lawsuit, as well as individual authors, raised significant objections to this settlement. The settlement was subject to court review and, in February 2011, Judge Chin threw it out.[18]

---

[12]Stephen Castle (6 May 2005), "Google Book Project Angers France," *The Independent (London)*, p. 33. Accessed via Lexis|Nexis.

[13]Edward Wyatt (25 May 2005), "Challenging Google," *New York Times*, E2. Accessed via Lexis|Nexis.

[14]Yuki Noguchi (13 August 2005), "Google Delays Book Scanning; Copyright Concerns Slow Project," *Washington Post*, D01.

[15]Edward Wyatt (25 May 2005), "Challenging Google," *New York Times*, E2. Accessed via Lexis|Nexis.

[16]Edward Wyatt (20 October 2005), "Publishers Sue Google over Scanning," *New York Times*, Finance 13.

[17]Miguel Helft and Motko Rich (30 October 2008), "Google Settles Suit over Putting Books Online," *New York Times*, Finance 20.

[18]See http://www.nysd.uscourts.gov/cases/show.php?db=special&id=115.

If Google was a commercial enterprise, universities saw value in digitizing books: they could be preserved longer, the search index was useful, and scholars could derive significant big data benefits from having all this knowledge together into one place. With these intentions in mind, a group of universities (12 in the American Midwest, plus the University of California system) announced in late 2008 that they would take volumes previously digitized by Google, as well as some of their own, and pool them into a collective trust: HathiTrust. It was an apt name, as the *New York Times* put it: "Hathi is Hindi for 'elephant,' an animal that is said to never forget."[19] They had lofty goals: "The partners aim to build a comprehensive archive of published literature from around the world and develop shared strategies for managing and developing their digital and print holdings in a collaborative way." A similar lawsuit was forthcoming a few years later when the Authors Guild and other groups and individual authors launched a case over "unauthorized" scans. Instead of damages, however, they simply asked "that the books be taken off the HathiTrust servers and held by a trustee."[20]

With the basic contours of the Google Print/Books and HathiTrust cases established, we should pause to discuss what this means for historians engaging in big data-related research. While media coverage understandably focused on the competing rights of authors and Google, these cases also lie at the heart of the ability of historians and others being able to conduct truly transformative, paradigm-shifting big data research. This argument was developed in an *amicus curiae* ("friend of the court") filing made by digital humanities and legal scholars, written by the aforementioned author of *Macroanalysis*, Matthew Jockers, and two law professors, Matthew Sag and Jason Schultz. As they noted, the "court's ruling in this case on the legality of mass digitization could dramatically affect the future of work in the Digital Humanities."[21]

---

[19] For more information on HathiTrust itself, see http://www.hathitrust.org/partnership. The *New York Times* article is found at http://bits.blogs.nytimes.com/2008/10/13/an-elephant-backs-up-googles-library/?_r=0. See also the overview at Heather Christenson (2011), "HathiTrust," *Library Resources & Technical Services*, **55**(2), 93–102.

[20] Julie Bosman (13 September 2011), "Lawsuit Seeks the Removal of a Digital Book Collection," *New York Times*, B7.

[21] See Matthew L. Jockers, Matthew Sag and Jason Schultz (3 August 2012), "Brief of Digital Humanities and Law Scholars as Amici Curiae in Authors Guild v. Google," *Social Science Research Network*, http://papers.ssrn.com/sol3/papers.cfm?abstract_id=2102542, accessed 26 July 2013.

Their highly-readable argument is essential reading for digital historians wondering about the future state of large-scale textual analysis as discussed in this book. After recounting several successful projects, such as the previously discussed culturomics and the findings of *Macroanalysis*, the brief notes that these methods have both "inspired many scholars to reconceptualise the very nature of humanities research," or more simply the "role of providing new tools for testing old theories, or suggesting new areas of inquiry."[22] The authors then make a very powerful statement (emphasis is theirs):

> **None of this**, however, can be done in the Twentieth-Century context if scholars cannot make nonexpressive uses of underlying copyrighted texts, which (as shown above) will frequently number in the thousands, if not millions. Given copyright law's objective of promoting "the Progress of Science," it would be perversely counterintuitive if the promise of Digital Humanities were extinguished in the name of copyright protection.

Without digital historians being active participants in copyright discussions, much of the promise of digital history will go unrealized for decades. This has had the effect of skewing digital historical research towards the 19th century: one recent author has characterized repositories like Google Books "as a place of scholarly afterlives, where forgotten authors and discarded projects are enjoying a certain reincarnation."[23] Digital investigations allow researchers to move beyond established canons of texts, discovering forgotten works through textual analysis. Unfortunately, while the 20th century is dominated by vast arrays of typewritten and born-digital sources, copyright rules have minimized the potential that these sources offer at present. In any case, copyright belongs in the pantheon of essential terms for digital historians.

Delving into Big Data

So far we have been looking at the overall contour of why going digital matters, now we want to transition towards what you can do with all of this information! In this respect, **textual analysis** and **basic visualizations**

---

[22] Ibid.
[23] Paula Findlen, "How Google Rediscovered the 19th Century," *Chronicle of Higher Education: The Conversation Blog*, 22 July 2013, http://chronicle.com/blogs/conversation/2013/07/22/how-google-rediscovered-the-19th-century/, accessed 13 August 2013.

need to be part of your toolkit. While we will go into depth about these terms, we first want to provide a brief sketch of some of the basic techniques that underlie the rest of the book. These techniques include, as a very basic and gentle introduction:

- **Counting words.** How often does a given word appear in a document? We can then move beyond that and see how often a word appears in dozens, or hundreds, or even thousands of documents, and establish change over time.
- **Ngrams, or phrase frequency.** When counting words, we are technically counting unigrams: frequency of strings of one word. For phrases, we speak of Ngrams: bigrams, trigrams, quadgrams, and fivegrams, although one could theoretically do any higher number. A bigram can be a combination of two characters, such as "bi", two syllables, or two words. An example: "canada is". A trigram is three words, quadgram is four words, and a fivegram is five words, and so on.
- **Keyword-in-context.** This is important. Imagine that you are looking for a specific term that also has a broader name, such as the *Globe and Mail* newspaper, colloquially referred to as the *Globe*. If you wanted to see how often that newspaper appeared, a search for *Globe* would capture all of the appearances you were looking for, but also others: globe refers to three-dimensional models of the Earth, or perhaps Earth, or sphere-shaped objects, cities like Globe, Arizona, or a number of newspapers around the world. So in the following case:

he	read	the	globe	and	mail	it
picked	up	a	globe	newspaper	in	toronto
jonathan	studied	the	globe	in	his	parlour
favourite	newspaper	the	globe	and	mail	smelled
the	plane	to	globe	arizona	was	late

In the middle, we have the keyword we are looking for (globe) and on the left and right we have the context. Without requiring sophisticated programming skills, we can see in this limited sample of five that three probably refer to the *Globe and Mail*, one is ambiguous (one could study a globe of the Earth or the newspaper in one's parlour), and one is clearly referring to the city of Globe, Arizona.

None of these terms are meant to be intimidating, but rather a gentle introduction to some of the major issues that you may encounter as you move forward in this area of research. Copyright matters, open access matters, and basic visualization terms can help you make sense of what other digital humanists are doing.

Why We're All Digital Now

You do not have to be a self-declared Digital Historian to be a digital historian. Indeed, almost all historians are digital today. While there are undoubtedly a few laggards, most historians use search engines to find sources (both online and in conventional print archives). A smaller, yet still significant, number take digital photographs at archives to review when they get home. Perhaps most significantly, historians increasingly rely on online databases to find relevant journal and newspaper articles: from JSTOR to ProQuest to regional or national undertakings like the Canadian province of Ontario's Scholars Portal database. The previous three keywords all apply to these practices: copyright influences what is and what is not available (especially important for newspapers) and to who, some databases are open access and others are not (as paywalls remind us), and — critically — computational textual analysis underscores these search databases. Our research is being shaped every day by these forces. Once a historian begins to conceptualize her everyday activities as being part of the digital turn, the leap towards the whole-scale manipulation and exploration of digital materials is not so big a gulf after all.

Beyond anecdote, we have increasingly sophisticated data on how historians are responding to this digital turn. In late 2012, the consulting firm ITHAKA S+R (owned by the parent company of the JSTOR database) carried out an exhaustive report on historians' research practices. Their summary shows the widespread impact of digital methods:

> Even if the impact of computational analysis and other types of new research methods remains limited to a subset of historians, new research practices and communications mechanisms are being adopted widely, bringing with them both opportunities and challenges.[24]

Historians begin with Google, find sources online, work with online databases, go to archives and take digital photographs, and digitally view

---

[24]Roger C. Schonfeld and Jennifer Rutner (7 December 2012), "Supporting the Changing Research Practices of Historians," *ITHAKA S+R*, http://www.sr.ithaka.org/research-publications/supporting-changing-research-practices-historians, accessed 30 July 2013.

these representations of analog materials on their home or office computers. Despite the antimodernist presentation of a historian in stock images and in parts of the popular consciousness, historians have been no less affected by the digital turn. The issue at hand is that while historians have adopted digital tools, to some degree they have adopted them uncritically.

Search engines need to be considered critically. As the authors of the important *Web Dragons: Inside the Myths of Search Engine Technology* note, we need to complicate our understanding of the Web as "the universal key to information access" for a number of reasons, including the fact that the "rich get richer." Websites that are linked to by more people go up in the search rankings, and as people use the search rankings to find websites, this compounds; it can be hard to break in.[25] In 2007, after noting the issues of why many websites receive no links and how they become hidden, the authors note that one mitigating factor is that "fortunately, we do not all favour the same dragon [search engine]."[26] While this was true, Google is now the uncontested victor of the search engine wars, maintaining a whopping 67.1% share of the search engine market.[27] Ted Underwood, a literary scholar at the University of Illinois, has argued that:

> The internal mathematics of full-text search also has more in common with data mining than with bibliographic retrieval. If I do a title search for Moby-Dick, the results are easy to scan. But in full-text search, there are often too many matches for the user to see them all. Instead, the algorithm has to sort them according to some measure of relevance. Relevance metrics are often mathematically complex; researchers don't generally know which metric they're using; in the case of web search, the metric may be proprietary.[28]

In short, if you Google something even seemingly particular like "Canadian history", you'll receive 273,000,000 results. You are probably not going to read result 270,000, or even result 100. What makes something get onto

---

[25] Ian H. Witten, Marco Gori and Teresa Numerico (2007), *Web Dragons: Inside the Myths of Search Engine Technology*, San Francisco, CA: Morgan Kaufmann, pp. 182–183.

[26] Ibid., p. 185.

[27] Jennifer Slegg (21 May 2013), "Google's Market Share Drops as Bing Passes 17%," *Search Engine Watch*, http://searchenginewatch.com/article/2269591/Googles-Search-Market-Share-Drops-as-Bing-Passes-17, accessed 31 July 2013.

[28] Ted Underwood (Summer 2014), "Theorizing Research Practices We Forgot to Theorize Twenty Years Ago," *Representations*, **127**(1), 65.

that first or second page? These are the questions that scholars begin to ask as we adopt digital tools on a widespread scale.

Consider the problem of using online newspaper databases.[29] They seem orderly, advanced, and comprehensive. Instead of using a microfilm reader to navigate an old newspaper, one logs into a newspaper database through a library portal. A keyword search for a particular event, person, or cultural phenomenon brings up a list of research findings. While date-by-date searching is also available, it seems clunky and slow; keyword searching, however, offers something *new*, something potentially transformative. Each result is often broken down by date, newspaper page number, the section it appears in, and a further click-through brings you to the entire page, scanned at a decently high resolution, search terms highlighted for convenience. The surrounding context of the page, advertisements, and the original layout are all preserved. Previously impossible or implausible research projects can now be approached, especially when they involve wide swaths of social or cultural terrain.

In the Canadian context, this was a particularly important issue: Canada was the first country to have its two major newspapers digitized in 2002: the *Toronto Star* (Canada's largest circulation newspaper) was fully searchable before even the *New York Times*, followed by the *Globe and Mail* (by some accounts the "paper of record" for Canada).[30]

Research done by Ian Milligan demonstrated that, dating back to 2002, researchers have disproportionately cited what they find online. Drawing on a collection of every history dissertation uploaded to ProQuest between 1997 and 2010, he discovered dramatic increases: comparing 1998 to 2010 saw a 991% increase in citations to the *Toronto Star*, as opposed to minor increases and even decreases for other newspapers. This has had two dramatic impacts. First, in a country with regional identities and histories, this had the effect of centralizing studies towards the metropoles and away from the peripheries — to the extent that studies of events in smaller cities with regional newspapers were recounted using Toronto-based newspapers.

Secondly, and perhaps most importantly, search engines have a necessarily skewing effect on our research: something that is true for Google

---

[29]This problem has been addressed in depth by one of the co-authors, in Ian Milligan (December 2013), "Illusionary Order: Online Databases, Optical Character Recognition, and Canadian History, 1997–2010," *Canadian Historical Review*, **94**(4).

[30]For background on the project, Cold North Wind has a fairly detailed website. Please visit "About Paper of Record," https://paperofrecord.hypernet.ca/default.asp (accessed 21 June 2012).

searches, to searching within electronic books, through to the *Toronto Star* online. Yet the issues of poor OCR in these databases make this a very pressing and significant issue. Something like newspaper digitization is both simple and complicated. Let us use the case of the *Toronto Star* as a pertinent example. At a speed of roughly one million pages of newspaper per month, digitization was carried out from microfilm originals. From the microfilm, each individual page was subsequently produced as a decently high-resolution PDF document, averaging approximately 700 KB. Every page was put through an OCR scanner, producing a text file of the text found; when a user enters a search term, he or she is searching their query against the text file. Once a match is found, the PDF is made available to the user.

However, OCR means that some data are lost. OCR is primarily concerned with commercial markets and users: the massive digitization and transcription of large arrays of typewritten documents, often in corporate, legal, and governmental settings. Applying this technology to historical documents is tricky, as we are taking a tool and applying it to a closely related yet far from identical task. In a comprehensive article, a team of three researchers has outlined the major problems facing OCR routines as they tackle historical documents and newspapers.[31] These include non-standard fonts (historical newspapers did not use standard typefaces); printing noise (the small errors, betraying the printer's hand on the actual paper); unequal line and word spacing; line-break hyphenation (if a word transgresses a column, frequent due to small historical columns, it is lost if the algorithm did not expect such cases), and the inherent data loss of medium transformation.

We use this extended example for two main reasons: firstly, to encourage readers to think about how big data (in the form of newspaper and journal databases) already structures their research activities. Yes, there is something distinctive about explicitly using computational methods to tackle new or existing research questions, but it now underpins all facets of our scholarly experience. Second, to illustrate some of the pitfalls that all scholars now have to look out for. We need to consider the underlying *structure* of databases: how they were constructed, what assumptions went into them, and how the data are formatted. For historians, as we work with digitized primary sources, we need to always consider the quality of the

---

[31]Maya R. Gupta, Nathaniel P. Jacobson and Eric K. Garcia (2007), "OCR Binarization and Image Pre-Processing for Searching Historical Documents," *Pattern Recognition: The Journal of the Pattern Recognition Society*, **40**, 389.

text. How was it constructed? Was it double-blind entered, like the *Old Bailey Online*? Or did commercial OCR algorithms, intended for law firms and applied to this application for which it was not designed, scan it? We need to cite the format that we use: if we are citing a newspaper article from a Lexis|Nexis database search, it should be cited as such; a book from Google Books, viewed in snippet form, needs to be treated and documented differently than the full e-book or the physical copy itself. Citing the digital matters, both for intellectual honesty as well as recognizing the algorithms that underlie these databases.

In any event, almost all historians (if not all) are in some ways digital. We have amazing amounts of information at our fingertips, via Google and JSTOR, and that information is delivered to us through a series of complicated mathematical and linguistic algorithms. With that in mind, going down the digital path should not seem daunting, but rather an opportunity to do what we do better. In the next section, we discuss the toolkit that historians can build to help them be explicit digital historians and bring some of the power of big data into their own hands.

Building the Historian's Toolkit

Let's begin to delve into things, shall we? We like the (rather common) metaphor of a "toolkit" for historians beginning to tackle big data problems: an assortment of various software programs that can each shed new light on the past. Some of these programs have explicit tool-like names: MALLET, the MAchine Learning for LanguagE Toolkit; others, more methods-based names such as Voyant, the Stanford Topic Modeling Toolbox; others, more whimsical names such as Python, a programming language named after the 1970s British comedy series *Monty Python's Flying Circus*.[32] They all have two shared characteristics: they are free and open source, and historians have fruitfully employed them. We will introduce several tools throughout this book, but there are more of course. Some other useful places to explore are the DiRT directory of Digital Research Tools at http://dirtdirectory.org/ and the Text Analysis Portal for Research (TAPoR) at http://tapor.ca/. We find TAPoR especially useful as it provides good write-ups of digital tools, provides historical context,

---

[32] "Why is it Called Python?" *Python documentation*, last updated 31 July 2013, http://docs.python.org/2/faq/general.html#why-is-it-called-python, accessed 31 July 2013.

and helps one learn about the broader field as you click around the various sites.

In Stephen King's *On Writing, A Memoir of the Craft*, he tells us a story about his Uncle Oren. It's an instructive story for historians. The screen door was broken. Uncle Oren lugged the enormous toolbox that had once belonged to his father to the door, found that only a small screwdriver was required, and fixed the door. In response to his young nephew's question about why he didn't just grab the screwdriver in the first place, Uncle Oren said, "I didn't know what else I might find to do once I got out here, did I? It's best to have your tools with you. If you don't you're apt to find something you didn't expect and get discouraged." Working with digital materials is a bit like King's suggestions for writing. You want to have a variety of tools handy, in order to ask different kinds of questions, and to see different kinds of patterns. There is no "canon" of big data tools, but the ones we mention in this chapter and the next are increasingly becoming part of the standard fluency of digital historians.

One tool that we highly suggest that historians use, whether they primarily engage with big data research or with conventional work, is the research tool Zotero. Developed by the Roy Rosenzweig Center for History and New Media at George Mason University, Zotero is a one-click shop for gathering, organizing, sharing, and citing sources. Available at https://www.zotero.org/ as either an extension for the open source Mozilla Firefox browser (it runs as a program within the browser) or as a standalone application, Zotero is a good platform to begin using and saving your material. Once you have it installed, you can automatically begin to extract source information. If you go to an article or book listing on Amazon.com, for example, or your institution's library website, a little picture of a book will appear in the address bar of your website — one click, and the information is added to your database. Even more promising, if you are in a repository like *JSTOR*, one click will also add the full text of the article and then index it for searching.

Finally, once you want to cite material, you can add citations in Word or OpenOffice through Zotero, in the citation format that you want. No more painstaking by-hand changing from Chicago Style footnotes to MLA-style embedded notes! While Zotero is invaluable, it does occasionally have some problems when interacting with other programs. It works quite well with Microsoft Word, for example, but sometimes applications built within its ecosystem can break. Still, the ever-present reminder of the Zotero icon in the upper right-hand corner of a Firefox browser, or in the start-up menu

---

Zotero — https://www.zotero.org/

General Principles

Zotero is a tool that lets you "collect, organize, cite, and share your research sources." Integrating with your web browser and your word processor, Zotero lets you collect bibliographic metadata from various sources that you stumble across. It downloads the PDF full text of articles, for example, or preserves snapshots of websites that you are using. Zotero can effectively run your research life.

Description

It is a simple database that runs either within the Mozilla Firefox browser or as a standalone program. It is an easy installation at https://www.zotero.org/.

Critique

Zotero does a great job of doing what it wants to do. Sometimes, however, it does not play well with plugins — updates can break them. The core competencies are well designed, but it is not always the most robust platform to build addons for.

How to Use It

It is very easy to use! Simply navigate to https://www.zotero.org and click on the big red "Download Now" button. If you use Firefox, click on "Zotero 4.0 for Firefox." If you want to use it as a standalone application, download that option instead. It has a straightforward installation procedure.

---

of a desktop computer, reassures you that your research database is always at hand.

There is also the problem of "link rot."[33] The ecosystem of links that pins digital materials together is prone to decay. If you searched for "http://geocities.com/" in, for instance, Google Books (perhaps you are interested

---

[33]For many issues concerning the Web, Internet, their underlying architectures, governance, and so on, Wikipedia is actually one of the best sources for gaining that initial understanding to help make sense of what else you might find. In this case, the article on "link rot," Wikipedia contributors, "Link rot," *Wikipedia, The Free Encyclopedia*, http://en.wikipedia.org/w/index.php?title=Link_rot&oldid=615587779, accessed 8 July 2014.

in the early history of the World Wide Web, a time when it seemed everyone had a "home page" hosted on GeoCities), the results you retrieve will contain links to pages that are now dead. Zotero has a function that allows you to keep a "snapshot" of any webpage you visit, and to store it within your library as part of its citation (it stores the snapshot locally on your computer, or any other computer on which you've installed Zotero). The problem is *no one else* can see this snapshot. Another service, called "WebCite" can be used to create a permanent citation to that web resource for you, which you can then share. In essence, WebCite creates a copy and provides a permanent address for it. Even if the original is taken offline, a copy will live at http://www.webcitation.org/. Finally, archived versions of websites exist in many corners of the online world, from Google's cache (click on the down arrow beside a search result to see the cached version; this is typically only the most recent version of the page indexed by Google's spiders), to the Internet Archive Wayback Machine.[34] There are others, but the Memento service (http://www.mementoweb.org/) brings these together into a portal service. While we will return to Zotero once or twice in the chapters that follow, to point you towards specific plugins that can enhance it for big data research, we believe that any historian can fruitfully benefit from having it installed, and from being aware of these other services.[35]

The tools we use all presuppose different ways of looking at the world, and many of them have a bias towards American datasets and linguistic constructions. Wolfram Alpha (the so-called "computational knowledge engine"), for instance, allows one to parse text automatically, assigning each name it finds a gender tag.[36] But what of the name "Shawn"? Is that a male

---

[34]Which can be found at http://archive.org/web/. See also Ian Milligan (11 February 2013), "Exploring the Old Canadian Internet: Spelunking in the Internet Archive" *ianmilligan.ca*, http://ianmilligan.ca/2013/02/11/exploring-the-old-canadian-internet-spelunking-in-the-internet-archive/.

[35]Many tutorials for getting the most out of Zotero exist; the *Profhacker* column in *The Chronicle of Higher Education* for instance has written about Zotero several times and contains many useful pointers to tutorials, videos, tablet and smartphone apps that extend the functions of Zotero, making it even more useful. See http://chronicle.com/blogs/profhacker/tag/zotero.

[36]As discussed in Ian Milligan (28 July 2013), "Quick Gender Detection Using Wolfram|Alpha," *ianmilligan.ca*, available online, http://ianmilligan.ca/2013/07/28/gender-detection-using-wolframalpha/. Lincoln Mullen provides a repository with tools for gender detection of names using the R statistical package (we discuss R in more depth in subsequent chapters). For more, see http://lincolnmullen.com/blog/analyzing-historical-history-dissertations-gender/.

name, or a female name? Shawn Graham (male), Shawn Colvin (female). Who compiled the list of names for this tool? How were they tagged? Who decides that "Shawn" is a male or female name? What about names that at one point were predominantly male (Ainsley) but are now more typically used by females? Alison Prentice, in her brave *mea culpa* "Vivian Pound was a man?" discusses how her research into the history of women members of the University of Toronto's Physics Department revolved around the figure of Vivian Pound, whom she thought was a woman[37]:

> ... it was certainly a surprise, and not a little humbling, to learn in the spring of 2000 that Pound, a physicist who earned a doctorate from the University of Toronto in 1913, was not a female of the species, as I had thought, but a male. In three essays on early twentieth-century women physicists published between 1996 and 1999, I had erroneously identified Vivian Pound not only as a woman, but as the first woman at the University of Toronto to earn a Ph.D. in physics.[38]

In Prentice's case, the dataset she was using — simple lists of names — led her to erroneous outcomes. Her work demonstrates how to reflect and build outwards from such reflection. For as we use computational analysis, a list of names might become a "tool" to use: and tools are rarely straightforward and neutral. This is an essential component to using digital tools (indeed, tools of any kind). In later chapters we will discuss in more detail how the worldviews built into our tools can lead us similarly astray.

Automatic Retrieval of Data

First, however, we need data. How can historians find big data repositories to work on? As with everything, this depends on your unique needs. We want to use a few different examples that scale in difficulty. At its easiest, the document is sitting there on one or two webpages and can be downloaded with a few clicks of your mouse, as in the case of second American president John Adams' diary. With a little more effort, we can automatically access large collections from the exhaustive Internet Archive. And with some added effort and a few more lines of commands, we can access

---

[37] Alison Prentice (2001), "Vivian Pound was a Man? The Unfolding of a Research Project," *Historical Studies in Education/Revue d'histoire de l'éducation*, **13**(2), 99–112, http://historicalstudiesineducation.ca/index.php/edu_hse-rhe/article/view/1860/1961.
[38] Ibid., 99.

even larger collections from national institutions including the Library of Congress and Library and Archives Canada.

Have you ever sat at your computer, looking at a long list of records held at a place like Library and Archives Canada, the British Library, or the Library of Congress, right-clicking and downloading each record-by-painstaking-record? Or have you pulled up a query in the Internet Archive that brings up hundreds of results? Perhaps not, but chances are that you have Googled for historical sources relating to your research interests, used online finding aids, and perhaps wondered how to access them in a quicker, more straightforward way. There are tools to ease this sort of work. There is a bit of a learning curve, in that the first download might actually take longer to do than if you did it manually, but there is a cumulative saving: the next collection will download far quicker, and from then on, you are saving time with every query.

Wget

General Principles

Wget runs on your computers' command line and lets you do sophisticated and automated downloading. You could, for example, decide to download an *entire copy* of an entire webpage with one command. If you are sitting at your computer, right-clicking page after page to download it, Wget can save you a lot of time.

Description

It is a text-based program that has a relatively steep learning curve, involving several different "flags" that modify the operation of the program.

Critique

It is difficult to use and for those unfamiliar with the command-line environment, it is initially relatively inaccessible. If you make a mistake, it is unforgiving and will not run properly.

How to Use It

The best way to learn how to use it is to consult the lesson at the *Programming Historian*, found at http://programminghistorian.org/lessons/automated-downloading-with-wget.

One of the most powerful ways for a historian to download data is the free and open source program **Wget**, available on every platform. It lets you set up some rules and automatically download data. If you ever find yourself staring at a list, right-clicking and downloading each individual file in a repetitive way, fear not: this is the situation that something like Wget was designed for.

Unlike many other software programs that you may be familiar with, Wget runs on a **command-line interface**. If you were a computer user in the 1980s or early 1990s, this will be familiar: MS-DOS was a command-line interface. If not, however, this may seem somewhat foreign. Most users today interact with computer systems through a graphical-user interface, which lets you navigate files and programs through images (icons, pictures, and rendered text). Several of the tools discussed in this book use the command line. While this has a bit of a learning curve, it offers a degree of precision and — eventually — speed that compensates for the initial difficulty.

In this section, we want to show you how you could install Wget on your system using the command line. While we do not provide this level of detail for every program in this handbook, we think that this can help demystify things. Playing on the command line is not just for "hackers" — with some introductions, you can begin functioning there as well. Let's begin. Because operating systems differ from system to system, you will see different instructions below. There is also another guide to using the command line at the *Programming Historian*, if you visit http://programminghistorian.org/lessons/intro-to-bash.

Wget can be relatively easily installed on your system. **Linux users** will have it pre-installed by default. **Mac users** have a slightly more complicated procedure (if you are a Windows user, please skip to the paragraph beginning "for Windows users"). From the App Store or from the Apple website itself, install "XCode." Once it has installed, install the "Command Line Tools" kit from the "Preferences" tab in the program. With that complete, a popular package manager named *Homebrew* can help you install Wget in a few lines of code. Open your "Terminal" window, which is by default found in the "Utilities" folder within your "Applications," and type the following as a single line to install *Homebrew*:

```
ruby -e "$(curl -fsSL
https://raw.github.com/Homebrew/homebrew/go/install)"
```

It might ask you for your password — don't worry, this is a normal stage in installing software (you often have to type in your password when installing software in your normal graphical operating system; if this line still doesn't work, try typing `sudo` at the start of the command). Get it configured to make sure it works by typing:

```
brew doctor
```

And then install Wget with the following easy command:

```
brew install wget
```

Wget will download and install itself on your system.

For Windows users, the easiest way is to download Wget for Windows. You simply download the file (wget.exe) to your C:\windows directory so you can access it from anywhere else on your system.[39] Then it is as easy as opening up your command line (which is "cmd.exe" and can be found by searching for that term through your Start Menu or finding it under "Accessories"). If you have downloaded wget.exe into the C:\windows directory, typing wget into that box will work.

You can open the command line within any directory in Windows by holding the shift key and right-clicking in the folder. A contextual menu box will open. Select "open command window here." This can save you some hassle as it is usually easier to navigate your files and folders using Windows Explorer than by manually changing directories using the "cd" command.

All together now (Mac, Windows, and Linux) — **let's quickly use it:** Before we turn back to the main body of the lesson, since we have gone so far as to install Wget, let's quickly use it. For more instructions, you might want to check out Ian Milligan's "Automated Downloading with Wget" lesson at the *Programming Historian* at http://programming historian.org/lessons/automated-downloading-with-wget. But, in short, the command is:

```
wget <any modifiers> <the site or page you want to download>
```

Let us try it on the example of the *Macroscope* page pertaining to this lesson. Type:

```
wget http://www.themacroscope.org/?page_id=330
```

---

[39] For example, at "WGET for Windows (Win32)," http://users.ugent.be/~bpuype/wget/, accessed 31 July 2013.

If you download this and then open it up with your web browser (using the file menu → open command in your browser), you will see a copy of that page! We can do more advanced things with this, such as mirroring an entire website or downloading entire arrays of documents. For your convenience, the previously mentioned Programming Historian lesson goes through several of these cases.

How to Become a Programming Historian, A Gentle Introduction

While there is certainly less stigma than there used to be, the idea of a "programming historian" can lead to a piqued eyebrow or two, or an easy laugh line at times.[40] Of course, as Chapter 1 discussed, historians have been actively programming since the 1970s as part of the first two waves of computational history. The difference with the third wave (open source software, powerful computing, and big data) is that the barriers to entry have never been lower. This is most obvious with the open source, open-access textbook the *Programming Historian* and its sequel, the aptly-named *Programming Historian 2* (now simply the *Programming Historian* once again). In short, the *Programming Historian* has a simple goal: to teach the basics of programming, drawing on historical examples and with an emphasis on bringing you up to speed quickly and practically. It is not a computer science course: it is instead a series of hands-on examples, focused on the what and how rather than the underlying architecture that drives programming languages. It's also a challenge to conventional forms of publishing, being a "community-driven collaborative textbook," soliciting submissions, constantly refining, and inviting comments at all stages. While you do not get an official certificate for completing the book, the skills you learn can move you quickly into the computational side of the digital humanities.

In early May 2008, the first iteration of the book went online, co-authored by two historians from the University of Western Ontario, William J. Turkel and Alan MacEachern. They came at it with varying levels of experience: Turkel, a life-long programmer, and MacEachern, who began programming only on New Year's Day 2008. Their argument behind why historians need to program was both extensive and disarmingly simple. In

---

[40]William J. Turkel and Alan MacEachern (May 2008), "The Programming Historian: About this Book," available online, http://niche-canada.org/wp-content/uploads/2013/09/programming-historian-1.pdf, accessed 12 August 2013.

short, as they put it, "if you don't program, your research process will always be at the mercy of those who do . . . programming is for digital historians what sketching is for artists or architects: a mode of creative expression and a means of exploration."[41] This book, and its second iteration as a collaboratively authored textbook, is one of the easiest ways for a historian to learn the basics of historical programming (the others include, as mentioned in the preface, unconferences like THATCamp or other physical gatherings of supportive people).

The *Programming Historian* uses all open source software: the Python programming language, the Komodo Edit editing environment, the Omeka digital exhibit platform, or the MAchine Learning for LanguagE Toolkit (MALLET). The most important lessons, in keeping with the textbook's name, involve the Python programming language. Beginning with the simple steps of installing the language itself onto your system, be it Linux, OS X, or Windows, it then moves through increasingly complicated lessons: automatically retrieving data, breaking it down into constituent parts, counting words, and creating basic visualizations. In short, in a few hours a user moves from having no knowledge to being able to programmatically interact with the exhaustive holdings of the *Old Bailey Online*.

In our experience as researchers and teachers, the word "programming" occasionally raises hackles. Beyond practical concerns of not having sufficient digital fluency to feel up to the task, there is the issue that programming can seem antithetical to the humanistic tradition. The lessons contained within the *Programming Historian*, however, as well as those in this book, show that programming should fundamentally be understood as a creative undertaking. Humanistic assumptions underlie the decisions that you will be making, and give us more control over the processes that produce results that we then parse into our narratives. Yes, it requires an attention to detail — a misplaced bracket here or there can throw off your program until you find the error — but for the most part we believe that it is a rewarding experience. Indeed, there's something to be said about a process that gives you immediate feedback — your program works or crashes! — as opposed to the long cycles of feedback that we and our students are used to.

This section does not intend to replicate the *Programming Historian*, which is both freely available online and continually updated to incorporate

[41]William J. Turkel and Alan MacEachern (May 2008), *Programming Historian*, ch. 2, http://niche-canada.org/wp-content/uploads/2013/09/programming-historian-1.pdf, accessed 12 August 2013.

changes in operating systems, plugins, and even best practices. Instead, we introduce you to what we consider are the basic conceptual lessons needed by a humanist, as well as providing context around why these issues are important. We encourage you to visit the *Programming Historian* as well as beginning to explore the very basic lessons discussed below.

Basic Scraping: Getting Your Data

There are a number of ways to grab existing big historical data. Sometimes, if we are lucky, the data that we wish to explore will already be provided to us in a format that we can use. Consider this fruitful example of a scholar sharing his or her research. Peter Holdsworth, an MA student at Carleton University, uploaded all of his raw data as Excel spreadsheets to the research data sharing website *Figshare*.[42] *Figshare* occupies an important niche in the ecosystem of scholarly publishing, especially as historians begin to grapple with larger and larger datasets that cannot possibly be described or effectively communicated in our traditional print journals. *Figshare* provides a unique digital identifier for every file that a researcher chooses to share on the site, which may be cited. Here for instance is Holdsworth's network dataset from his research:

Holdsworth, Peter (2013): Holdsworth 1902 Organizational Network. figshare http://dx.doi.org/10.6084/m9.figshare.727770.

Figshare also provides an "application programming interface" (API) which allows other websites or software to access the files held in *Figshare* (one could write a program that visualizes the location of all data concerned with a particular geographic region, for instance). Using APIs is a kind of "scraping" in the sense that APIs provide a formal protocol for the sharing, reuse, and remixing of data, automatically. Using APIs is not overly difficult (the *Programming Historian* explains how to use the Zotero reference and research environment API) but for now we want to explore ways of obtaining information automatically using free software tools.

Wget is a useful tool when the information we want is well formed and well organized as a series of pages in a static website (see Wget box above). Many sites are prearranged for retrieving information in such a way that we can use it for our own analysis. Imagine visiting the website of a historical society that has transcribed a series of newspaper articles onto a

---

[42] Peter Holdsworth, "Author page," *Figshare*, http://figshare.com/authors/Peter_Holdsworth/402385.

single webpage. The page is well laid out: every date is clearly offset from the text, the text is nicely arranged for reading... we might want to scrape that information into a spreadsheet file (comma-or tab-separated values). We could "save as" the page to our desktop and manually grab everything, cutting and pasting. That would be an enormous waste of effort. Since the browser knows how to visualize the information for us to read it, we can use those tags — the HTML (Hypertext Markup Language) markup for headers and tables and so on — and get the computer to automatically put it into a table for us. *The Programming Historian* has a number of lessons explaining how to do this in Python. Here, we describe a way of using three different pieces of software to achieve the same thing. While we would certainly recommend that learning how to do this using Python should be on your to-do list, using browser-based tools can make things easier in the beginning.

The first tool that we sometimes use is called "Outwit Hub," available at http://www.outwit.com/. We will revisit it in Chapter 4 when we discuss topic modeling, and show how you can use it to grab specific data from an American primary source to subsequently visualize it. It is not freeware, but it does come in a basic, free version that is quite useful if occasionally a bit limited.

Outwit Hub, as with many other pieces of software programs that find information on the Web, finds information by parsing the "soup" of HTML markup tags to download elements of interest. HTML is a markup language that dictates how a webpage should appear. Think of when you edit — or "mark up" — a document on paper: when something should be in italics, maybe you circle it and write "italics"; or if something should be emphasized, you underline it. This is what a markup language is. The HTML document contains two things: the content, but also the instructions on how the content should be displayed. So you might have a document like:

```
<HTML>
    <body>
    <h1>The diary of Professor Smith.</h1>
        <h2>13 December 2013</h2>
            <em>This is the diary entry.</em>
        <h2>14 December 2014</h2>
            <em>This is a second entry.</em>
    </body>
</HTML>
```

This document would appear like so:

The diary of Professor Smith.

13 December 2013

This is the diary entry.

14 December 2014

This is a second entry.

So in this case, while it isn't visible to the naked eye, the dates are all encapsulated within the <h2> (or Header, Level 2) tags, the title is within the <h1> tag, and the entries are all within the italics, or <em> tags. So if we wanted to quickly get a list of the dates, we would point Outwit Hub at the <h2> tags, to get information between <h2> and </h2> .

Download and install the free version. Outwit Hub looks rather like a web browser. That's because it contains one within it. To use, simply put the address of the website you are interested in into the address bar. Outwit will load the page. You then click on the "source" button in the menu on the left side of the screen. This shows you the underlying markup for the page. Scroll down through this material, taking note of the tags that embrace the kinds of information that you are interested in, for instance:

```
<h3> {the date of the entry} </h3>.
```

Here are some example data that you might see:

```
<h3>15 January 1945</h3>
<p>It was a cold day in New York City today. I wish I had a
coat.</p>
<h3>16 January 1945</h3>
<p>I am still cold. I really wish I had a coat.</p>
```

In the following example, we will use Outwit Hub to extract the dates — in this case, 15 and 16 January 1945 — as well as the entries, relating to our poor friend being cold in New York City. We could then make a spreadsheet out of them: one column with dates, the second with the entries themselves. This is giving some structure to otherwise seemingly unstructured data, which will let computational tools interact with them. The above HTML code should seem familiar! It is a bit different than the first example we gave, but similar enough to begin to parse.

In Outwit Hub, click on the "scrapers" item on the left side of the screen, within the menu bar. In the free version, you are limited to the number of scrapers you may design, and the number of rows of material that they will scrape (the maximum is 100). A new subwindow opens in the screen. Click "new" in the bottom frame to start a new scraper. You are now ready to begin.

At the bottom of the screen is a table that allows you to construct your scraper. Double-click in the first blank field under "Marker Before." You can put the first part of the tag that embraces the information you want in here, e.g. <h3> or the date tag in our example above. Double-click in the next column over (under "Marker After") and put in the closing tag, e.g. </h3> . If you then clicked "execute," the bottom part of the screen would fill up with a table with a single column, with the list of dates. In your scraper, you could input a second criterion (say, everything embraced by <p> and </p> , or *paragraph*) and when you hit the "execute" button your table would contain *both* the date and the text for that date as a nicely formed table. You then hit the "export" button at the bottom of the screen to save your "catch" (as Outwit Hub terms it) as an .XLS or .CSV or other output. Our diary has been painlessly exported! We will return to Outwit Hub in Chapter 4 in more detail. It requires some tinkering because every website is different, but in general if there's some structure in the website, Outwit can grab it for you.

What is a CSV file, you may be asking? You have probably heard of XLS files — those are the proprietary formats that a program like Microsoft Excel uses to show a spreadsheet. A CSV file is a "comma-separated value" file, and it is just that: a file that has a bunch of information organized by different commas. Consider the following spreadsheet of data:

31-Mar-14   I am looking forward to catching up with my colleagues Scott and Shawn.

01-Apr-14   It was April Fools' Day! My good colleagues fooled me good.

In a CSV format it would be:

```
31-Mar-14, I am looking forward to catching up with my
colleagues Scott and Shawn.
1-Apr-14, It was April Fools' Day! My good colleagues fooled
me good.
```

It is plain text, separated by commas, which lets a computer program read it and know where fields should be broken.

Now, Outwit Hub can do much more than this simple scrape, but this in essence is what the program does. You "train" it to recognize the data you are interested in, a step that we will discuss below, and then you set it to grab those data. There are far more sophisticated things you could set it to do. You could give it a particular pattern to look for over a number of sites, or within x number of links of a site, or a particular kind of data file; you can set it to guess automatically as to the kind of data a site might have; you can speed up or slow down the speed with which it asks websites for data (you do not want to over tax someone else's server). The full documentation of what the program can do is provided on the website and through numerous video tutorials provided by users.

A second option is still in "beta" — or undergoing a public release with the expectation of finding bugs or issues with the program — but, as of writing, seems to hold much promise. Called "import.io", it is similarly a standalone piece of software (with related plugins for the Chrome browser) that allows sophisticated crawling and scraping of data from websites and APIs. It allows not just the scraping of data, but the ability to mix data together from various sources and APIs, to share those data via unique URI (universal resource identifier), and to visualize real-time streams of data. The Chrome plugin will alert the user if a scraper for a particular website already exists (install it and then visit *The Guardian* newspaper online, for example). Import.io works as a standalone browser. Like Outwit Hub, you have to train it (or you can have it guess, with mixed results) on the kind of data that you are looking for in a page. The browser provides much contextual help and step-by-step instructions to guide the user through the process of building and executing a scraper, and so this might be a good option for researchers new to scraping.[43] Import.io is currently free but it may develop "premium" features. Its creators write that they will always have a free tool available for scraping and exporting the data.[44]

Finally, the Chrome browser web store has a number of plugins for scraping websites that require varying degrees of fluency with a query language

---

[43] A useful tutorial by Mike Klaczynski scrapes movie titles from a database https://www.tableausoftware.com/public/blog/2013/08/importio-2088. Keep in mind, however, that some of these steps (or perhaps all) could become obsolete if Import.io changes materially once it is formally launched (that is, no longer in "beta").

[44] See http://import.io/pricing for more information.

called "xpath." The easiest to use is simply called "Scraper."[45] Scraper, once installed, provides a "Scrape Similar" contextual menu item (install it, then right-click on any piece of text on a webpage to bring up the contextual menu). When you click this, a window opens that shows you the results of what Scraper grabbed, as well as an "xpath" query window showing the pattern of data that it searched for. Xpath is query language for HTML and XML. In essence, the query is a list of the nested tags that describe the data that you are looking for. Chrome has a built-in tool called the "inspect element," again available from the contextual menu. When you click on this, an inspector window opens at the bottom of the browser showing the underlying source code. You can then click on the element in the source copy and select "copy xpath." This can then be put in the xpath query window, for instance. Scraper is integrated with Google Drive, so anything you collect can be sent instantly to Google's spreadsheet (and thence exported to a CSV or Excel file).

Splitting a CSV file into separate text files

Sometimes it might be necessary to break one of these CSV files into separate text files, in order to do the next stage of your analysis. For instance, imagine that you had scraped John Adams' diaries into a single CSV file, but what you really wanted to know was the way his views on governance changed over time. This might be a question for which topic modeling (see Chapter 4) could be well suited; many topic modeling tools require each document (here, a diary entry) to be in its own text file.

On a Mac, this can be done in a single command! For instance, we did scrape John Adams' diaries into a single CSV file — our file has 1025 rows, one row per entry. (You can find a copy of this file on our companion website, http://themacroscope.org). We open a terminal window, and at the prompt, type:

```
split -a 3 -l 1 johnadams-diary.csv
```

This command, "split", will take our CSV file, and split it one line, one file (which is what -l 1 means). You'll notice that the files that are created are named "aaa", "aab", "aac", and so on. This is because of the "-a 3" part of the command: aaa. If we wrote "-a 1", then only 26 files could be

---

[45] A tutorial by Jens Finnas gives detailed instructions at http://dataist.wordpress.com/2012/10/12/get-started-with-screenscraping-using-google-chromes-scraper-extension/. Also note that Finnas maintains a useful list of resources for "Data Journalism" at http://datajournalistik.se/ (in Swedish).

split from our original source, since split names things alphabetically. With "-a 3", we are making sure we have enough unique file names to cover all 1025 rows of the CSV file. Using "-a 2" would give us an error, because 26×26 gives us 676 rows, or not enough. The split command can do other interesting things, such as splitting files by their size rather than the number of lines. At the terminal, type "man split" to read the manual entry for the command.

There's one last command though that would be useful. These newly split files do not have file extensions! Again, a single command can do the trick:

```
find . -type f -exec mv '{}' '{}'.csv
```

This command finds, recursively within the folder (which is what the period means), all the files, to which it appends the CSV file extension.

Unfortunately, PC users do not have it so easy. We are still left with the original problem of getting our CSV file split apart. It's not even clear where we would begin!

One route to explore, when we don't know exactly how to achieve what we're trying to do, is to examine the question and answer site StackOverflow, available at http://stackoverflow.com/. It is a repository of questions posed and answered by users, and is a great place to learn the basics of programming. Chances are that if you have run into a problem, somebody else has run into it as well and discussed it on this site. There is no need to reinvent the wheel when it comes to digital work.

We went to StackOverflow and typed our question into its search box: "how do I break an Excel spreadsheet into single files for each row?" We found that a user named Eke had asked a similar question: "how do I write each Excel row to new .TXT file with ColumnA as file name?" This captures what we're trying to do, so let's look at that discussion.

If you examine his question on StackOverflow, Eke has precisely described what it is he's trying to achieve, he has cited other threads on the forum that seem relevant to his question, even if they are not exactly what he wants, and he has given examples of his data and his ideal output. Go visit the specific site at http://stackoverflow.com/questions/15554099/write-each-excel-row-to-new-txt-file-with-columna-as-file-name/15665756#15665756 or — for those who want to avoid long links — try http://bit.ly/1yweKHz. This is a very good example of how to get the most out of this (or indeed any) forum. We provide this example so you can see how we learn to tackle complicated problems as well!

If we examine the thread, we see a lot of back and forth with various users as suggestions are made and Eke reports back his results. A good citizen of the site, Eke also posts his complete code once he finds the solution that works best for him. You do not need to reinvent the wheel: **the code is already here!**

PC users, let's copy and paste that code. To use this script, we have to make a new macro in Excel and then edit it. In Excel, find the Macros button for your version (it may be hidden under the "tools" menu bar in more recent versions of the spreadsheet suite), click view macros, and then click "create." (Sometimes, the "create" button is grayed out. If this is true for you, click "record new macro" instead, hit the start then stop button and the new macro will appear on the list. You can then click "edit.") A new window opens with "Microsoft Visual Basic" in the title. You can now copy and paste Eke's code into your window. You don't need to hit save, as anything you do in this window will save automatically.

Go back over to your normal Excel spreadsheet that contains your table of data. Click on Macros, select the one now listed as "SaveRowsasTXT" and the macro will automatically copy and paste each row into a new worksheet, save it as a txt file, close that new worksheet, and iterate down to the next row. If you get an out-of-range error, make sure your worksheet in Excel is named "Sheet1", so that this line in the script is correct:

```
set wsSource = ThisWorkbook.Worksheets("Sheet1")
```

Note the line that reads

```
filePath = "C:\Users\Administrator\Documents\TEST\
```

You will want to change everything after the quotation mark to point to the location where you want your separate files stored.[46]

---

[46] In later chapters we describe the statistical programming language R and how to accomplish various text-mining tasks within it. Code written in R works on PC or Mac or Linux without issue, provided you have the latest version of the R language installed on your machine. R is extremely versatile. Once you become familiar with it, you will see that you can accomplish many of these kinds of "helper" tasks within R itself, which is advantageous since you can do all of your analyses within the one environment. Ben Marwick has written a "script" for R (in essence, a recipe of commands) to separate the rows in a single Excel file into separate text files, which is available at https://gist.github.com/benmarwick/9278490. If you'd like to use this script right away, skip ahead to our sections on R in Chapter 4 to get a sense of the basics, and then follow Ben's instructions. We thank Ben for writing and contributing this, and several other pieces, of R code. Eke's code is also available

Whichever tool you use, or whether you build one from scratch, being able to scrape websites for information for your research is a key ability of doing digital historical research. When using free software, be certain to read the terms of service and understand the implications of what you are doing.

Normalizing and Tokenizing Data

Imagine that you're using a computer to explore the *Old Bailey Online*, trying to train it to find things out that you would find if you read it yourself. There are questions that you may take for granted that we need to lay out for the computer. For example:

- Do you want to pay attention to **cases**? If we are counting words, should we treat "hello" and "Hello" the same, or treat them differently? What if certain words are capitalized, such as those at the beginning of a chapter, or names? The *Old Bailey Online*, for example, capitalizes names at times (i.e. BENJAMIN BOWSEY's at one point, but perhaps "Bowsey's" elsewhere).
- What about **punctuation**? Should "Benjamin's" and "Benjamin" be treated the same, or differently?
- Do you want to count **common words**? If you count all the words in a document, chances are that words like "the", "it", "and", and so forth will appear frequently. This may occlude your analysis, and it may thus be best to remove the words: they do not tell you anything particular about the case itself.

In general, when counting words or doing more complicated procedures such as topic modeling, we go through these steps and decide to **normalize**, or make normal, all of the text. Text is all made lower case (a simple Python command), punctuation is stripped out, and common words are removed based on a stopwords ("the", "it", etc.) dictionary.

For historians, there are no simple answers: we work with diverse source bases, and thus a conceptual understanding of normalization is more

---

http://themacroscope.org/2.0/code/. Try it yourself on John Adams' diary (which you can download at http://themacroscope.org/2.0/datafiles). Incidentally, having the CSV broken into separate files *arranged in chronological order* (so, sort them by date written before running the macro) means that, when the zipped folder of these files is uploaded to Voyant Tools, you can explore trends over time, reading from left (older) to right (newer), in the basic Voyant Tools interface.

important than knowing the specific code. The trick is to understand your documents and to be prepared to do this a few times. For some cases, the solution can be as simple as a "find-and-replace," either using Python (this is taught by the *Programming Historian*) or even in your favorite word processor.

Here are some places where normalization will be essential, from simple to more complicated. On a simple level, perhaps you are studying shifting mentions to newspapers. Take the Canadian newspaper, the *Globe and Mail*. If in a document it is mostly spelled *Globe and Mail*, but occasionally *Globe & Mail*, and even more infrequently *G & M*, you would want to capture all three of those under one category. A find-and-replace could help fold those together in a document. A slightly more complicated case would be currency: $20, twenty dollars, twenty bucks, $20.00, 20$, and other colloquial usages. If you are interested in financial flows, you do not want to miss these things — and a computer will unless it is normalized. Finally, on a more complicated level, comes stemming: reducing words down to their core concept: i.e. "buying"/"bought"/"buy" to "buy", or "sold"/"selling"/"sell" to "sell".

Tokenization is another key concept. It involves taking a sentence and breaking it down to the smallest individual parts, which can then be easily compared to each other. Let's take the short phrase, as used in the *Programming Historian* after basic normalization: "it was the best of times it was the worst of times it was the age of wisdom it was the age of foolishness." If we turn the sentence into tokens, based on word boundaries, we get the following single tokens: "it", "was", "the", "best", "of", "times", "it", "was", "the", "worst" ... and so on.

Why does it matter that we've taken a straightforward sentence and turned it just into a bunch of individual words? These are now easy to count, and we can tally up the number of times they appear: "times" twice, "best" once, "was" four times. From this, one can apply a list of common words and remove them. More importantly, this stage is a crucial one to catch any normalization errors that might have crept in: does "can" appear frequently as well as "t" — maybe you're breaking up "can't" and creating two word tokens where only one should be, which may throw off your analysis. When a computer is counting words, it is tokenizing them before counting them. Making sure to tokenize them yourself ensures that you catch these niggling little errors. You may want to tokenize contractions so "can't" appears together. More importantly, you may want to treat URLs as http://macroscope.org rather than "http", "macroscope", and "org".

With a large enough corpus, meaningful information can be retrieved by counting data. But if data are not normalized and tokenized, it is easy to miss something.

Bringing it All Together: What's Ahead in the Great Unread

In this chapter we have introduced you to the key terms that define the digital humanities, have advanced an argument that we are all digital historians now as we use a variety of tools from Google to newspaper databases, and have provided cautionary notes and then showed some of the unplumbed depths stretching out before us. These issues all have implications for how historians study the past: how more information, and the tools we now have to study them, affects our research practices.

Franco Moretti, in his ground-breaking 2005 *Graphs, Maps, Trees*, sketched out the potential that this field had for the study of English literature. Scholars had generally focused on a canon of around 200 novels, which Moretti pointed out was a mere fraction of the sheer output of 19th century novels:

> [C]lose reading won't help here, a novel a day every day of the year would take a century or so. ... And it's not even a matter of time, but of method: a field this large cannot be understood by stitching together separate bits of knowledge about individual cases, because it *isn't* a sum of individual cases: it's a collective system, that should be grasped as such, as a whole.[47]

This has been described, elsewhere by Margaret Cohen, as the "great unread."[48] In this lies the important metaphor of the macroscope: A way to pull back, to find broader structures within data, while keeping one's inquiries firmly rooted in the humanistic tradition. As noted, this does not produce "truth" or more scientific outcomes, but rather provides a new process of studying the past. There are "great unreads" everywhere, with potential implications for the pre-digital past.

Grappling with these datasets is not new. For historians, the census is probably the best traditional example of a "great unread." It is an

---

[47]Franco Moretti (2005), *Graphs, Maps, Trees: Abstract Models for Literary History*, London, New York: Verso, p. 4.
[48]Margaret Cohen (1999), *The Sentimental Education of the Novel*, Princeton, NJ: Princeton University Press, p. 23.

assemblage of traces of the past without parallel — a record of every person recorded by the census takers: names, birth dates, occupations, locations, and so forth. This record of millions of people who lived in the past has been studied in parts and chunks: initially case studies of individual cities, or painstaking tabulations, using statistical methods, of other dimensions. The computational wave of the 1960s and 1970s allowed for rudimentary computational processing of ever-increasing datasets. Finally, new digital methods within the last few years have seen the application of Natural Language Processing (NLP) methods to these bodies of data: finding individuals who moved districts, changed occupations, beginning to sketch out complicated models of change over time with millions of people. While a person can probably identify within a margin of error that a 20-year-old man named Frank Smith with a wife named Marie and two children is the same person, ten years later, as a 30-year-old man named Frank Smith, a wife named Marie, and three children, a computer has difficulty. This is due to OCR constraints, having to identify minor issues, but also the numerous inferences and rules needed.

These "great unreads" are everywhere, presenting alluring topics for scholars. Entire annals of parliamentary records, in varying states of transcription and OCR, stretch back centuries or more. Certainly, historians have an understanding of many of the "important speeches:" the lofty invocations that launched or settled wars, connected nations, or began political scandals or other skulduggery. Much of what happens in a legislature, however, is routine, casting light on the people sitting inside of it and the broader society. In Australia and Canada, for example, private members spend a not inconsequential amount of time giving private statements: the accomplishments of local sports teams, notable citizens, entrepreneurs, infrastructure deficiencies, birthdays, wedding anniversaries, and other issues of local concern. There would be an ebb and flow in these.

Big data will accelerate this process, as the arrays of data being generated are being created on a previously unimaginable scale. As historians begin to turn their attention to the 1990s and 2000s, as the Internet and the World Wide Web become in many cases primary sources for understanding the social and cultural past, exploring this "great unread" will become necessary. Internet comments, blogs, tweets, and everything will combine to present an indispensable source. If newspapers form the foundational source for much of 20th century historiography, an accelerating process as they go online, these networks of communication will be equally important as we begin to study the 21st. Could you, we rhetorically ask, even do justice to many topics situated in the 1990s and beyond, without drawing on the World Wide Web? In the next two chapters, we specifically focus on what one could learn from large quantities of text. In this chapter, we have learned how to collect it and how to begin to use it; in the next, let us put it to good use.

Chapter 3

Text Mining Tools:
Techniques and Visualizations

In this chapter, we set up and explore some basic text mining tools and consider the kinds of things these can tell us. We move on to more complex tools (including how to set up some of them on your own machine rather than using the web-based versions). Regular expressions are an important concept to learn that will aid you greatly; you will need to spend some time on that section.

Now that we have our data — whether through Wget or by using Outwit Hub or some other tool — we have to start thinking about what to do with it! Luckily, we have many tools that will help us take a large quantity of information and "mine" it for the information that we might be looking for. These can be as simple as a word cloud, as we begin our chapter with, or as complicated as sophisticated topic modeling (the subject of Chapter 4) or network analysis (Chapters 6 and 7). Some tools are as easy to run as clicking a button on your computer and others require some under-the-hood investigation. This chapter aims to introduce you to the main contours of the field, providing a range of options, and also to give you the tools to participate more broadly in this exciting field of research. A key rule to remember is that there is no "right" or "wrong" way to do these forms of analysis: they are tools and, for most historians, the real lifting will come once you have the results. Yet we do need to realize that these tools shape our research: they can occasionally occlude context or mislead us. These questions are at the forefront of this chapter.

Basic Text Mining: Word Clouds, their Limitations, and Moving Beyond

Having large datasets does not mean that you need to jump into programming right away to extract meaning from them: far from it. There are three approaches that, while each have their limits, can shed light on your research question very quickly and easily. In many ways, these are "gateway drugs" into the deeper reaches of data visualization. In this section then,

---

Word Clouds — multiple locations, but we use http://wordle.net

General Principles

A word cloud lets you see a graphical representation of how often phrases appear in a body of text. If the word President appears 500 times, and the word Choice appears 200 times, the former word will appear larger than the latter. Do this on a large enough scale and you can *perhaps* get a sense of recurring concepts.

Description

Words are laid out, usually with different colors (often chosen aesthetically rather than to provide information), in patterns that can resemble a jumble or a shape. They are often pleasing to the eye.

Critique

The big issue is the lack of *context*. As we note, the word "taxes" might appear in a speech 100 times. But does that mean the candidate was in favor of them, or opposed to them? You only have the ability to learn about simple word frequency.

How to Use It

It is very easy to use! Visit http://wordle.net, click on "create," paste in your text — the portal supports very large datasets — and watch the results appear before your eyes.

How to Analyze the Results

The naked eye is necessary to analyze the results. You can download the picture and embed it in your document or website.

we briefly explore word clouds (via Wordle), as well as the comprehensive data analysis suite Voyant Tools. There are alternatives, of course, that can do many of the same kinds of analysis, including Many Eyes (http://many-eyes.com), an IBM product. While also very simple to use — one simply copies and pastes one's text or numeric data into a text box on the website, and fairly smart algorithms take care of the rest — the price for this simplicity is the transference of intellectual property rights of your data to IBM. The data also become available to any other user. For these reasons we will not go into any deeper discussion.

The simplest data visualization is a **word cloud**. In brief, they are generated through the following process. First, a computer program takes a text and counts how frequent each word is. In many cases, it will normalize the text to some degree, or at least give the user options: if "racing" appears 80 times and "Racing" appears five times, you may want it to register as a total of 85 times to that term. Of course, there may be other times when you do not, for example if there was a character named "Dog" as well as generic animals referred to as "dog". You may also want to remove stopwords, which add little to the final visualization in many cases. Second, after generating a word frequency list and incorporating these modifications, the program then puts them into order, sizing by frequency and begins to print them. The word that appears the most frequently is placed as the largest (and, usually, in the center). The second most frequent a bit smaller, the third most frequent a bit smaller than that, and continuing on to dozens of words. While, as we shall see, word clouds have strong critics, they are a very useful entryway into the world of basic text mining.

Try to create one yourself using the web site http://wordle.net. You simply click on "Create," paste in a bunch of text, and see the results. For example, you could take the plain text of Leo Tolstoy's novel *War and Peace* (a synonym for an overly long book, with over half a million words) and paste it in: you would see major character names (Pierre, Prince, Natasha who recur throughout), locations (Moscow), themes (warfare and nations such as France and Russia), and at a glance get a sense of what this novel might be about (Fig. 3.1). As English speakers, we have elected to use a translated version of the text.

Yet with such a visualization the main downside becomes clear: we lose context. Who are the protagonists? Who are the villains? As adjectives are separated from other concepts, we lose the ability to derive meaning. For example, a politician speaks of "taxes" frequently: but from a word cloud, it is difficult to learn whether they are positive or negative references. With

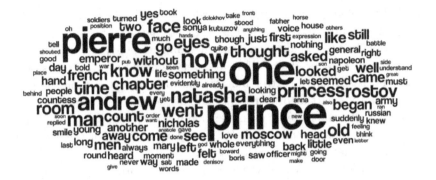

Fig. 3.1   *War and Peace* as a word cloud. Made with Wordle.net.

these shortcomings in mind, however, historians can find utility in word clouds. If we are concerned with change over time, we can trace how words evolved in historical documents. While this is fraught with issues — words change meaning over time, different terms are used to describe similar concepts, and we still face the issues outlined above — we can arguably still learn something from this.

Take the example of a dramatically evolving political party in Canada: the New Democratic Party (NDP), which occupies similar space on the political spectrum as Britain's Labour Party. While we understand that most of our readers are not Canadian, this will help with the example. It had its origins in agrarian and labour movements, being formed in 1933 as the Co-Operative Commonwealth Federation (CCF). Its defining and founding document was the "Regina Manifesto" of that same year, drafted at the height of the Great Depression. Let's visualize it as a word cloud (Fig. 3.2).

Stop! What do you think that this document was about? When you have a few ideas, read on for our interpretation.

At a glance, we argue that you can see the main elements of the political spirit of the movement. We see the urgency of the need to profoundly change Canada's economic system, with the boldness of "must," an evocative call that change needed to come immediately. Other main words such as "public," "system," "economic," and "power" speak to their critique of the economic system, and words such as capitalist, socialized, ownership, and worker speak to a socialist frame of analysis. You can piece together key components of their platform from this visualization alone.

For historians, though, the important element comes in change over time. Remember, we need to keep in mind that words might change. Let's

Fig. 3.2   The Regina Manifesto as a word cloud. Made with Wordle.net.

take two other major documents within this singular political tradition. In 1956, the CCF, in the context of the Cold War, released its second major political declaration in Winnipeg. Again, via a word cloud, Fig. 3.3:

Fig. 3.3   The CCF's Winnipeg Declaration of 1956 as a word cloud. Made with Wordle.net.

New words appear, representing a new thrust: "opportunity," "freedom," "international," "democratic," "world," "resources," and even "equality." Compared to the more focused, trenchant words found in the previous declaration, we see a different direction here. There is more focus on the international, Canada has received more attention than before, and most importantly, words like socialized have disappeared. Indeed, the CCF here was beginning to change its emphasis, backing away from overt calls for socialism. But the limitations of the word cloud also rear their head: for example, the word "private." Is private good? Bad? Is opportunity good, bad? Is freedom good, or bad? Without context, we cannot know from the image alone. But the changing words are useful.

For a more dramatic change, let's compare it to modern platforms. Today's New Democratic Party grew out of the CCF in 1961 and continues largely as an opposition party (traditionally a third party, although in 2012 it was propelled to the second-party Official Opposition status). By 2012, what do party platforms speak of? Fig. 3.4 gives us a sense:

Fig. 3.4   NDP platform for the 2012 Canadian General Election as a word cloud. Made with Wordle.net.

Taxes, families, Canada (which keeps building in significance over the period), work, employment, funding, insurance, homes, and so forth. In three small images, we have seen the evolution of a political party morph from an explicitly socialist party in 1933, to a waning of that during the Cold War climate of 1956, to the mainstream political party that it is today.

Thus, while they need to be used with caution, we believe that word clouds *can* tell us something. On his blog, digital historian Adam Crymble ran a quick study to see if historians would be able to reconstruct the contents of documents from these word clouds — could they look at a word cloud of a trial, for example, and correctly ascertain what the trial was about. He noted that, while substantial guesswork is involved, "an expert in the source material can, with reasonable accuracy, reconstruct some of the more basic details of what's going on."[1] It also represents the inversion of the traditional historical process: rather than looking at documents that we think may be important to our project and pre-existing thesis, we are looking at documents more generally to see what they might be about. With big data, it is sometimes important to let the sources speak to you, rather than looking at them with preconceptions of what you might find.

Word clouds need to be used cautiously. They do not explain context. This is the biggest shortcoming of word clouds, but we still believe that they are a useful entryway into the world of data visualization. Complementary to wider reading and other forms of inquiry, they present a quick and easy way into the world of data visualization. Once we are using these, we're visualizing data, and it's only a matter of how. In the pages that follow, we move from this very basic stage, to other basic techniques including AntConc and Voyant Tools, before moving into more sophisticated methods involving text patterns (or regular expressions), spatial techniques, and programs that can detect significant patterns and phrases within your corpus.

AntConc

AntConc is an invaluable way to carry out some forms of textual analysis on datasets. While it does not scale to the largest datasets terribly well, if you have somewhere in the ballpark of 500 or even 1,000 newspaper-length articles you should be able to crunch data and receive tangible results. AntConc can be downloaded online from Dr. Laurence Anthony's personal webpage at http://www.antlab.sci.waseda.ac.jp/software.html. Anthony, a researcher in corpus linguistics among many other varied pursuits, has created this software to carry out detailed textual analysis. Let's take a quick tour.

Installation, on all three operating systems, is a snap: one downloads the executables directly for OS X or Windows, and on Linux the user needs to change the file permissions to allow it to run as an executable. Let's explore a quick example to see what we can do with AntConc.

---

[1] Adam Crymble (5 August 2013), "Can We Reconstruct a Text from a Word-cloud?" *Thoughts on Digital and Public History,* http://adamcrymble.blogspot.ca/2013/08/can-we-reconstruct-text-from-wordcloud.html.

Once AntConc is running, you can import files by going to the File menu and clicking on either Import File(s) or Import Dir, which would allow you to import all the files within a directory. In the screenshot below, we opened up a directory containing plain text files of Toronto heritage plaques. The first visualization panel is "Concordance." We type in the search term "York", the old name of Toronto (pre-1834) and visualize the results (Fig. 3.5).

In this case, we can see various contexts in which "York" is being used: North York (a later municipality until 1998), ties to New York state and city, various companies, other boroughs, and so forth. A simple search for

---

Concordances — multiple ways to generate, but we use AntConc (http://www.laurenceanthony.net/software.html)

General Principles

A concordance allows you to see words on either side of your selected keyword, which can let you explore change over time, or simply to see the *context* in which a given word appears. For example, if you select "taxes" you might see

```
to raise taxes is good
to lower taxes is bad
```

And get a sense of what the speaker referred to when discussing taxes.

Description

Words are laid out in a string, with the selected word generally in the middle, followed by related words to either side.

Critique

They can be manually intensive to explore, and are not suited for all research questions. Concordances are also very good with relatively circumscribed corpuses — once you have hundreds or thousands, you need to find another tool to make sense of the concordances themselves!

How to Use It

AntConc is easy to use, as discussed here. You can also manually generate keyword-in-contexts by following the lessons at the *Programming Historian.*

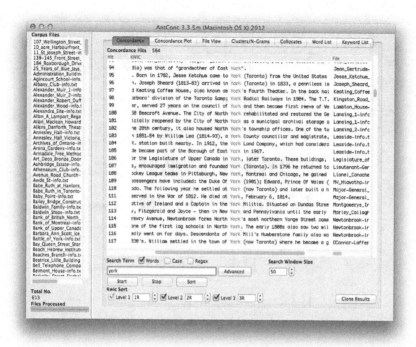

Fig. 3.5   The AntConc interface. Courtesy Laurence Anthony.

the keyword "York" would reveal many plaques that might not fit our specific query.

The other possibilities are even more exciting. The Concordance Plot traces where various keywords appear in files, which can be useful to see the overall density of a certain term. For example, in the below visualization of newspaper articles, we trace when frequent media references to "community" in the old Internet website GeoCities declined (Fig. 3.6).

It was dense in 1998 and 1999, but declined dramatically by 2000 — and even more dramatically as that year went on. It turns out, upon some close reading, that this is borne out by the archival record: Yahoo! acquired GeoCities, and discontinued the neighborhood and many internal community functions that had defined that archival community.

Collocates are an especially fruitful realm of exploration. Returning to our Toronto plaque example, if we look for the collocates of "York" we see several interesting results: "Fort" (referring to the military installation Fort York), "Infantry," "Mills" (the area of York Mills), "radial" (referring to

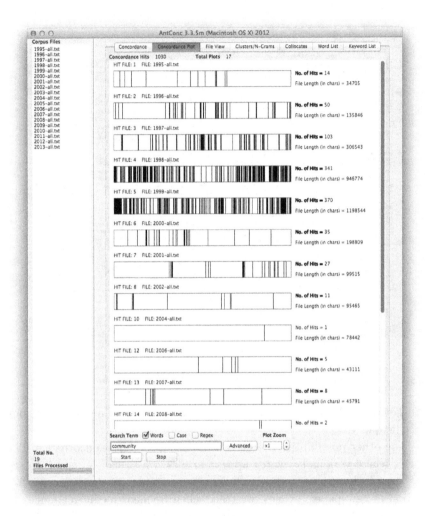

Fig. 3.6   Concordance plot tool in AntConc. Courtesy Laurence Anthony.

the York Radial Railway), and even slang such as "Muddy" ("Muddy York" being a Toronto nickname). With several documents, one could trace how collocates change over time: perhaps early documents refer to Fort York and subsequently we see more collocates referring to North York? Finally, AntConc also provides options for overall word and phrase frequency, as well as specific Ngram searching.

A free, powerful program, AntConc deserves to be the next step beyond Wordle for many undergraduates. It takes textual analysis to the next level. Finally, let's move to the last of our three tools that we explore in this section: Voyant Tools. This set of tools takes some of the graphical sheen of Wordle and weds it to the underlying, sophisticated, textual analysis of AntConc.

Voyant Tools — http://voyant-tools.org/

General Principles

Voyant Tools combines several of the tools that we have discussed so far. Users provide it with a corpus of text and are presented with a word cloud, word frequency information broken down into a table, frequency over time as a graph, and keyword-in-context information.

Description

Users have a workbench to do their work with: it is customizable and reasonably intuitive. If you have larger datasets, you can download and run the program on your own computer. For most applications, you can simply visit the website to use it.

Critique

The individual components face the same shortcomings as before, mitigated to some degree by having different tools all presented together (you can click on a word in the word cloud and see the context in which it appears, for example). The website can occasionally go down and data saved on it are not reliably retained.

How to Use It

It is very easy to use! Visit http://voyant-tools.org/ and paste in the text that you want to analyze. If you want to run your own server, keep reading.

How to Analyze the Results

While you will generally analyze results within the Voyant workbench, you can export any of the results by clicking on the "gear" icon in the upper right portion of the data panels. You can also click the "save" icon to embed a panel from the program into a document, or even your own website!

Voyant Tools

With your tongue whetted, you might want to have a more sophisticated way to explore large quantities of information. The suite of tools known as Voyant provides this. It provides complicated output with simple input. Growing out of the Hermeneuti.ca project,[2] Voyant is an integrated textual analysis platform. Getting started is quick. Simply navigate to http://voyant-tools.org/ and either paste a large body of text into the box, provide a website address, or click on the "upload" button to load text or PDF files into the system.

Voyant works on a single document or on a larger corpus. For the former, just upload one file or paste the text in; for the latter, upload multiple files at that initial stage. After uploading, the workbench will appear as demonstrated in Fig. 3.7. The workbench provides an array of basic visualization and text analysis tools at your disposal. For customization or more options, remember that for each of the smaller panes you can click on the "gear" icon to get advanced icons, including how you want to treat cases (do you want upper and lower case to be treated the same) and whether you want to include or exclude common stopwords.

With a large corpus, you can do the following things:

- In the "Summary" box, track words that rise and fall. For example, with multiple documents uploaded in order of their year, you can see what words see significant increases over time, or significant decreases.
- For each individual word, see how its frequency varies over the length of the corpus. Clicking on a word in the text box will generate a line chart in the upper right. You can control for case.
- For each individual word, you can also see the "keyword-in-context" in the lower right-hand — by default, three words to the left and the three words to the right.
- Track the distribution of a word by clicking on it and seeing where it is located within the document alongside the left-hand of the central text column.

If you press Ctrl and click on multiple words, you can compare words in each of these windows.

---

[2]Stéfan Sinclair and Geoffrey Rockwell. *Hermenutic.ca — The Rhetoric of Text Analysis*, http://hermeneuti.ca.

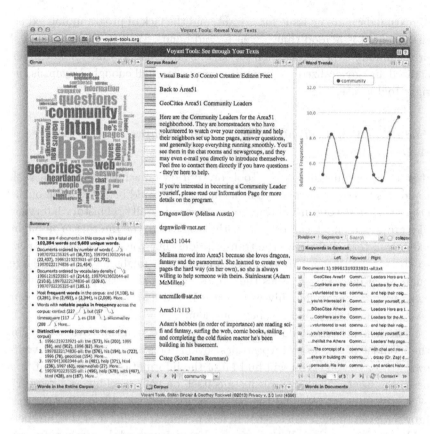

Fig. 3.7   The standard Voyant Tools interface screen. Courtesy Stéfan Sinclair and Geoffrey Rockwell.

These are all useful ways to interpret documents, and a low barrier to entering this sort of textual analysis work. Voyant is ideal for smaller corpuses of information or classroom purposes.

Voyant, however, is best understood — like Wordle, albeit far more sophisticated — as a "gateway drug" when it comes to textual analysis. This default version is hosted on the McGill University servers, which limits the ability to process very large datasets. They do offer a home server installation as well, discussed shortly.

None of this, however, is to minimize the importance and utility of Voyant Tools, arguably the best research portal in existence. Even the most seasoned big data humanist can turn to Voyant for quick checks, or when they are dealing with smaller (yet still large) repositories. A few megabytes of textual data are no issue for Voyant, and the lack of programming expertise required is a good thing, even for old hands. We have several years of programming experience amongst us and often use Voyant for both specialized and generalized inquiries: if a corpus is small enough, Voyant is the right tool to use.[3]

Installing Voyant Tools on your own machine: A Quick Aside

It is possible to install Voyant Tools on your own machine. You might wish to do this to keep control of your documents. It could be a condition of the ethics review at your institution, for instance, that all oral history interview files are stored on a local machine without access to the Internet. You might like to run text analysis on the transcriptions, but you cannot upload them to the regular Voyant Tools server. Finally, you might have a very large quantity of data that crashes the Voyant Tools online site, but that your own computer could handily work with. If you had Voyant Tools on your own machine, this would not be a problem.

The instructions could change with newer versions of Voyant, but for the moment if you go to http://docs.voyant-tools.org/resources/run-your-own/voyant-server/, you will find all of the information and files that you need. In essence, Voyant Tools installs itself on your machine as a "server" — it will serve up files and the results of its analysis to you via your web browser, even though you are not in fact pulling anything over the Internet.

It is a very easy installation process. If you download the server software, unzip it, and then execute the VoyantServer.jar file, a control console will open, and when you click "start server," your browser will also appear. In the control console, you can change how much memory Voyant Tools can access to perform its operations. By default, it will use one gigabyte

---

[3]There are more tools available in Voyant by clicking on the "save" icon in the top-right side of the page in the blue "Voyant Tools: Reveal Your Texts" title bar. This icon opens a pop-up with five different export options. The first, "a URL for this tool and current data" will provide you with a direct URL to your corpus which you may then share with others or return to at a later time; the final option, "a URL for a different tool/skin and current data" will open another menu allowing you to select which tool you'd like to use. If you selected "RezoViz" (a tool for constructing a network with organizations, individuals, and place names extracted from your texts), you would end up with a URL like this: http://voyant-tools.org/tool/RezoViz/?corpus=1394819798940.8347. The string of numbers is the corpus ID for your texts. If you know the name of another tool, you can type it in after /tool/ and before /?corpus.

of memory. This should be enough for most of your text analysis, but if you get an error saying you need more memory — if you are putting in lots of data, for example — you can increase this. When you are done with Voyant, you can click "stop server" and it will close.

In the browser, you will see this address in the address bar: http://127.0.0.1:8888. This means that the page is being served to you locally, through port 8888. You do not need to worry about that, unless you are running other servers on your machine at the same time.

Clustering Data to Find Powerful Patterns with Overview

Journalists have recently taken to big data and data visualization, as a response to the massive data dumps occasioned by such things as Wikileaks or the Snowden revelations. The Knight Foundation, for instance, has been promoting the development of new tools to help journalists and communities deal with the deluge. Past winners of the Knight News Challenge have included crowd-mapping applications such as Ushahidi (http://ushahidi.com/), or DocumentCloud (http://documentcloud.org/home). Indeed, some historians have used these applications in their own work, and historians could usefully repurpose these projects to their own ends.[4]

A recent project to emerge from the Knight News Challenge is "Overview." Overview has some affinities with topic modeling, discussed in the following chapter, and so we suggest it here as a more user-friendly approach to exploring themes within your data.[5] Overview can be installed for free on your own computer.[6] However, if your data warrants it (i.e. there are no privacy concerns), you can go to **http://overviewdocs.com/** and upload your materials to their servers and begin exploring.

---

[4]See Shawn Graham, Guy Massie and Nadine Feurherm (2013), "The HeritageCrowd Project: A Case Study in Crowdsourcing Public History," in *Writing History in the Digital Age*, Jack Dougherty and Kristen Mawrotszki (eds), Ann Arbor, MI: University of Michigan Press, available at http://dx.doi.org/10.3998/dh.12230987.0001.001.

[5]Jonathan Stray has written an excellent piece on using Overview as part of a "data journalism" workflow, many points of which are appropriate to the historian. See Jonathan Stray (14 March 2014), "You Got the Documents. Now What? — Learning — Source: An OpenNews Project," *Source*, https://source.opennews.org/en-US/learning/you-got-documents-now-what/.

[6]The documentation for Overview may be found at http://overview.ap.org/; the software itself can be downloaded at https://github.com/overview/overview-server/wiki/Installing-and-Running-Overview.

Overview Project — https://www.overviewproject.org/

General Principles

Overview is designed to identify order within large sets of documents, using powerful search and natural language processing routines to file documents into nested folders of progressively greater and greater similarity.

Description

Users can upload PDFs, CSV, DOC and HTML files via a standard document upload page. Overview sorts the documents according to their topical similarity. The user can then jump back and forth between this visualization and the source documents, using this jump as a way of performing both "close" and "distant" readings.

Critique

Overview's interface can become cluttered quite quickly once a number of tags are created.

How to Use It

It is very easy to use! Visit https://www.overviewproject.org/, create an account, and then upload your documents. If you want to run your own server, keep reading.

How to Analyze the Results

The user may add tags to the folders, to impose semantic order on it, and export the tagged documents to a spreadsheet for further analysis. The visualization of the folder tree will use the colors of the tags to show how many documents with that tag exist in a particular folder. One can also quickly discover "outliers," or subfolders with documents that do not fit the broader corpus. Using complex searches for terms and then tagging the results, the user can trace themes and ideas within the documents across the collection.

Overview explores word patterns in your text using a rather different process than topic modeling, which you will learn about in the next chapter. It looks at the occurrence of words in every pair of documents. "If a word appears twice in one document, it's counted twice... we multiply the frequencies of corresponding words, then add up the results."[7] (The technical phrase is "term frequency-inverse document frequency".) Documents are then grouped together using a clustering algorithm based on this similarity of scores. It categorizes your documents into folders, subfolders, sub-subfolders. Let's say that we are interested in the ways historical sites and monuments are recorded in the city of Toronto. We upload the full text of these historical plaques (614 texts) into Overview (Fig. 3.8).

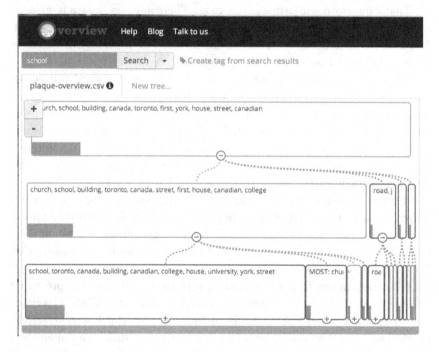

Fig. 3.8 The Overview interface sorting the text of historical plaques from Toronto. Courtesy Jonathan Stray, *et al.*, Overview Project.

Overview divides the historical plaques, at the broadest level, of similarity into the following groups:

'church, school, building, toronto, canada, street, first, house, canadian, college (545 plaques),

---

[7]http://overview.ap.org/blog/2013/04/how-overview-can-organize-thousands-of-documents-for-a-reporter/.

'road, john_graves, humber, graves_simcoe, lake, river, trail, plant' (41 plaques)

'community' with 'italian, north_york, lansing, store, shepard, dempsey, sheppard_avenue', 13 documents

'years' with 'years_ago, glacier, ice, temperance, transported, found, clay, excavation', 11 documents.

That's interesting information to know. There appears to be a large division between what might be termed "architectural history" — first school, first church, first street — and "social history." Why does this division exist? That would be an interesting question to explore.

Overview is great for visualizing patterns of similar word use across sets of documents. Once you've examined those patterns, assigning tags for different patterns, Overview can export your texts with those descriptive labels as a CSV file, that is, as a table. Thus, you could use a spreadsheet program to create bar charts of the count of documents with an "architecture" tag or a "union history" tag, or "children," "women," "agriculture," etc. We might wonder how plaques concerned with "children," "women," "agriculture," "industry," etc. might be grouped, so we could use Overview's search function to identify these plaques by searching for a word or phrase and applying that word or phrase as a tag to everything that is found. One could then visually explore the way various tags correspond with particular folders of similar documents.[8]

Using tags in this fashion, comparing with the visual structure presented by Overview, is a dialogue between a close and distant reading. Overview thus does what it set out to do: it provides a quite quick and relatively painless way to get a broad sense of what is going on within your documents.

Manipulating Text with the Power of Regular Expressions

A regular expression (also called regex) is a powerful tool for finding and manipulating text.[9] At its simplest, a regular expression is just a way of looking through texts to locate (case sensitive) patterns. A regular

---

[8] As in this example http://overview.ap.org/blog/2013/07/comparing-text-to-data-by-importing-tags/.

[9] Regex expressions are sometimes instantiated differently depending on which program you are working with. They simply do not work in Microsoft Word. For best results, try TextWrangler (on Mac) or Notepad++ (in Windows).

Regular Expressions — aka Regex http://www.regexr.com/

General Principles

You no doubt have used find-and-replace in a word processor, but have run into the frustration of wanting to replace, say, a day-month-year date into a month-day-year format. Wouldn't it be good if you could just automatically search for a date, and rearrange the month and day automatically? Normal find-and-replace can't do that: but regular expressions can. Instead of specifying *what* to search for, you describe the *pattern* instead.

Description

Regex emerges from the early days of computer science when the UNIX system was dominant. Text editors and development environments that support regex have a built-in processor that parses the pattern the user specifies. There are various "flavors" of regex; we use a cheat sheet to help us, depending on which system we happen to be working on: http://www.regular-expressions.info/.

Critique

The learning curve with regular expressions, since they describe a *pattern* for the machine to look for, can be formidable.

How to Use It

Regex is not easy. We recommend practising first with something like http://www.regexr.com/. You can paste some of your data into this tool, write a regex, and test to see if it does what you want it to do. If it does, you can then go back to your text editor and run the regex on your actual data. **Save often** when doing regex text manipulations. TextWrangler (Mac) and Notepad++ (PC) can do regex searches.

---

expression can help you find every line that begins with a number, or every instance of an email address, or whenever a word is used even if there are slight variations in how it's spelled. As long as you can describe the pattern you're looking for, regular expressions can help you find it. Once you've found your patterns, they can then help you manipulate your text so that it fits just what you need. Regular expressions can be difficult, but they are worth it.

This section will explain how to take a book scanned and available on the Internet Archive, *Diplomatic correspondence of the Republic of Texas*, and manipulate the raw text into a format that you can use in the Gephi network visualization package. We will end with a correspondence network. In this section, we begin with a simple unstructured index of letters and then use regular expressions to turn the text into a spreadsheet that can be edited in a program like Excel.

Regular expressions can look pretty complex but once you know the basic syntax and vocabulary, simple "regexes" will be easy. **Regular expressions can often be used right inside the "find-and-replace" box in many text and document editors, such as Notepad++ on Windows, or TextWrangler on OS X. You cannot use regex with Microsoft Word, however!** You can find Notepad++ at http://notepad-plus-plus.org/ or TextWrangler at http://www.barebones.com/products/textwrangler/. Both are free and well worth downloading, depending on the platform that you use. This lesson is designed to work with these editors. Results may differ with other editors.

You type the regular expression in the search bar, press "find," and any words that match the pattern you're looking for will appear on the screen. On TextWrangler, select the "grep" box to enable regular expressions. For Notepad++, select the "regular expressions" tab. As you proceed through this section, you may want to look for other things. In addition to the basics provided here, you will also be able to simply search regular expression libraries online: for example, if you want to find all postal codes, you can search "regular expression Canadian postal code" and learn what "formula" to search for to find them.

Let's start with the basics and say you're looking for all the instances of "cat" or "dog" in your document. When you type the vertical bar on your keyboard (it looks like |, shift+backslash on Windows keyboards), which means "or" in regular expressions. So, if your query is dog|cat and you press "find," it will show you the first time either dog or cat appears in your text. Open up a new file in your editor and write some words that include "dog" and "cat" and try it out (also include "Dog" and "Cat" — your query won't find those words, as regular expressions know the difference between D and d!)

If you want to replace every instance of either "cat" or "dog" in your document with the world "animal", you would open your find-and-replace box, put dog|cat in the search query, put animal in the "replace" box, hit "replace all," and watch your entire document fill up with references to animals instead of dogs and cats.

The astute reader will have noticed a problem with the instructions above; simply replacing every instance of "dog" or "cat" with "animal" is bound to create problems. Simple searches don't differentiate between letters and spaces, so every time "cat" or "dog" appear within words, they'll also be replaced with "animal". "catch" will become "animalch"; "dogma" will become "animalma"; "certificate" will become "certifianimale". In this case, the solution appears simple: put a **space** before and after your search query, so now it reads:

```
dog | cat
```

With the spaces, "animal" replaces "dog" or "cat" only in those instances where they're definitely complete words; that is, when they're separated by spaces.

The even more astute reader will notice that this still does not solve our problem of replacing every instance of "dog" or "cat". What if the word comes at the beginning of a line, so it is not in front of a space? What if the word is at the end of a sentence or a clause and thus followed by a punctuation mark? Luckily, in the language of regex, you can represent the beginning or end of a word using special characters.

```
\b
```

means the beginning of a word. So if you search for \bcat it will find "cat", "catch", and "catsup" but not "copycat", because your query searched for words beginning with "cat". For patterns at the end of the line, you would use:

```
\b
```

again. If you search for:

```
cat\b
```

it will find "cat" and "copycat" but not "catch", because your query searched for words ending with -"cat".

Regular expressions can be mixed, so if you wanted to find words only matching "cat", no matter where in the sentence, you'd search for:

```
\bcat\b
```

which would find every instance. And, because all regular expressions can be mixed, if you searched for:

```
\bcat\b|\bdog\b
```

and replaced all with "animal", you would have a document that replaced all instances of "dog" or "cat" with "animal", no matter where in the sentence they appear.

You can also search for variations within a single word using parentheses. For example if you were looking for instances of "gray" or "grey", instead of the search query

`gray|grey`

you could type

`gr(a|e)y`

The parentheses signify a group, and like the order of operations in arithmetic, regular expressions read the parentheses before anything else. Similarly, if you wanted to find instances of either "that dog" or "that cat", you would search for:

`(that dog)|(that cat)`

Notice that the vertical bar | can appear either inside or outside the parentheses, depending on what you want to search for.

The period character . in regular expressions directs the search to just find any character at all. For example, if we searched for:

`d.g`

the search would return "dig", "dog", "dug" and so forth.

Another special character from our cheat sheet, the plus + instructs the program to find any number of the previous character. If we search for

`do+g`

it would return any words that looked like "dog", "doog", "dooog", and so forth. Adding parentheses before the plus would make a search for repetitions of whatever is in the parentheses, for example querying

`(do)+g`

would return "dog", "dodog", "dododog", and so forth.

Combining the plus "+" and period "." characters can be particularly powerful in regular expressions, instructing the program to find any amount of any characters within your search. A search for

`d.+g`

for example, might return "dried fruits are g", because the string begins with "d" and ends with "g", and has various characters in the middle.

Searching for simply ".+" will yield query results that are entire lines of text because you are searching for any character and any amount of them.

Parentheses in regular expressions are also very useful when replacing text. The text within a regular expression forms what's called a group, and the software you use to search remembers which groups you queried in order of their appearance. For example, if you search for

```
(dogs)( and )(cats)
```

which would find all instances of "dogs and cats" in your document, your program would remember "**dogs**" as group 1, " **and** " as group 2, and "**cats**" as group 3. Your text editor remembers them as "\1", "\2", and "\3" for each group, respectively.

If you wanted to switch the order of "dogs" and "cats" every time the phrase "dogs and cats" appeared in your document, you would type

```
(dogs)( and )(cats)
```

in the "find" box, and

```
\3\2\1
```

in the "replace" box. That would replace the entire string with group 3 ("cats") in the first spot, group 2 (" and ") in the second spot, and group 1 ("dogs") in the last spot, thus changing the result to "cats and dogs".

The vocabulary of regular expressions is pretty large, but there are many cheat sheets for regex online (one that we sometimes use is http://regexlib.com/CheatSheet.aspx. Another good one is at http://docs.active state.com/komodo/4.4/regex-intro.html).

To illustrate, we've included an example of searching using regular expressions that draws from these cheat sheets, to provide a sense of how you would use it to form your own regular expressions. It uses a corpus of diplomatic correspondence in 19th century Texas. Using regular expressions, we will turn an unformatted index of correspondences, drawn from a book, into a structured file that can be read in Excel or any of a number of network analysis tools. A portion of the original file, drawn from the Internet Archive, looks like this:

```
Sam Houston to A. B. Roman, September 12, 1842 101
Sam Houston to A. B. Roman, October 29, 1842 101
Correspondence for 1843-1846 ---
Isaac Van Zandt to Anson Jones, January 11, 1843 103
```

By the end of this workflow, it will look like this:

```
Sam Houston, A. B. Roman, September 12 1842
Sam Houston, A. B. Roman, October 29 1842
Isaac Van Zandt, Anson Jones, January 11 1843
```

While the changes appear insignificant, it will allow us to turn this index into something that a network analysis program (for instance) could read and make visual sense of. It is, in fact, turning an OCR'd page of text into a CSV file!

Begin by pointing your browser to the document listed below.[10] With your web browser, visit https://archive.org/stream/diplomaticcorre33 statgoog/diplomaticcorre33statgoog_djvu.txt. Please then copy and paste the text into your text editor, either Notepad++ (PC) or TextWrangler (Mac).[11] You can do this by pressing Ctrl+A (Windows) or Cmd+A (Mac). It'll look a bit messy, but that's where the next step comes in.

Remember to save a spare copy of your file before you begin — this is very important because you're going to make mistakes that you won't be sure how to fix.

Now delete everything but the index where it has the list of letters. Look for this in the text, as depicted in Fig. 3.9, and delete everything that comes before it (what you're looking for begins at approximately line 260 and continues until line 2,670, depending on how carefully you selected the text when you copied and pasted). This can be a bit time-consuming, so feel free to skip this step and download our online version at http://themacroscope.org/2.0/datafiles/raw-correspondence.txt. If you run into problems, try using our "raw-correspondence.txt" file, found in the footnote below, instead of copying and pasting from your browser.

If you want to do it yourself, however, you're looking for the table of letters, starting with "Sam Houston to J. Pinckney Henderson, December 31, 1836 51" and ending with "Wm. Henry Daingerfield to Ebenezer Allen, February 2, 1846 1582". There are, before we clean them, approximately 2,400 lines worth of entries indexed in this table.

Notice that there is a lot of text that we are not interested in at the moment: page numbers, headers, footers, or categories. We're going to use

---

[10]We have lodged a copy of this file also at http://themacroscope.org/2.0/datafiles/source-texas-correspondence.txt.

[11]Notepad++ (for Windows) can be downloaded at http://notepad-plus-plus.org/. Text wrangler (for Mac) can be found at http://www.barebones.com/products/textwrangler/.

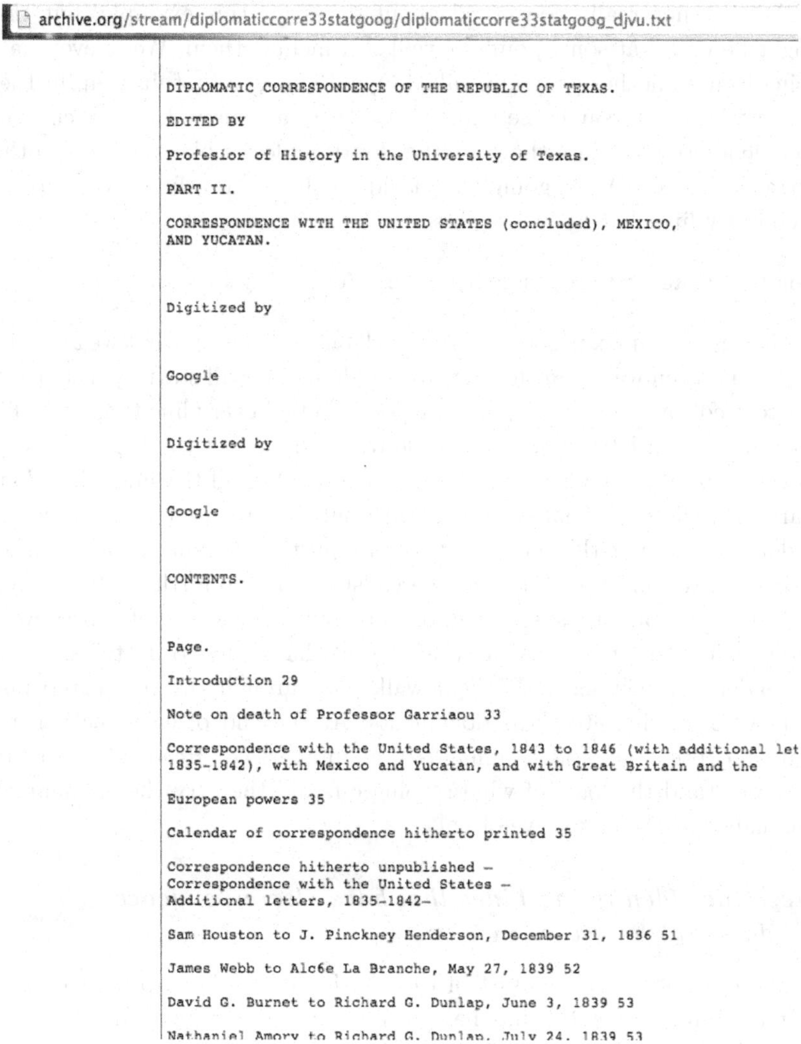

archive.org/stream/diplomaticcorre33statgoog/diplomaticcorre33statgoog_djvu.txt

```
DIPLOMATIC CORRESPONDENCE OF THE REPUBLIC OF TEXAS.

EDITED BY

Profesior of History in the University of Texas.

PART II.

CORRESPONDENCE WITH THE UNITED STATES (concluded), MEXICO,
AND YUCATAN.


Digitized by


Google


Digitized by


Google


CONTENTS.


Page.

Introduction 29

Note on death of Professor Garriaou 33

Correspondence with the United States, 1843 to 1846 (with additional let
1835-1842), with Mexico and Yucatan, and with Great Britain and the

European powers 35

Calendar of correspondence hitherto printed 35

Correspondence hitherto unpublished —
Correspondence with the United States —
Additional letters, 1835-1842—

Sam Houston to J. Pinckney Henderson, December 31, 1836 51

James Webb to Alc6e La Branche, May 27, 1839 52

David G. Burnet to Richard G. Dunlap, June 3, 1839 53

Nathaniel Amory to Richard G. Dunlap, July 24, 1839 53
```

Fig. 3.9 Screenshot of the metadata to delete in the archive.org file on the diplomatic correspondence of the Republic of Texas.

regular expressions to get rid of them. Our end goal is to end up with a CSV file, which when opened in a spreadsheet would have three columns called:

Sender, Recipient, Date

We are not really concerned about dates for this example, but they might be useful at some point so we'll still include them. We're eventually going to use another program, called OpenRefine, to fix things up further.

Scroll down through the text. Notice there are many lines which don't include a letter because they're either header info, or blank, or some other extraneous text. We're going to get rid of all of those lines. We want to keep every line that looks like this:

```
Sender to Recipient, Month, Date, Year, Page
```

This is a complex process, so first we'll outline exactly what we are going to do, and then walk you through how to do it. We will start by instructing our text editor, using a regular expression, to find every line that looks like a reference to a letter and put a tilde (a ~ symbol) at the beginning of it so we know to save it for later. Next, we get rid of all the lines that don't start with tildes, so that we're left with only the relevant text. After this is done, we format the remaining text by putting commas in appropriate places, so we can import it into a spreadsheet and do further edits there.

There are lots of ways we can do this, but for the sake of clarity we're going to just delete every line that doesn't have the word "to" in it (as in sender TO recipient). We will walk you through the seven-step plan of how to manipulate these documents. At the end of each section, the regular expressions and commands are summarized. Read the step first to understand the logic of what's going on, and then try the summarized commands at the end. Save often!

Step One: Identifying Lines that have Correspondence Senders and Receivers in them

Move your cursor to the start of the file. In Notepad++, press Ctrl-F or search → find to open the find dialogue box. In that box, go to the "Replace" tab and check the radio box for "Regular expression" at the bottom of the search box. In TextWrangler, hit command+F to open the find-and-replace dialogue box. Tick off the "grep" radio button (which tells TextWrangler that we want to do a regex search) and the "wraparound" button (which tells TextWrangler to search everywhere).

Remember from earlier that there's a way to see if the word "to" appears in full. Type

```
\bto\b
```

in the search bar. This will find every instance of the word "to" (and not, for instance, also "pota**to**" or "**to**morrow").[12]

We don't just want to find "to", but the entire line that contains it. We assume that every line that contains the word "to" in full is a line that has relevant letter information, and every line that does not is one we do not need. You learned earlier that the query ".+" returns any amount of text, no matter what it says. If your query is

`.+\bto\b.+`

your search will return every line which includes the word "to" in full, no matter what comes before or after it, and none of the lines which don't (it would not find lines that began with "to", which is good in this case; for future reference, if you did want to do that, you could just remove the first ".+\b").

As mentioned earlier, we want to add a tilde ~ before each of the lines that look like letters, so we can save them for later. This involves the find-and-replace function, and a query identical to the one before but with parentheses around it, so it looks like

`(.+\bto\b.+)`

and the entire line is placed within a parenthetical group. In the "replace" box, enter

`~ \1`

which just means replace the line with itself (group 1), placing a tilde before it. Make sure you use the digit '1' not the letter 'l'. In short, that's:

> **STEP ONE COMMANDS:**
>
> **Find:** `(.+\bto\b.+)`
>
> **Replace:** `~ \1`
>
> **Click "Replace All".**

---

[12]Remember, these are markers for "word boundaries." See http://www.regular-expressions.info/wordboundaries.html.

Step Two: Removing Lines that Aren't Relevant

After running the find-and-replace, you should note your document now has most of the lines with tildes in front of it and a few which do not. The next step is to remove all the lines that do not include a tilde. The search string to find all lines that don't begin with tildes is

\n[^~].+

A \n at the beginning of a query searches for a new line, which means it's going to start searching at the first character of each new line.

However, given the evolution of computing, it may well be that this won't quite work on your system. Linux based systems use \n for a new line (which refers to a "line feed" character), while Windows often uses \r\n (the \r. refers to a "carriage return"), and older Macs just use \r. These are the sorts of things that digital historians need to keep in mind! Since this will likely cause much frustration, your safest bet will be to save a copy of what you are working on and then experiment to see what gives you the best result. In most cases, this will be:

\r\n[^~].+

Within a set of square brackets [ ] the caret ^ means search for anything that isn't within these brackets; in this case, the tilde ~. The .+ as before means search for all the rest of the characters in the line as well. All together, the query returns any full line which does not begin with a tilde; that is, the lines we did not mark as looking like letters.

By finding all \r\n[^~].+ and replacing it with **nothing**, you effectively delete all the lines that don't look like letters. What you're left with is a series of letters and a series of blank lines.

STEP TWO COMMANDS (SAVE before you run this command so you can undo if necessary!):

Find: \r\n[^~].+

(Remember, you may need to search something like: \n[^~].+ instead, depending on your system)

Replace:

Click "Replace All".

Step Three: Removing the Blank Lines

We need to remove those surplus blank lines. The find-and-replace query for that is:

> **STEP THREE COMMANDS:**
>
> **Find:** \n\r
>
> (In TextWrangler on OS X): ^\r
>
> **Replace:**
>
> **Click "Replace All".**

Step Four: Beginning the Transformation Into a Spreadsheet

Now that all the extraneous lines have been deleted, it's time to format the text document into something you can import into and manipulate with Excel as a *.CSV, or a comma-separated-value file. A *.CSV is a text file which spreadsheet programs like Microsoft Excel can read, where every comma denotes a new column and every line denotes a new row.

To turn this text file into a spreadsheet, we'll want to separate it out into one column for sender, one for recipient, and one for date, each separated by a single comma. Notice that most lines have extraneous page numbers attached to them; we can get rid of those with regular expressions. There's also usually a comma separating the month-date and the year, which we'll get rid of as well. In the end, the first line should go from looking like:

~Sam Houston to J. Pinckney Henderson, December 31, 1836 51

to

Sam Houston, J. Pinckney Henderson, December 31 1836

such that each data point is in its own column.

Start by removing the page number after the year and the comma between the year and the month-date. To do this, first locate the year on each line by using the regex:

[0-9]{4}

In a regular expression, [0-9] finds any digit between 0 and 9, and {4} will find four of them together. Now extend that search out by appending .+ to the end of the query; as seen before, it will capture the entire rest of the line. The query

```
[0-9]{4}.+
```

will return, for example, "1836 51", "1839 52", and "1839 53" from the first three lines of the text. We also want to capture the comma preceding the year, so add a comma and a space before the query, resulting in

```
, [0-9]{4}.+
```

which will return ", 1836 51", ", 1839 52", etc.

The next step is making the parenthetical groups which will be used to remove parts of the text with find-and-replace. **In this case, we want to remove the comma and everything after year, but not the year or the space before it**. Thus our query will look like:

```
(,)( [0-9]{4})(.+)
```

with the comma as the first group "\1", the space and the year as the second "\2", and the rest of the line as the third "\3". Given that all we care about retaining is the second group (we want to keep the year, but not the comma or the page number), the find-and-replace will look like this:

STEP FOUR COMMANDS:

Find: (,)([0-9]{4})(.+)

Replace: \2

Click "Replace All".

Step Five: Removing Tildes

The next step is easy; remove the tildes we added at the beginning of each line, and replace them with nothing to delete them.

STEP FIVE COMMANDS:

Find: ~

Replace:

Click "Replace All".

Step Six: Separating Senders and Receivers

Finally, to separate the sender and recipient by a comma, we find all instances of the word "to" and replace it with a comma. Although we used \b to denote the beginning and end of a word earlier in the lesson, we don't exactly do that here. We include the space preceding the "to" in the regular expression, as well as the \b to denote the word ending. Once we find instances of the word and the space preceding it, " to\b", we replace it with a comma ",".

STEP SIX COMMANDS:

Find: to\b

Remember, there's a space in front of "to\b"

Replace: ,

Click "Replace All".

Step Seven: Cleaning Up Messy Data

You may notice that some lines still do not fit our criteria. Line 22, for example, reads "Abner S. Lipscomb, James Hamilton and A. T. Bumley, AugUHt 15, ". It has an incomplete date; these we don't need to worry about for our purposes. More worrisome are lines like 61 "Copy and summary of instructions United States Department of State, " which include none of the information we want. We can get rid of these lines later in Excel.

The only non-standard lines we need to worry about with regular expressions are the ones with more than two commas, like line 178, "A. J. Donelson, Secretary of State [Allen,. arf interim], December 10 1844". Notice that our second column, the name of the recipient, has a comma inside it. If you were to import this directly into Excel, you would get four columns — one for sender, two for recipient, and one for date — which would break any analysis you would then like to run. Unfortunately these lines need to be fixed by hand, but happily regular expressions make finding them easy. The query:

.+,.+,.+,

will show you every line with more than two commas because it finds any line that has any set of characters, then a comma, then any other set, then another comma, and so forth.

STEP Seven COMMANDS:

Find: .+,.+,.+,

Fix the line by hand, and then click "Find Next".

Celebrate! You're almost done!

After using this query, just find each occurrence (there will be 13 of them) and **replace the appropriate comma with another character that signifies it was there, like a semicolon**. While you're searching, you may find some other lines, like 387, "`Barnard E. Bee, James Treat, April 28, 1`≫`40 665`", which are still not quite perfect. If you see them, go ahead and fix them by hand so they fit the proper format, deleting the lines that are not relevant. There will also be leftover lines that are clearly not letters; delete those lines. Finally, there may be snippets of text left over at the bottom of the file. Highlight these and delete them.

At the top of the file, add a new line that simply reads "Sender, Recipient, Date". These will be the column headers.

Go to file → save as, and save the file as `cleaned-correspondence.csv`.

Congratulations! You have used regular expressions to extract and clean data. This skill alone will save you valuable time. A copy of the cleaned correspondence file is available at http://themacroscope.org/2.0/datafiles/cleaned-correspondence.csv. Note that the file online has been fixed by hand, so it is well formatted. The file you worked on in this walkthrough still needs some additional cleaning, such as the removal of lines like 61 "`Copy and summary of instructions United States Department of State,`".

Cleaning Data with OpenRefine

OpenRefine is a powerful tool that originated within Google. Since 2012, it has become a free, open source tool under continual community development. It allows users to get a quick overview of their data, find the messy bits, and start to transform the data into a usable format for further analyses. At the OpenRefine webpage, there are numerous tutorials, background information, and manuals that we strongly recommend any historian to explore. Here, we continue our example from above and use OpenRefine to clean up the data that we extracted using the regex (like in our section above about installing Voyant Tools locally, OpenRefine runs as a server on your own computer).

Download OpenRefine from http://openrefine.org/download.html. Follow the installation instructions. Start OpenRefine by double-clicking on its icon. This will open a new browser window, pointing to http://127.0.0. 1:3333. This location is your own computer so, even though it looks like it's running on the Internet, it isn't. The "3333" is a "port," meaning that OpenRefine is running much like a server, serving up a webpage via that port to the browser.

Start a new project by clicking on the "create project" tab on the left-hand side of the screen. Click on "choose files" and select the CSV file created in the previous section. This will give you a preview of your data. Name your project in the box on the top right side and then click "create project." It may take a few minutes.

Once your project has started, one of the columns that should be visible in your data is "sender." Click on the arrow to the left of "Sender" in OpenRefine and select Facet → Text Facet. Do the same with the arrow next to "Recipient." A box will appear on the left side of the browser showing all 189 names listed as senders in the spreadsheet (Fig. 3.10).

The spreadsheet itself is nearly a thousand rows, so immediately we see that, in this correspondence collection, some names are used multiple times. You may also have noticed that many of the names suffered from errors in the text scan (OCR errors), rendering some identical names from the book as similar, but not the same, in the spreadsheet. For example the recipient "Juan de Dios Cafiedo" is occasionally listed as "Juan de Dios CaAedo". Any subsequent analysis will need these errors to be cleared up, and OpenRefine will help fix them.

Within the "Sender" facet box on the left-hand side, click on the button labeled "Cluster." This feature presents various automatic ways of merging values that appear to be the same.[13] Play with the values in the drop-down boxes and notice how the number of clusters found changes depending on

---

[13]This is described in more detail here https://github.com/OpenRefine/OpenRefine/wiki/Clustering-In-Depth.

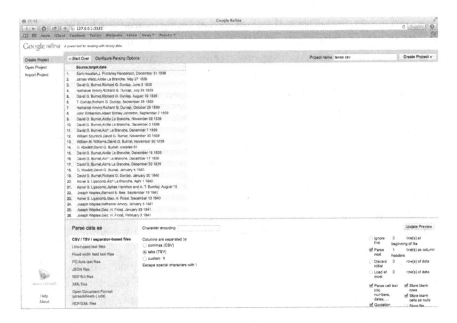

Fig. 3.10   The regex search results imported into OpenRefine.

which method is used. For example, the first "method" that it will suggest is Key Collision, which provides two suggestions. You might then want to attempt the Nearest Neighbor approach, which will find several more as well. Try out the two different distance functions as well. Keep playing. Because the methods are slightly different, each will present different matches that may or may not be useful. If you see two values which should be merged, e.g. "Ashbel Smith" and ". Ashbel Smith", check the box to the right in the "Merge" column and click the **"Merge Selected & Re-Cluster"** button below.

Go through the various cluster methods one-at-a-time, including changing number values, and merge the values that appear to be the same. "Juan de Dios CaAedo" clearly should be merged with "Juan de Dios Cafiedo", however "Correspondent in Tampico" probably should not be merged with "Correspondent at Vera Cruz". If you are not an expert of this period, use your best judgement. By the end, you should have reduced the number of unique Senders from 189 to around 150. Repeat these steps with Recipients, reducing unique Recipients from 192 to about 160. To finish the automatic cleaning of the data, click the arrow next to "Sender" and

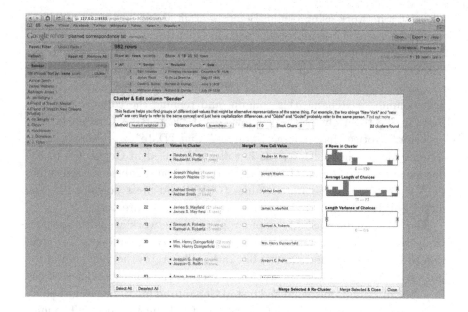

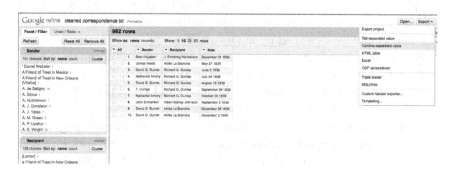

Fig. 3.11   The output of using OpenRefine to clean our data.

select "Edit Cells → Common transforms → Trim leading and trailing whitespace." Repeat for "Recipient." The resulting spreadsheet will not be perfect, but it will be much easier to clean by hand than it would have been before taking this step (Fig. 3.11). Click on "export" at the top right of the window to get your data back out as a .CSV file.

We discuss the network analysis and visualization tool Gephi in more depth in later chapters, but right now you will see how easy it can be to visualize a network using Gephi. Before we talk about how to import data for Gephi, there is one more step to do in OpenRefine.

In order to get these data into Gephi, we will have to rename the "Sender" column to "source" and the "Recipient" column to "target". In the arrow to the left of Sender in the main OpenRefine window, select Edit column → Rename this column, and rename the column "source". Now, in the top right of the window, select "Export → Custom tabular exporter." Notice that "source," "target," and "Date" are checked in the content tab; uncheck "Date," as it will not be used in Gephi. Go to the download tab and change the download option from "Tab-separated values (TSV)" to "Comma-separated values (CSV)" and press download.[14] The file will likely download to your automatic download directory.

Gephi is an increasingly popular piece of network visualization and analysis software. This next section is not meant to be an in-depth introduction to Gephi (that comes later!) but rather illustrates the final step in the process that began when we started looking at the correspondence of the Republic of Texas. Download and install Gephi from http://gephi.github.io. Now open Gephi by double-clicking its icon. Click "new project." The middle pane of the interface window is the "Data Laboratory," where you can interact with your network data in spreadsheet format. This is where we can import the data cleaned up in OpenRefine.

In the Data Laboratory, select "Import Spreadsheet." Press the ellipsis "..." and locate the CSV you just saved in the download directory. Make sure that the Separator is listed as "Comma" and the "As table" is listed as "Edges table." Press "Next," then "Finish."

Your data should load up. Click on the "overview" tab and you will be presented with a tangled network graph. You can save your work here and return to it after reading Chapter 5! Don't worry; we will explain what to do with it then.

Congratulations. You've downloaded a body of historical materials, used regular expressions to parse this material, trimming it to remove extraneous information that wasn't of use to you, used OpenRefine to clean it further, and loaded it into a software package for further analysis and visualization.

---

[14]It's worth pointing out that once you have cleaned data in CSV or TSV format, your data can be imported into a variety of other tools or be ready for other kinds of analysis. Many online visualization tools like Raw (http://app.raw.densitydesign.org/) and Palladio (http://palladio.designhumanities.org/) accept and expect data in these formats.

With these skills, you will be able to handle very big historical data indeed! On the website for this book, we have also included some further exercises and tutorials exploring some further things one could do with these data, such as parsing the text for place names ("Named Entity Recognition") or visualizing the pattern of correspondence over time as a dynamic network.

Quickly Extracting Tables from PDFs

Much of the historical data that we would like to examine that we find online comes in the cumbersome form of the PDF, "the portable document format." Governments especially love the PDF because they can quickly be generated in response to freedom of information requests, and because they preserve the look and layout of the original paper documents. Sometimes, a PDF is little more than an image; the text shown is just a pattern of dark and light dots. Other times, there is a hidden layer of machine-readable text that one can select with the mouse by clicking and dragging and copying. When we are dealing with tens or hundreds or thousands of pages of PDFs, this is not a feasible workflow. Journalists have this same problem and have developed many tools that the historian may wish to incorporate into her own workflow. Recently, the "data journalist" Jonathan Stray has written about the various free and paid tools that can be wrangled to extract meaningful data from thousands of PDFs at a time.[15] One in particular that Stray mentions is called "Tabula," which can be used to extract tables of information from PDFs, such as may be found in census documents.

Tabula is open source and runs on all the major platforms. You simply download it from http://tabula.nerdpower.org/, install it, and then double-click on the icon; it loads up inside your browser at address http://127.0.0.1:8080.[16] If for some reason it does not appear, try typing that address into the address bar directly. Once Tabula is running, you load your PDF into it. When the PDF appears, draw boxes around the tables that you are interested in grabbing. Tabula will then extract that table cleanly, allowing

---

[15]Jonathan Stray (14 March 2014), "You Got the Documents. Now What? — Learning — Source: An OpenNews Project," *Source*, https://source.opennews.org/en-US/learning/you-got-documents-now-what/.

[16]Since it is open source, you can make and maintain your own copy, in the event that the original "Tabula" website goes offline. Indeed, this is a habit you should get into. (This is called "forking" on github; you create an account on github, login, then go to the repository you wish to copy. Click "fork" and you've got your own copy!)

you to download it as a CSV or tab-separated file, or paste it directly into something else.

For instance, say you're interested in the data that Gill and Chippindale compiled on neolithic Cycladic figurines and the art market.[17] If you have access to the database JSTOR, you can find it here http://www.jstor.org/stable/506716. There are a lot of charts so it is a good example to play with. You would like to grab those tables of data to perhaps compile with data from other sources to perform some sort of meta study about the antiquities market.

Download the paper, open it in your PDF reader and then feed it into Tabula. Let's look at Table 2 from the article in your PDF reader. You could just highlight this table in your PDF reader and hit Ctrl+C to copy it, but when you paste that into your spreadsheet, you'd get everything in a single column. For a small table, maybe that's not such a big issue. But let's look at what you get with Tabula. With Tabula running, you go to the PDF you are interested in and draw a bounding box around the table. Release the mouse and you will be presented with a preview that you can then download as a CSV. You can quickly drag the selection box around every table in the document and hit download just the one time.

Since you can copy directly to the clipboard, you can paste directly into a Google Drive spreadsheet (thus taking advantage of all the visualization options that Google offers) or into something like Raw from Density Design, exploring the data and their patterns through a variety of quickly generated visualizations.[18]

Conclusion

This chapter has covered a lot of ground: we have moved from the relatively simple province of word clouds to the more sophisticated world of Overview, regular expressions, and hinted at even more advanced techniques that lurk

---

[17]David W. Gill and Christopher Chippindale (October 1993), 'Material and Intellectual Consequences of Esteem for Cycladic Figures,' *American Journal of Archaeology*, **97**(4), 601.

[18]Another open source project, "Raw," lets you paste your data into a box on a webpage and then render that data using a variety of different kinds of visualizations. You can download it at http://app.raw.densitydesign.org/. Raw does not send any data over the Internet; it performs all calculations and visualizations within your browser, so your data stay secure. It is possible (but not easy) to install Raw locally on your own machine, if you wish. Follow the links on the Raw website to its github code repository.

in the shadows. They all share the same goal, however: how to take a lot of information and explore it in ways that a person could not. How can we use our computers — these powerful machines sitting on our desks or laps — for more than just word processing, to tap their computational potential? As we will note in the next chapter, however, a potential pitfall of this is that we — in most of these cases — still needed to know what we were looking for. Data do not "speak" for themselves: they require interpretation, and — as we will see in more depth in the chapter after next — they require conscientious visualization.

Scholars often learn by reading and sifting: looking through archival boxes, reading literature, not with an eye on a particular research outcome but with a goal to holistically understand the field, approached from a particular perspective (theory). We can do the same with big data repositories, trying to get a macroscopic view of the field through methods including topic modeling and network analysis. In the next chapters, we build on our more targeted investigations here with a full-scale implementation of our historian's macroscope.

Chapter 4

Topic Modeling:
A Hands-On Adventure
in Big Data

In this chapter, we discuss different ways of building topic models of the patterns of discourse in your source documents. We explore what "topic models" are, how topic modeling works, and explore why some tools might be better in certain circumstances than others.

Keywords have their limitations, in that they require us to know what to search for. Topic modeling, on the other hand, allows us to come in with an open mind. Instead, in this approach, the documents "tell" us what topics they contain. The "model" in a topic model is the idea of how texts get written: authors compose texts by selecting words from a distribution of words (or "bag of words" or "bucket of words") that describe various thematic topics. Got that? In the beginning there was the topic. The entire universe of writing is one giant warehouse wherein its aisles are bins of words — here are the bins of Canadian History, there are the bins for major league sports (a very small aisle indeed). All documents (your essay, my dissertation, this book) are composed of words plucked from the various topic bins and combined. If that describes how the author actually writes, then this process is reversible: it is possible to decompose from the entire collection of words the original distributions held in those bags and buckets.

In this section, we explore various ways of creating topic models, what they might mean, and how they might be visualized. We work through a number of examples, so that the reader might find an approach to adapt to his or her own work. The essence of a topic model is in its input and its output: a corpus — a collection — of text goes in and a list of topics that comprise the text comes out the other side. Its mechanism is a deeply flawed assumption about how writing works, and yet the results of this mechanism are often surprisingly cogent and useful.

What is a topic, anyway? If you are a literary scholar, you will understand what a "topic" might mean perhaps rather differently than how a librarian might understand it: as discourses rather than as subject headings. Then there is the problem of how do the mathematicians and computer scientists understand what a "topic" might be? To the developers of these algorithms, a "document" is simply a collection of words that are found in differing proportions (thus it could be, in the real world, a blog post, a paragraph, a chapter, a ledger entry, an entire book). To decompose a document to its constituent "topics," we have to imagine a world in which every conceivable topic of discussion exists and is well defined, and each topic is perfectly represented as a distribution of particular words. Each distribution of words is unique, and thus you can infer a document's topicality by carefully comparing its distribution of words to the set of ideal topics we already know exist.

Topic Modeling by Hand

Let's look at the Gettysburg Address:

> Four score and seven years ago our fathers brought forth on this continent a new nation, conceived in liberty, and dedicated to the proposition that all men are created equal.
>
> Now we are engaged in a great civil war, testing whether that nation, or any nation so conceived and so dedicated, can long endure. We are met on a great battlefield of that war. We have come to dedicate a portion of that field, as a final resting place for those who here gave their lives that that nation might live. It is altogether fitting and proper that we should do this.
>
> But, in a larger sense, we can not dedicate, we can not consecrate, we can not hallow this ground. The brave men, living and dead, who struggled here, have consecrated it, far above our poor power to add or detract. The world will little note, nor long remember what we say here, but it can never forget what they did here. It is for us the living, rather, to be dedicated here to the unfinished work which they who fought here have thus far so nobly advanced. It is rather for us to be here dedicated to the great task remaining before us — that from these honored dead we take increased devotion to that cause for which they gave the last full measure of devotion — that we here highly resolve that these dead shall not have died in vain — that this nation, under God, shall have a new birth of freedom — and that government of the people, by the people, for the people, shall not perish from the earth.

This is a single document. How many topics are present, and what are their most significant words? Let us generate a topic model by hand. We have used this exercise in class as an introduction to text analysis more generally, but it can also highlight the differences in the ways computers "know" something versus the ways historians "know."

Take out some highlighters, and mark up this passage (print out a readily accessible copy online if you do not want to sully this book). Use one color to highlight words related to "war" and another for words related to "governance." You might find that some words get double-marked. As you do this, you are doing some rather complicated inferences. What are "war" words anyway? Have someone else do this exercise at the same time. Depending on your experience with 19th century rhetoric, or politics, or history, your marked up pages will be subtly different. One person will see that "field" perhaps ought to be part of the "war" topic, while another will not make that connection. What makes the difference? Fundamentally, given our individual backgrounds, it comes down to a matter of probability.

Then, list the "war" words down one side of a page and the "governance" words on the other. Have a "count" column beside your list in which you will display the number of times the word appears. You might like to do this using a spreadsheet, so you can then sort your lists so that the words that appear most often are at the top. The Gettysburg Address, as reproduced here, has 271 words. The most frequently occurring word, "that", is found 13 times, or roughly 5%. Add up your "counts" column and figure out the proportion that those words, these topics, account for your total document by dividing by 271. (Incidentally, if you visualize your results as a histogram, swapping out the bars in the chart for the words themselves, you have more or less created a word cloud.)

Hollis Peirce, an undergraduate student at Carleton University, created the following spreadsheet, working this out for himself (Fig. 4.1).

His count looks like this:

War Words Count	
	Struggled 1
Dead 3	Remember 1
War 2	Never 1
Gave 2	Forget 1
Living 2	Fought 1

War Words Count

Have 2	Nobly 1
Engaged 1	Advanced 1
Battlefield 1	Honoured 1
Field 1	Take 1
Final 1	Cause 1
Resting 1	Died 1
Place 1	Vain 1
Lives 1	Perish 1
Live 1	
Hallow 1	Total: 35
Ground 1	
Brave 1	35/271= 9%

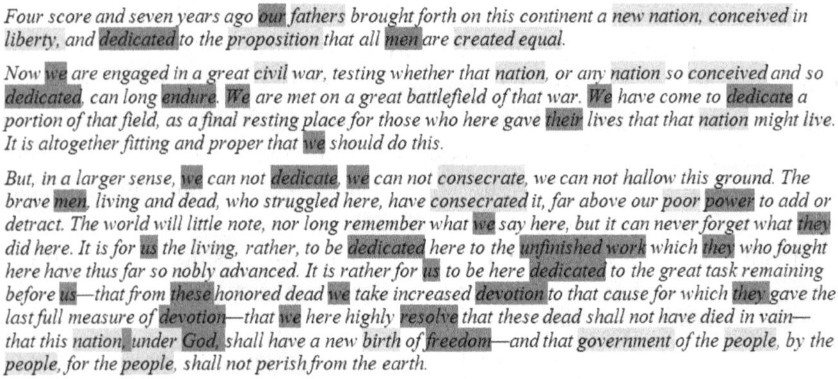

Four score and seven years ago our fathers brought forth on this continent a new nation, conceived in liberty, and dedicated to the proposition that all men are created equal.

Now we are engaged in a great civil war, testing whether that nation, or any nation so conceived and so dedicated, can long endure. We are met on a great battlefield of that war. We have come to dedicate a portion of that field, as a final resting place for those who here gave their lives that that nation might live. It is altogether fitting and proper that we should do this.

But, in a larger sense, we can not dedicate, we can not consecrate, we can not hallow this ground. The brave men, living and dead, who struggled here, have consecrated it, far above our poor power to add or detract. The world will little note, nor long remember what we say here, but it can never forget what they did here. It is for us the living, rather, to be dedicated here to the unfinished work which they who fought here have thus far so nobly advanced. It is rather for us to be here dedicated to the great task remaining before us—that from these honored dead we take increased devotion to that cause for which they gave the last full measure of devotion—that we here highly resolve that these dead shall not have died in vain— that this nation, under God, shall have a new birth of freedom—and that government of the people, by the people, for the people, shall not perish from the earth.

Fig. 4.1 Hollis Peirce's marked up Gettysburg address. Yellow (light) represents "war" words, green (grey) represents "governance", red (dark) represents words that could be either.

This was Hollis' handmade topic model, but the magical, computational part — deciding what constituted a topic — was done in his head. We decided, *a priori*, that there were two topics in this document and that they dealt specifically with "war" and "governance." We poured over the words and fitted them probabilistically into one or the other topic (and sometimes, both). The finished list of words and their counts is the distribution-over-words that characterizes a topic; the proportion that those words account for in the entire document demonstrates the document's topical composition. If we had several more documents, we could use our lists that we've generated as a guide to color-code, to mark up, these other documents. In the argot of topic modeling, this would be a "trained" topic model (we use our intuition about the Gettysburg Address to find patterns in other documents). We can run the same process from scratch on each of our new documents, and then iterate again through our lists, to understand the latent or hidden structure of our corpus as a whole. We should point out that — while "document" in everyday use means a diary entry, a single speech, an entire book — for the purpose of data mining, a document could be just every paragraph within that book or every 1,000 words.

When the computer does the work for us, it pays close attention to those words that might appear in multiple documents. Ted Underwood asks us to think about the word "lead" which might be a verb, and thus part of a topic related to leadership, (i.e. *he took the lead in the charge*) or it might be a noun, and thus part of a topic related to environmental contamination (i.e. *lead in the pipes was responsible for the poisoning*). How can we know the difference? That is, how can we encode our understanding of the semantic differences and word usage in a series of steps for the computer to undertake? We ask the computer to figure out the probability that "lead" belongs in a given topic, versus other topics. Additionally, we start by initially assigning words to topics at random. Hollis already knew that some words were more likely to be about war than governance; the computer does not.

Instead, we instruct the computer to pick topics for us, and it begins with a series of blind guesses, assigning words to bins at random. The computer knows a warehouse full of word bins exists but it cannot see inside it. The topic model is the computer's attempt at inferring the contents of each bin by looking at each document and working backwards to the topic bins it likely drew from. The computer starts from the assumption that, if several documents contain the same groups of words, those words likely form a "topic." As the computer scans through the text over and over again, it reorganizes its initially random bins into closer and closer approximations of what it guesses the "real" topic bins must look like. Internally, the computer is optimizing for this problem: given a distribution of words over an entire collection of documents, what is the probability that this distribution of words within a document belongs to a particular topic?

This is a Bayesian approach to probability. Thomas Bayes was an 18th century clergyman who dabbled in mathematics. He was interested in problems of conditional probabilities, in light of prior knowledge.[1] The formula which now bears Bayes' name depends on assigning a *prior probability* and then re-evaluating that probability in the light of what it finds. As the computer goes through this process over and over for each word in the collection, it changes its assumptions about the distribution. In his book *The Signal and the Noise*, statistician Nate Silver's example examines the chances that you are being cheated on when you discover a pair of underwear in your house *not* belonging to your partner.[2] To estimate the chances that you are being cheated on, you have to decide (or estimate) three conditions.

1. What are the chances that the underwear is there because you *are* being cheated on (call this "*y*")?
2. What are the chances that the underwear is there because you *are not* being cheated on (call this "*z*")?
3. And what would you have estimated, before finding the underwear, that your partner would have been prone to cheat (call this "*x*," the *prior probability*)?

The formula is:

$$xy \, / \, xy + z(1\text{-}x)$$

You can do the math for yourself. You can also feed your result back into the equation, changing your prior probability as new information comes to light.

Is this what topic modeling does? Yes, in essence, though the maths are a bit more complicated than this. Underwood writes,

> [. . . As we iterate our estimates, adjusting our probabilities, fitting words into topics, fitting topics across documents], a) words will gradually become more common in topics where they are already common. And also, b) topics will become more common in documents where they are already common. Thus our model will gradually become more consistent as topics focus on specific words and documents. But it can't ever become perfectly consistent, because words and documents don't line up in one-to-one fashion. [. . .] the tendency for topics to concentrate on

---

[1]Thomas Bayes and Mr. Price (1763), "An Essay towards solving a Problem in the Doctrine of Chances," *Philosophical Transactions of the Royal Society of London*, **53**, 370–418.

[2]Nate Silver (2012), *The Signal and the Noise: Why so Many Predictions Fail — but Some Don't*, New York, NY: Penguin Press, 243–247.

particular words and documents will eventually be limited by the actual, messy distribution of words across documents.

That's how topic modeling works in practice. You assign words to topics randomly and then just keep improving the model, to make your guess more internally consistent, until the model reaches an equilibrium that is as consistent as the collection allows."[3]

There is a fundamental difficulty however. When we began looking at the Gettysburg Address, Hollis was instructed to look for two topics that we had already named "war" and "governance." When the computer looks for two topics, it does not know beforehand that there are two topics present, let alone what they might mean in human terms. In fact, we as the investigators have to tell the computer "look for two topics in this corpus of material," at which point the machine will duly find two topics. At the moment of writing, there is no easily-instantiated method to automatically determine the "best" number of topics in a corpus. For the time being, the investigator has to try out a number of different scenarios to find out what's best. This is not a bad thing, as it forces the investigator continually to confront (or even, close-read) the data, the model, and the patterns that might be emerging.

The late statistician George Box once wrote, "Essentially, all models are wrong, but some are useful."[4] A topic model is a way of fitting semantic meaning against a large volume of text. The researcher has to generate many models against the same corpus until she finds one that reaches Box's utility.[5] We create topic models not to prove that our idea about phenomenon

---

[3]Ted Underwood (7 April 2012), "Topic Modeling made just simple enough." *The Stone and the Shell*, http://tedunderwood.com/2012/04/07/topic-modeling-made-just-simple-enough/.

[4]George E.P. Box and Norman R. Draper (1987), *Empirical Model-Building and Response Surfaces*, New York: Wiley, p. 424.

[5]When we describe topic modeling here, we have in mind the most commonly used approach, "Latent Dirichlet Allocation" (LDA). There are many other possible algorithms and approaches, but most usages of topic modeling amongst digital humanists and historians treat LDA as synonymous with topic modeling. It is worth keeping in mind that there are other options, which might shed useful light on your problem at hand. A special issue of the *Journal of Digital Humanities* treats topic modeling across a variety of domains and is a useful jumping off point for a deeper exploration of the possibilities (http://journalofdigitalhumanities.org/2-1/). The LDA technique was not the first technique now considered topic modeling but it is by far the most popular. The myriad variations of topic modeling have resulted in an alphabet soup of techniques and programs to implement them that might be confusing or overwhelming to the uninitiated; for the beginner it is enough to know that they exist. MALLET primarily utilizes LDA.

x in the past is true, but rather to generate new ways of looking at our materials, to deform it. In fact there is a danger in using topic models as historical evidence; they are configurable and ambiguous enough that, no matter what you are looking for, you just might find it. Remember, a topic model is in essence a statistical model that describes the way that topics are formed. *It might not be the right model for your corpus.* It is, however, a starting point and the topics that it finds (or fails to find) should become a lens through which you look at your material, reading closely to understand this productive failure. Ideally, you would then re-run the model, tweaking it so that it better describes the kind of structure you believe exists. You generate a model to embody your instincts and beliefs about how the material you are working on was formed. Your model could represent ideas about syntax, or ideas about the level of "token" (Ngrams of a particular length, for instance) that is appropriate to model. Then you use the algorithm to discover that structure in your real collection. And then repeat.[6]

If the historian used it on a series of political speeches, for example, topic modeling tools would return a list of topics and the keywords composing those topics. Each of these lists is a topic according to the algorithm. Using the example of political speeches, the list might look like:

```
1. Job Jobs Loss Unemployment Growth
2. Economy Sector Economics Stock Banks
3. Afghanistan War Troops Middle-East Taliban Terror
4. Election Opponent Upcoming President
5. ... etc.
```

There are many dangers that face those who use topic modeling without fully understanding it.[7] For instance, we might be interested in word-use as a proxy for placement along a political spectrum. Topic modeling could certainly help with that, but we have to remember that the proxy is not in itself the thing we seek to understand — as Andrew Gelman demonstrates in his mock study of zombies using Google Trends.[8]

---

[6]David Blei (2012), "Topic modeling and the digital humanities," *Journal of Digital Humanities*, **2**(1), http://journalofdigitalhumanities.org/2-1/topic-modeling-and-digital-humanities-by-david-m-blei/.

[7]Scott Weingart (6 May 2012), "The Myth of Text Analytics and Unobtrusive Measurement," *scottbot.net*, http://www.scottbot.net/HIAL/?p=16713.

[8]Andrew Gelman (March 31, 2010), "'How Many Zombies Do You Know?' Using Indirect Survey Methods to Measure Alien Attacks and Outbreaks of the Undead," *arXiv*:1003.6087 [physics], http://arxiv.org/abs/1003.6087/.

The tools we discuss below are organized in order of their progressive difficulty-of-use. The trade-off is of course that the easier to use the tool, the less powerful (in certain regards) the tool. When we introduce topic modeling in our own classes, we like to begin with the *GUI Topic Modeling Tool* to hook our students and then, depending on the nature of the materials we're working with, move to MALLET on the command line *or* the Stanford Topic Modeling Toolbox. Finally, in our own research, we find that we are more and more often using the various topic modeling tools afforded in the R statistical programming environment (which we access through "R Studio") since R also allows us to manipulate and transform the results with (comparative) ease. Which tool to use, and how to use it, is always dependent on where you wish to go.

Topic Modeling with the GUI Topic Modeling Tool

The *GUI Topic Modeling Tool* (GTMT) is an excellent way to introduce topic modeling to classroom settings and other areas where technical expertise may be limited (our experience is that this is a good entryway into simple topic modeling), or if you wish to quickly explore a body of materials. Because it is a Java-based program, it also has the advantage of being natively cross-platform: it has been tested and will work on Windows, Mac OS X, and even Linux systems.

Available in a Google Code repository at https://code.google.com/p/topic-modeling-tool/, the GTMT provides quick and easy topic model generation and navigation. With a working Java instance on any platform, simply download the GTMT program and double-click on its icon to run it. Java will open the program, which will present you with a menu interface (Fig. 4.2). You then click on "Select Input File or Dir" to select the materials you wish to fit a topic model to, select an output location for the output, identify the number of topics you are looking for, and click "Train Topics." The actual topic modeling is done using the topic modeling routines incorporated from the MALLET toolkit (see below), although you do not need to install MALLET separately — it comes included!

Let's work through an example. Imagine that we were interested in knowing how discourses around the commemoration of heritage sites played out across a city (so we want to know not just what the topics or discourses are, but also if there are any spatial or temporal associations too). The first part of such a project would be to topic model the text of the historical plaques. The reader may download the full text of 612 heritage plaques in

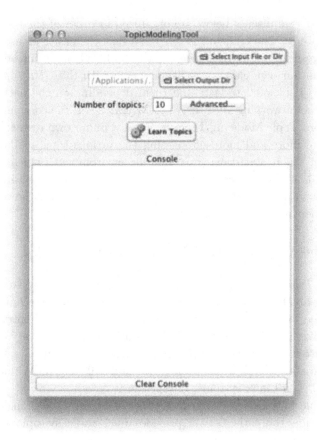

Fig. 4.2   The GUI Topic Modeling Tool.

Toronto as a zip file from http://themacroscope.org/2.0/datafiles/toronto-plaques.zip to follow along. Unzip that folder, and start the GTMT.

Select the data to be imported by clicking the "Select Input File or Dir" button, which allows you to pick an individual file or an entire directory of documents. You tell the system where you want your output to be generated (by default it will be where you have the GTMT installed, so beware if you're running it out of your "Applications" folder as it can get a bit cluttered), note the number of topics, and then click "Learn Topics" to generate a topic model. The advanced settings are important as well, as they can let you remove stopwords, normalize text by standardizing case, and tweak your iterations, size of topic descriptors, and the threshold at which you want to cut topics off (Fig. 4.3).

Fig. 4.3   The GUI Topic Modeling Tool settings.

Let's run it! When you click Learn Topics, you'll see a stream of text in the program's console output. Pay attention to what happens. For example, you might notice that it finishes very quickly. In that case, you may need to fiddle with the number of iterations or other parameters.

In the directory you selected as your output, you will now have two folders: output_csv and output_html. Take a moment to explore them. In the former, you will see three files: DocsInTopics.csv, Topics_Words.csv, and TopicsInDocs.csv. The first one will be a big file, which you can open in a spreadsheet program. It is arranged by topic, and then by the relative ranks of each file within each topic. For example, using our sample data, you might find:

topicId	rank	docId	filename
1	1	5	184_Roxborough_Drive-info.txt
1	2	490	St_Josephs_College_School-info.txt
1	3	328	Moulton_College-info.txt
1	4	428	Ryerson_Polytechnical_Institute-info.txt

In the above, we see that in topic number 1, we have a declining order of relevant documents, which are probably about education: three of the plaques are obviously educational institutions. The first (184 Roxborough) is the former home of Nancy Ruth, a feminist activist who helped found the Canadian Women's Legal Education Fund. By opening the Topics_Words.csv file, our suspicions are confirmed: topic #1 is school, college, university, women, toronto, public, institute, opened, association, residence.

GTMT shines best, however, when you explore the HTML output. This allows you to navigate all of the information in an easy-to-use interface. In the output_html folder, open up the file all_topics.html. It should open in your default browser. The results of our model are visualized below (Fig. 4.4).

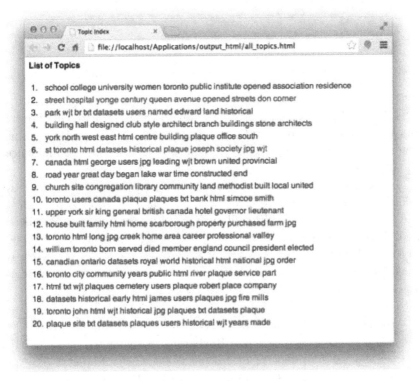

Fig. 4.4   Sample HTML output from the GUI Topic Modeling Tool.

Fig. 4.5   Top-ranked documents in a topic, generated HTML output from the GUI Topic Modeling Tool.

This is similar to the Topics_Words.csv file, but the difference is that each topic can be explored further. If we click on the first topic, the school-related one, we see our top-ranked documents from before (Fig. 4.5).

We can then click on each individual document: we get a snippet of the text and also the various topics attached to each file (Fig. 4.6). These are each individually hyperlinked as well, letting you explore the various topics and documents that comprise your model. If you have your own server space, or use a service like Dropbox, you can easily move all these files online so that others can explore your results.

From beginning to end, then, we quickly go through all the stages of a topic model and have a useful graphical user interface to deal with. While the tool can be limiting, and we prefer the versatility of the command line, this is an essential and useful component of our topic modeling toolkit.

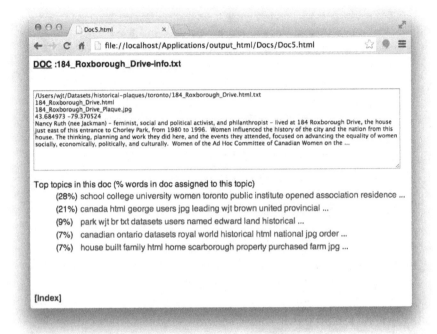

Fig. 4.6 Looking inside a document, using the HTML output from the GUI Topic Modeling Tool.

Building a topic model with MALLET

While the GTMT allows us to build a topic model quite quickly, there is very little tweaking or fine-tuning that can be done. For more in-depth analysis and modeling, the current standard solution to use is to employ directly the topic modeling routines of the MALLET NLP tool kit. There is an irony of course in naming the major topic modeling toolkit after a hammer, with all the caveats about the entire world looking like a nail once you have it installed.[9] For reference's sake, we explain here how to install MALLET, but we do not think it overly useful for you to invest too much time learning to use it from the command line. If you are so-inclined, please see our *Programming Historian* tutorial. Nevertheless, here we describe the most basic usage and how to get started with this tool.[10]

---

[9]Originally pointed out by Ben Schmidt, "When you have a MALLET, everything looks like a nail" on his wonderful blog *SappingAttention.com*. See http://sappingattention.blogspot.ca/2012/11/when-you-have-mallet-everything-looks.html.

To install MALLET on any platform, please follow these steps:

1. Go to the MALLET project page at http://mallet.cs.umass.edu/index. php, and download MALLET. (As of this writing, we are working with version 2.0.7.) Unzip it in your home directory — that is in C:/ on Windows, or the directory with your username in OS X (it should have a picture of a house).
2. You will also need the Java Development Kit, or JDK — that is, not the regular Java that one will find on every computer, but the one that lets you program things. You can find it at http://www.oracle.com/ technetwork/java/javase/downloads/index.html. Install this on your computer.

For computers running OS X or Linux, you're ready to go! For Windows systems, you have a few more steps:

3. Unzip MALLET into your C: directory. This is important: it cannot be anywhere else. You will then have a directory called C:\mallet-2.0.7 or similar. For simplicity's sake, rename this directory to just **mallet**.
4. MALLET uses an environment variable to tell the computer where to find all the various components of its processes when it is running. It's rather like a shortcut for the program. A programmer cannot know exactly where every user will install a program, so the programmer creates a variable in the code that will always stand in for that location. We tell the computer, once, where that location is by setting the environment variable. If you moved the program to a new location, you'd have to change the variable.

To create an environment variable in Windows 7, click on your Start Menu → Control Panel → System → Advanced System Settings. Click new and type MALLET_HOME in the variable name box. It must be like this — all caps, with an underscore — since that is the shortcut that the programmer built into the program and all of its subroutines. Then type the exact path (location) of where you unzipped MALLET in the variable value, e.g. `c:\mallet`

---

[10]We have previously published an online tutorial to help the novice install and use the most popular of the many different topic modeling programs available, MALLET, at programminghistorian.org. This section republishes elements of that tutorial but we recommend checking the online version in case of any upgrades or version changes.

MALLET is run from the command line, also known as a Command Prompt. If you remember MS-DOS, or have ever played with a Unix computer terminal (or have seen "hackers" represented in movies or on television shows), this will be familiar. The command line is where you can type commands directly, rather than clicking on icons and menus.

On Windows, click on your Start Menu → All Programs → Accessories → Command Prompt. On a Mac, open up your Applications → Utilities → Terminal.

You'll get the command prompt window, which will have a cursor at c:\user\user> for Windows or ∼ username$ on OS X.

On Windows, type cd .. (That is: cd-space-period-period) to change directory. Keep doing this until you're at the C:\. For OS X, type cd – and you'll be brought to your home directory.

Then type :

```
cd mallet
```

and you will be in the MALLET directory. Anything you type in the command prompt window is a command. There are commands like cd (change directory) and to see all the fields in a directory you could type dir (Windows) or ls (OS X). You have to tell the computer explicitly that "this is a MALLET command" when you want to use MALLET. You do this by telling the computer to grab its instructions from the MALLET bin, a subfolder in MALLET that contains the core operating routines. Type:

bin\mallet on Windows, or

./bin/mallet on OS X

at the prompt. If all has gone well, you should be presented with a list of MALLET commands — congratulations! If you get an error message, check your typing. Did you use the wrong slash? Did you set up the environment variable correctly? Is MALLET located at C:\mallet on Windows or in your home directory on OS X?

Creating a topic model on your data is now a two step process. In the first, you read your data into a single file for MALLET to process. In the second step, you specify how MALLET should generate the model based on that data. The command you type runs the command (found in MALLET's "bin" directory) and then tells the computer which functions to apply to the command. To read your data in you might type this in at the command prompt:

```
bin\mallet import-dir --input
pathway\to\the\directory\with\the\files --output mydata.mallet
--keep-sequence --remove-stopwords
```

(Mac users, your command would start a little differently: ./bin/mallet)

That command tells MALLET to use the "import-dir" command; the next flag, "–input" tells MALLET where to find your text files; the next flag "–output" tells MALLET what to call the file; and the last two flags tell MALLET to keep everything in the same order as in your original folder and to remove the stopwords. To generate the topic model, you might type this:

```
bin\mallet train-topics --input mydata.mallet --num-topics 20
--output-state topic-state.gz --output-topic-keys
mydata_keys.txt --output-doc-topics mydata_composition.txt
```

This instructs MALLET to run the "train-topics" command, feeding it the data you created in the sequence above; it instructs it to fit 20 topics; the entire output gets compressed into a .gz zip file; the key words in the topic model are written in the mydata_keys.txt, and the distribution of topics over documents is written in the mydata_composition.txt file. You can open these in a spreadsheet for examination or further transformation.

For more instructions on using MALLET from the command line and on OS X, please see our online tutorial at *The Programming Historian* (http://programminghistorian.org/lessons/topic-modeling-and-mallet). There are many options for fine-tuning your results, and one can build chains of commands as well (such as removing stopwords, or filtering out numbers or leaving them in).[11]

---

[11] One thing to be aware of is that, since many of the tools we are about to discuss rely on Java, changes to the Java run-time environment and to the Java development kit (as for instance when Oracle updates Java, periodically) can break the other tools. We have tested everything and know that these tools work with Java 7. If you are finding that the tools do not run, you should check what version of Java is on your machine. In a terminal window, type 'java --version' at the prompt. You should then see something like 'java version "1.7.0_05"'. If you're not seeing this, it *could* be that you need to install a different version of Java.

Topic Modeling with the Stanford Topic Modeling Toolbox

Different tools give different results even if they are all still "topic modeling" writ large. This is a useful way to further understand how these algorithms shape our research, and is a useful reminder to always be up front about the tools that you are using in your research. One tool that historians should become familiar with is the *Stanford Topic Modeling Toolbox*, (STMT), because its outputs make it easy to see how topics play out over time (it "slices" its output by the dates associated with each document). Indeed, while it is not easy to use this tool, this particular feature makes it a useful addition to our toolbox, which is why we are going into some depth about this tool. The STMT allows us to track the evolution of topics within a corpus at a much finer level, at the level of each individual entry. STMT is written in Java and requires the latest version of Java to be installed on your machine (available for free from https://www.java.com/en/download/). You can find it at http://nlp.stanford.edu/software/tmt/tmt-0.4/.

A brief review: scraping data from a website for the purposes of the STMT

Because the STMT is most useful for us as historians when we have documents with dates, let us consider the workflow for getting a digitized diary off a website and into the STMT. You may wish to skip this section; you can obtain the scraped data CSV from our website.

Visit one of the online pages showing Adams' diary entries (for example, http://www.masshist.org/digitaladams/archive/doc?id=D0). Right-click on the page in your web browser, select "view source" on the pop-up menu, and examine the tags used to mark up the HTML. Every so often, you will see something like:

```
<a id="D0.17530608"></a><div class="entry"><div
class="head">HARVARD <span title="College">
COLLEDGE</span> JUNE 8TH. 1753.</div><div
class="dateline"><span title="1753-06-08">8
FRIDAY.</span></div><div class="p">At <span
title="College">Colledge>/span>.
```

Using the scraper tool in Outwit Hub we can grab everything that falls within the "entry" class. We want to make sure we get the dates first. In this

Stanford Topic Modeling Toolbox

General Principles

STMT gives us a different perspective on our topic models by allowing us to see how topics and key words distribute over time within our model. It was developed for the Stanford Natural Language Processing Group www-nlp.stanford.edu by Daniel Ramage and Evan Rosen.

Description

The STMT requires that the user write a series of commands in a single file (a "script") to point it to the user's data, to describe the data ("here are dates, there is the actual text of the documents") and otherwise how to manipulate it.

Critique

From a usability perspective, modifying scripts can be quite daunting. The tool is no longer maintained.

How to Use It

Open a sample script from the website in a text editor, change certain lines in the script to point to your own data and to describe it correctly. Save the script. Open the STMT; increase the available memory in the memory option box. Load your script and then hit "run". The results will be written in the same folder.

How to Analyze the Results

The results can be visualized by opening the CSV files in Excel or another spreadsheet program. Using the tools of the spreadsheet, one can explore how word usage plays out across various user-defined groupings, especially over time.

case, we want the computer to find "1753-06-08" and grab it in a separate column. We see that every time a date appears, it is preceded by <div class="dateline"><span title=" and followed by >.

To do this, let's refresh how to use Outwit Hub. Load the program, and enter the URL http://www.masshist.org/digitaladams/archive/doc?id=D0 into Outwit's navigation bar. Hit enter and be brought to the page. Now, click "scrapers" in the left-hand column, and then "new" below. Our goal is to set up a scraper that can produce two columns: one with dates and the other one with entries.

In the "scrapers" section, we want to make this happen. We begin by double-clicking on empty fields in the table below, which allow us to enter information (Fig. 4.7). We type a descriptive label under "description" (so we can remember what is supposed to be scraped there) — which will either be "date" or "entry." We then peruse the HTML to again identify the relevant tag or "marker" before the information we want, and the marker afterwards, like so. So remember above, what we had before the date we want — 1753-06-08 — and what we have afterwards. Fill out the form like so:

description	marker before	marker after
Date	<div class="dateline"><span title="	">

Now it is time to grab the actual text of the diary entry. It's a bit messier. When we look at the HTML around entries, we see the following:

```
<a id="D0.17530608"></a><div class="entry"><div
class="head"> HARVARD <span title="College">
COLLEDGE</span> JUNE 8TH. 1753.</div> <div
class="dateline"><span title="1753-06-08"> 8
FRIDAY.</span></div><div class="p"> At <span
title="College"> Colledge</span> . ... </div></div>
```

(We added the elipses there!) There is a lot of text cut out of here, but in general, entries begin with the code <div class="entry"> and they end

Fig. 4.7 A scraper using Outwit Hub.

with two </div> </div> tags (**with two spaces between them**). In Outwit hub, then, we put the following as the next row in our scraper:

entry	class="entry">	</div> </div>

This is telling us to get everything that starts with that paragraph marker and ends with the beginning of the link. Don't worry, you'll see what we mean below.

The resulting output will look like this, opening in a new panel at the bottom of the screen when we hit the "execute" button and then the "catch" button (important: make sure to "catch" the data or you won't be saving it):

1753-06-08	At Colledge. A Clowdy Dull morning and so continued till about 5 a Clock when it began to rain moderately But continued not long But remained Clowdy all night in which night I watched with Powers.
1753-06-09	At Colledge the weather still remaining Clowdy all Day till 6 o'Clock when the Clowds were Dissipated and the sun brake forth in all his glory.
1753-06-10	At Colledge a clear morning. Heard Mr. Appleton expound those words in I.Cor.12 Chapt. 7 first verses and in the afternoon heard him preach from those words in 26 of Mathew 41 verse watch and pray that ye enter not into temptation

Perfect! We have a spreadsheet of that first online page of John Adams' diary thanks to the magic of Outwit Hub! The paid version of Outwit can crawl through the entire website automatically, exploring all subpages, matching your scraper against each page it finds, and saving the data to a single spreadsheet file.

Using the free version, you can manually page through the site, getting Outwit to add the new data to your spreadsheet. Beside the "catch" button there is a drop-down arrow. Set this to "auto-catch." Then, in the URL at the top of the screen, which ends with /doc?id=D0, you can page through the site by changing the 0 to 1, then to 2, then to 3... and so on. As an interesting exercise, one of these pages (the one ending id=D1) will be slightly broken and won't work — you won't get the date information. Click back on "scrapers," look at the code, and you'll see that for this one page alone there is a space between <div class="dateline"> and <span title=". While we debated omitting this point, this is what research "in the wild" presents you with. So for this page, change your scraper to have the space, execute it, and then change it back for subsequent ones.

Each time the subsequent pages load, Outwit will automatically apply the scraper and paste the data into your spreadsheet. You can then click on the "export" button at the bottom of the screen (the drop-down arrow beside export will let you choose your desired format). The free version is limited to 100 rows of data. When you push up against that barrier, you can hit the "empty" button (after exporting, of course!) and continue onwards, using a new file name.

After exporting, open your file in your spreadsheet program of choice (when you have more than one file, you can copy one and paste it into the other). Delete the first row (the one that reads URL, Date, and Entry). We then need to insert a column at the beginning of these data (in most spreadsheet programs, click "add column" in the "Insert" menu), so that each diary entry gets its own unique record number (you can do this by either manually inputting numbers, or by creating a quick formula in the first cell, and pasting it in the remaining cells):[12]

1	1753-06-08	At Colledge. A Clowdy Dull morning and so continued till about 5 a Clock when it began to rain moderately But continued not long But remained Clowdy all night in which night I watched with Powers.
2	1753-06-09	At Colledge the weather still remaining Clowdy all Day till 6 o'Clock when the Clowds were Dissipated and the sun brake forth in all his glory.
3	1753-06-10	At Colledge a clear morning. Heard Mr. Appleton expound those words in I.Cor.12 Chapt. 7 first verses and in the afternoon heard him preach from those words in 26 of Mathew 41 verse watch and pray that ye enter not into temptation

You might need to rearrange some of the columns, but the data are there: some wrangling will put them into the format you see. We save this as 'johnadams-for-stmt.csv'.[13] The STMT always imagines the data to be structured in three (or more) columns — a record id, a date, and the text itself (of course, it could be structured differently, but for our purposes here,

---

[12] Assuming you are using Excel, and the first cell where you wish to put a unique ID number is cell A1: put '1' in that cell. In cell A2, type =a1+1 and hit return. Then, copy that cell, select the remaining cells you wish to fill with numbers, and hit enter. Other spreadsheet programs will have similar functionality.

[13] Our version of this file may be found at http://themacroscope.org/2.0/datafiles/johnadams-for-stmt.csv.

this suffices). Make sure to save the file in the same directory that you are about to unzip the tmt-040.0.jar file to.

Installing the STMT and inputting the data

With our data extracted, we turn to the toolbox. Installing the STMT is a matter of downloading, unzipping, and then double-clicking the file named tmt-0.40.0.jar, which brings up this interface (Fig. 4.8):

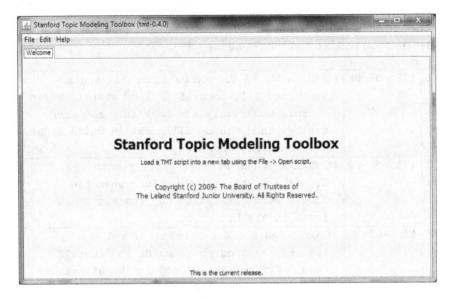

Fig. 4.8 Stanford Topic Modeling Toolbox. Courtesy Daniel Ramage.

The STMT operates by running various scripts the user creates. This allows a lot of flexibility, but it can also seem very daunting for the first time user. However, it is not as scary as it might first seem. The STMT uses scripts written in the Scala language. For our purposes, we can simply modify the sample scripts provided by the STMT team.[14] Just scroll down from the download page (http://nlp.stanford.edu/software/tmt/tmt-0.4/) to see them listed below.

The four scripts that are provided in the documentation show how to build up a workflow of several different operations into a single script. The

---

[14]If the scripts on the Stanford site are now different than what is recounted in this passage, please use the ones at http://themacroscope.org/2.0/code-stmt/.

scripts that we are interested in are Example 2 and Example 4. Example 2 creates a topic model; Example 4 slices it so that it can be visualized in a spreadsheet by various groupings (such as chronology).

Download the two scripts (example-2-lda-learn.scala, and example-4-lda-slice.scala), and make sure to save them with the .scala file extension. Save them in the same folder as your data CSV file. We will use these example scripts as building blocks to work with our own data!

Example 2 from the STMT website trains a topic model (http://nlp. stanford.edu/software/tmt/tmt-0.3/examples/example-2-lda-learn.scala). To see how it works, open this script using a text editor such as Notepad++ or TextWrangler, which will automatically provide line numbers (which are quite handy when examining code). We have used these programs earlier in the regular expression section.

The critical line is line 15:

```
15 val source = CSVFile("pubmed-oa-subset.csv") ~>
IDColumn(1);
```

This line is telling STMT where to find your data, and that the first column is the unique ID number. Change the example file name to whatever you called your data file (in our case, "johnadamsscrape.csv"). It should now read:

```
15 val source = CSVFile("johnadamsscrape.csv") ~>
IDColumn(1);
```

The next line to examine is line 28, in this block (in this language, comments are noted by the two forward slashes // which explain what each line is doing):

```
26 val text = {
27 source ~> // read from the source file
28 Column(4) ~> // select column containing text
29 TokenizeWith(tokenizer) ~> // tokenize with tokenizer
above
30 TermCounter() ~> // collect counts (needed below)
31 TermMinimumDocumentCountFilter(4) ~> // filter terms in
// filter out 60 most common terms
32 DocumentMinimumLengthFilter(5)// take only docs with >=5
terms
33 }
```

If you run the script as is, it will look for text in the fourth column — there are no data there, so you will get a java.lang.IndexOutOfBoundsException error message. You need to change line 26 so it reads like:

```
26 Column(3) ~> // select column containing text
```

This tells STMT to look in the third column for the actual **text** we wish to topic model (if, for example, you had the text in column 2 and the dates in column 3, you would have to change some of these lines). It is also extracting and filtering common words that might create noise; whether or not 60 is an appropriate number for this corpus is something with which we should experiment.

Finally, you may wish to examine line 38 and line 39:

```
val params = LDAModelParams(numTopics = 30, dataset =
dataset,
    topicSmoothing = 0.01, termSmoothing = 0.01);
```

Changing the numTopics allows you to change the number of topics fitted in the topic model. Save your script (we used the name "johnadams-topicmodel.scala"). In the STMT interface, select File → open script. Select your script. Your STMT interface will now look like Fig. 4.9:

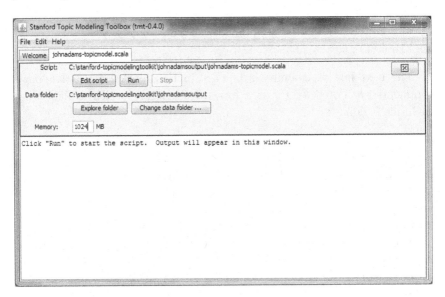

Fig. 4.9   Configuring the Stanford Topic Modeling Toolbox. Courtesy Daniel Ramage.

We find it useful to increase the memory available to the STMT to do its calculations by changing the number in the Memory box in the interface (the default is 256 MB; type in 1024 or another multiple of 256, as appropriate to your machine's available memory). This is because sometimes, if we are putting too much text in the system, we might run out of room in the system's memory!

Now click "run," and you should soon have a new folder in your directory named something along the lines of "lda-afbfe5c4-30-4f47b13a." Note that the algorithm for generating the topics is our old friend, LDA, as indicated in the folder name (the lda part of that long string).

Open this folder. There are many subfolders, each one corresponding to a progressive iteration of the topic model. Open the last one, labeled **"01000"**. There are a variety of .TXT files; you will want to examine the one called "summary.txt". The information within that file is arranged by topic and descending importance of words within each topic:

Topic 00	454.55948070466843
company	24.665848270843448
came	21.932877059649453
judge	14.170879738912884
who	13.427171229569737
sir	10.826043463533079

If you return to the folder, there is also a CSV file indicating the distribution of topics over each of the diary entries, which can be visualized or explored further in a variety of ways; one in particular worth looking at in more detail is STMT's ability to "slice" topics by time.

Slicing a topic model

The STMT allows us to "slice" a model to show its evolution over time and its contribution to the corpus as a whole. That is, we can look at the proportion of a topic at a particular point in time. To achieve a visualization comparing two topics (say) over the entire duration of John Adams' diary entries, one has to create a "pivot table report" (a summary of your data in aggregate categories in Excel or in a similar spreadsheet). The exact steps will differ based on which version of the spreadsheet you have installed; more on that in a moment.

In the code for the slicing script (http://nlp.stanford.edu/software/tmt/tmt-0.3/examples/example-4-lda-slice.scala), pay attention to line 16:

```
16 val modelPath = file("lda-59ea15c7-30-75faccf7");
```

Remember seeing a bunch of letters and numbers that looked like that before? Make sure the file name within the quotations is to the output folder you created previously. In line 24, make sure that you have the original CSV file name inserted so it reads like:

```
val source = CSVFile("johnadamscrape.csv") ~> IDColumn(1);
```

In line 28, make sure that the column indicated is the column with your text in it, i.e. Column 3 (by default you'll change it from 4 to 3 again). Line 36 is the key line for "slicing" the topic model by date:

```
36 val slice = source ~> Column(2);
37 // could be multiple columns with: source ~>
Columns(2,7,8)
```

Thus, in our data, Column 2 contains the year-month-day date for the diary entry (whereas Column 3 has the entry itself; check to make sure that your data are arranged the same way). By default, it just so happens that this script should work! One could have three separate columns for year, month, day, or indeed, whatever other slicing criterion. Once you've made your edits, save the script as johnadams-slicing.scala.

Once you load and run that script (same process as before), you will end up with a .CSV file that looks something like this. The location of it will be noted in the STMT window — for us, for example, it was lda-8bbb972c-30-28de11e5/johnadamsscrape-sliced-usage.csv:

Topic	Group ID	Documents	Words
Topic 00	1753-06-08	0.047680088	0.667521
Topic 00	1753-06-09	2.79E-05	2.23E-04
Topic 00	1753-06-10	0.999618435	12.99504
Topic 00	1753-06-11	1.62E-04	0.001781
Topic 00	1753-06-12	0.001597659	0.007988

...and so on for every topic, for every document ("Group ID"), in your corpus. The numbers under "documents" and "words" will be decimals, because in the current version of the topic modeling toolbox, each word in the corpus is not assigned to a **single** topic, but over a distribution of topics (i.e. "cow" might be .001 of Topic 4 — or 0.1%, but .23 or 23% of Topic 11). Similarly, the "documents" number indicates the total number of documents associated with the topic (again, as a distribution). Creating a pivot table report will allow us to take these individual slices and aggregate them in interesting ways to see the evolution of patterns over time in our corpus.

To create a pivot table (see Figs. 4.10–4.15)

1. Highlight all of the data on the page, including the column header (Fig. 4.10).
2. Select "pivot table" (under the "data" menu option). The pivot table wizard will open. You can drag and drop the various options at the top of the box to other locations. Arrange "topic" under "column labels," "Group ID" under row labels, and under "values" select *either* documents or words. Under "values", select the "i" and make sure that the value being represented is "**sum**" rather than "count" (Fig. 4.11).

You've now got a table, as in Fig. 4.12, that sums up how much the various topics contribute to each document. Let us now visualize the trends using simple line charts.

3. Highlight two columns: try "row labels" and "topic 00." Click charts, then line chart. You now have a visualization of topic 00 over time (Fig. 4.13).
4. To compare various topics over time, click the drop-down arrow beside column labels, and select the topics you wish to visualize. You may have to first unselect "select all," and then click a few. For example, Topics 04, 07, and 11 as in Fig. 4.14.
6. Your table will repopulate with just those topics displayed. Highlight row labels and the columns (don't highlight the "grand totals"). Select line chart — and you can now see the evolution over fine-grained time of various topics within the documents, as in Fig. 4.15.

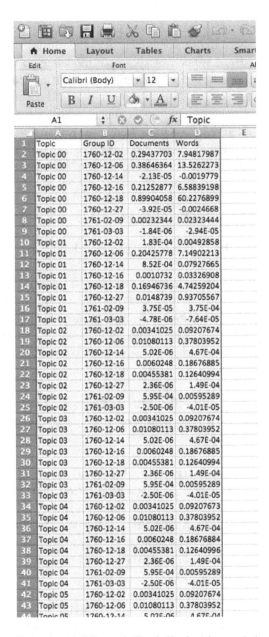

Fig. 4.10   Select all the data in Microsoft Excel. Used with permission from Microsoft.

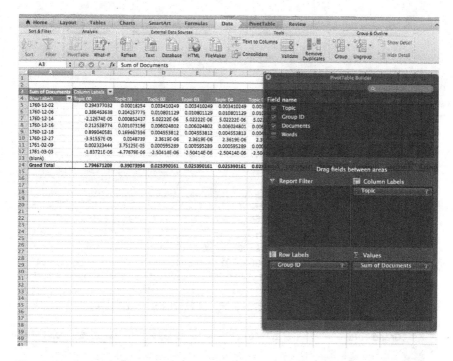

Fig. 4.11 Configure the pivot table wizard in Microsoft Excel. Used with permission from Microsoft.

Sum of Documents	Column Labels										
Row Labels	Topic 00	Topic 01	Topic 02	Topic 03	Topic 04	Topic 05	Topic 06	Topic 07	Topic 08	Topic 09	Topic 10
1760-12-02	0.294377032	0.00018254	0.003410249	0.003410249	0.003410249	0.003410249	0.003410249	0.012909833	0.003410249	0.003410249	0.000121431
1760-12-06	0.386463638	0.204257775	0.010801129	0.010801129	0.010801129	0.010801129	0.010801129	0.105276728	0.010801129	0.010801129	0.000522923
1760-12-14	-2.12674E-05	0.000852437	5.02222E-06	5.02222E-06	5.02222E-06	5.02222E-06	5.02222E-06	-2.99556E-05	5.02222E-06	5.02222E-06	8.12316E-05
1760-12-16	0.212528774	0.001073196	0.006024802	0.006024802	0.006024801	0.006024802	0.006024802	0.000694251	0.006024802	0.006024802	0.000759817
1760-12-18	0.899040581	0.169467356	0.004553812	0.004553812	0.004553813	0.004553812	0.004553812	6.34014E-05	0.004553812	0.004553812	0.411937545
1760-12-27	-3.91557E-05	0.0148739	2.3619E-06	2.3619E-06	2.3619E-06	2.3619E-06	2.3619E-06	-2.66842E-05	2.3619E-06	2.3619E-06	-1.11205E-05
1761-02-09	0.002323444	3.75125E-05	0.000595289	0.000595289	0.000595289	0.000595289	0.000595289	0.580778198	0.000595289	0.000595289	0.000214639
1761-03-03	-1.83721E-06	-4.77679E-06	-2.50414E-06	-2.50414E-06	-2.50414E-06	-2.50414E-06	-2.50414E-06	-2.00765E-07	-2.50414E-06	-2.50414E-06	-6.5647E-06
(blank)											
Grand Total	**1.794671209**	**0.39073994**	**0.025390161**	**0.025390161**	**0.025390161**	**0.025390161**	**0.025390161**	**0.699665571**	**0.025390161**	**0.025390161**	**0.413619901**

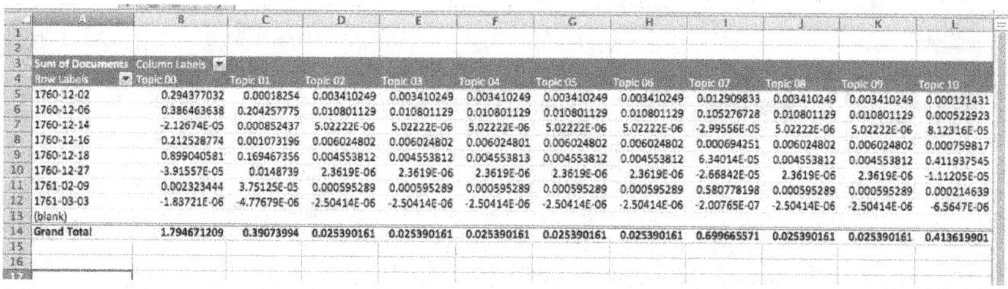

Fig. 4.12 The data now arranged as a pivot table in Microsoft Excel. Used with permission from Microsoft.

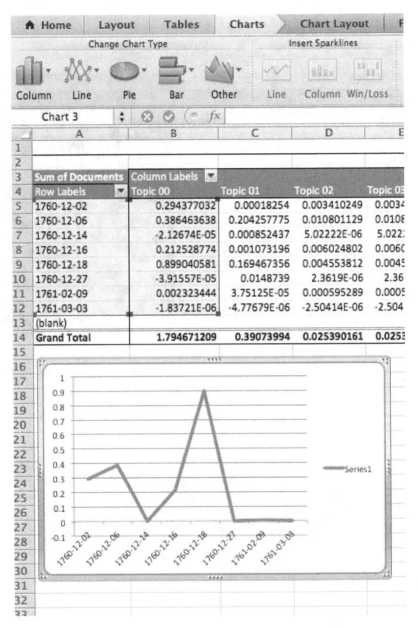

Fig. 4.13   Visualizing a single topic over time in Microsoft Excel. Used with permission from Microsoft.

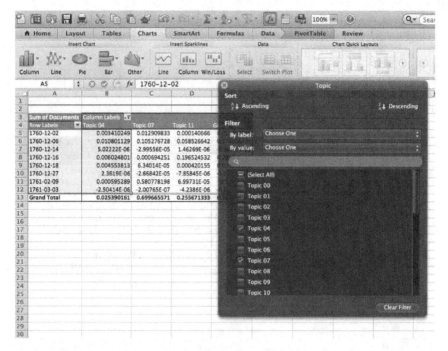

Fig. 4.14 Comparing topics over time in Microsoft Excel. Used with permission from Microsoft.

Let's look at our example topic model again. In our data, the word "congress" appears in three different topics:

```
Topic 10
    498.75611573955666
    town                16.69292048824643
    miles               13.89718543152377
    tavern              12.93903988493706
    [...]
    congress            6.1549912410407135
Topic 15
    377.279139869195
    should              14.714242395918141
    may                 11.427645785723927
    being               11.309756818192291
    [...]
    congress            10.652337301569547
```

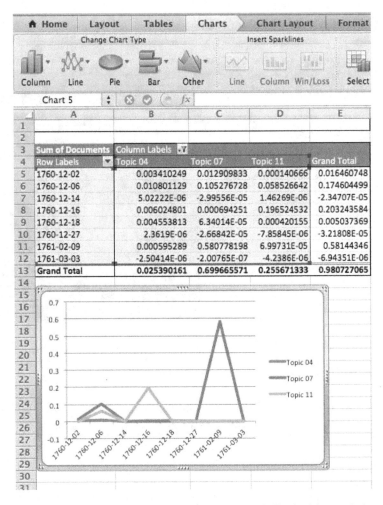

Fig. 4.15   Visualizing topics over time in Microsoft Excel. Used with permission from Microsoft.

Topic 18 (Continued)

```
385.6024287288036
french              18.243384948219443
written             15.919785193963612
minister            12.110373497509345
[...]
congress            8.043713670428902
```

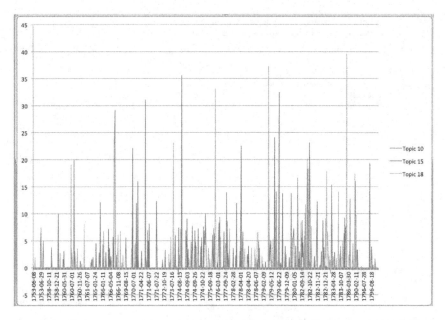

Fig. 4.16   Topics 10, 15, 18 over time in John Adams' diaries in Microsoft Excel. Used with permission from Microsoft.

These numbers give a sense of the general overall weight or importance of these words to the topic and the corpus as a whole. Topic 10 seems to be a topic surrounding a discourse concerning local governance, while Topic 15 seems to be about ideas of what governance, at a national scale, ought to be, and Topic 18 concerns what is actually happening, in terms of the nation's governance. Thus, we might want to explore how these three topics play out against each other over time to get a sense of how Adams' differing scales of "governance" discourses play out over time. Accordingly, we select Topic 10, 15, and 18 from the drop-down menu. The chart updates automatically, plotting the composition of the corpus with these three topics over time (Fig. 4.16).

The chart is a bit difficult to read, however. We can see a spike in Adams' "theoretical" musings on governance in 1774 followed by a rapid spike in his "realpolitick" writings. It would be nice to be able to zoom in on a particular period. On the drop-down arrow under the dates column, we can select the relevant periods. We could also achieve a dynamic time visualization by copying and pasting the entire pivot table (filtered for our three topics) into a new Google spreadsheet. At http://j.mp/ja-3-topics there is a publicly available spreadsheet that does just that (Fig. 4.17

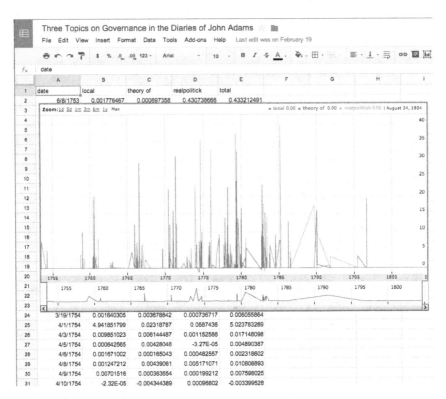

Fig. 4.17   Using Google Sheets to visualize time slices of documents and topics in John Adams' diaries.

is a screen shot). We copied and pasted the filtered pivot table into a blank sheet. Then we clicked on the "insert chart" button on the toolbar. Google recognized the data as having a date column and automatically selected a scrollable/zoomable time series chart. At the bottom of that chart, we can simply drag the time slider to bracket the period that we are interested in.

The ability to slice our topic model into time chunks is perhaps, for the historian, the greatest attraction of the Stanford tool. That it also accepts input from a CSV file, which we can generate from scraping online sources, is another important feature of the tool.

Working with scripts can be daunting at first, but the learning curve is worth the power that they bring us! We would suggest keeping an unchanged copy of the example scripts from the STMT website in their own folder. Then, copy and paste them to a unique folder for each dataset you will work with. Edit them in Notepad++ (or similar) to point to the particular dataset you wish to work with. Keep your data and scripts together, preferably in a Dropbox folder as a backup strategy. Folding Google spreadsheets in your workflow is also a handy tool, especially if you plan on sharing or writing about your work online.

Advanced Topic Modeling with R

Working with MALLET from the command line takes some getting used to. Its output is somewhat difficult to work with, as the user has to load it into Excel or another spreadsheet to manipulate it. The STMT allows us to manipulate our topic model to a degree for better visualization, but it presents its own challenges.

One thing we might like to do with the output is to create a table where our documents are down the side and our topics are arranged in order across the top, with the percentage composition filling out the cells. Once we have the data arranged this way, we will be able to use functions in MS Excel to work out which documents are correlated with which other documents, or which topics are correlated with what topics (the better to create network visualizations with, for instance). Such a matrix is not natively output by MALLET or the other tools we've discussed, and with larger datasets, can be quite time-consuming to create. It is possible (but not easy) to create a macro or a script in Excel that could do the work for you. In which case, we would suggest that you might wish to experiment with creating topic models within the R statistical programming environment. The key advantage here: R is *built* to deal with large matrices of data, to manipulate it, to rearrange it, and to visualize it. Many common tasks have already been packaged together such that, instead of programming them from scratch, you can invoke the package as its own command. R also enables someone else to *reproduce* what you have done, and thus introduces the idea that another historian could work with your data and extend or critique your argument on those grounds.

Getting started with R

To begin, we will need to download R as well as RStudio. R is the language; RStudio is a user interface that makes working in R a great deal easier. You can download R from http://cran.rstudio.com (select the appropriate version for your operating system), and then RStudio from http://www.rstudio.com/products/rstudio/download/ (make sure to select the free, open source version). Both have standard installation processes that you can run like any other piece of software.

RStudio uses a graphical interface that allows you to create "workspaces" for your project. You load your data into the workspace, run your commands, and keep your output in this workspace (all without altering your original data). The ability to save and reload workspaces allows you to pick up where you left off.

We do not intend this section to be a full-blown introduction to R and how to use the R environment. There are a number of excellent online tutorials available to get you started with R. Paul Torfs and Claudia Braur have a very good general introduction to R.[15] Fred Gibbs has a tutorial on computing document similarity with R that we highly recommend.[16] Ben Marwick also has a good tutorial that shows some of the ins and outs of using R, programmed in R itself.[17]

One thing to note is that, like Marwick, many people share their "scripts" for doing different tasks, via GitHub. To see this in action, navigate to Marwick's tutorial (https://gist.github.com/benmarwick/5403048) and click on the "download gist" button (there are three files within this gist). You will receive a zipped folder containing a file called "short-intro-R.R". Unzip that file to your desktop. Then, in the R environment select "file" → "open script". Browse to "short-intro-R.R" and select it. (Our vision here is to show you how to run other people's programs and make minor changes yourself.)

A new window will open containing the script. Within that script, any line beginning with a hash character is a comment line. R ignores all comment lines when running code. You can now run either every command in the script, or you can run each line one at a time to see what happens. To run each line one at a time, place the cursor at the beginning of the line, and hit Ctrl+R on Windows, or Command+Enter on OS X. You'll see the

---

[15] Paul Torfs and Claudia Brauer (3 March 2014), "A (very) Short Introduction to R," http://cran.r-project.org/doc/contrib/Torfs+Brauer-Short-R-Intro.pdf. Another very good interactive tutorial for R is available through codeschool.com at http://tryr. codeschool.com/.

[16] Fred Gibbs (4 June 2013), "Document Similarity with R," *fredgibbs.net*, http://fredgibbs.net/tutorials/tutorial/document-similarity-with-r/.

[17] Downloadable at https://gist.github.com/benmarwick/5403048. Another version is lodged at http://themacroscope.org/2.0/datafiles/gist5403048. The other files in this folder contain Marwick's notes to his class providing more context, and can be opened in RStudio.

line appear in the main console window. Since the first line in Marwick's script is led with a # (meaning, a comment), the line copies and nothing else happens. Hit Ctrl+R/Command+Enter so that the line

```
2 + 2
```

is copied into the console. R will return, directly underneath:

```
4
```

As you proceed through Marwick's script, you'll see other ways of dealing with data. In line 35, you create a variable called "a" and give it the value 2; in line 36 you create a variable called "b" and give it the value 3. Line 24 has you add "a + b", which will return "5." An excellent online, interactive tutorial that covers the basic ideas of R, which we also recommend, can be found at http://tryr.codeschool.com/.

Extending R with others' packages

Sometimes, you will see a line like this:

```
library(igraph)
```

This line is telling R to use a particular package that will provide R with more tools and algorithms to manipulate your data. If that package is not installed, you will receive an error message. If that happens, you can tell R to install the package quite easily:

```
install.packages("igraph")
```

R will ask you which download site you wish to use (which it calls a "mirror"); select one that is geographically close to you for the fastest download. These mirrors are the repositories that contain the latest versions of all the packages.

Using Mimno's MALLET wrapper in R

David Mimno has written a wrapper for MALLET in R. Mimno's wrapper installs MALLET's topic modeling tools directly inside R, allowing greater speed and efficiency, as well as turning R's full strength to the analysis and visualization of the resulting data. You do not have to have the command-line version of MALLET installed on your machine already to use Mimno's wrapper: the wrapper *is* MALLET, or at least, the part that does the topic modeling![18] Since MALLET is written in Java, the wrapper will install the rJava package to enable R to run it.

To use the MALLET wrapper in R, one simply types (remember, in R, any line with a # is a comment and so does not execute):

```
#the first time you wish to use it, you must install:
install.packages("mallet")
# R will then ask you which 'mirror' (repository) you wish
to install from. Select one that is close to you.
#any subsequent time, after you've installed it:
require(mallet)
```

If you find you're having trouble getting started, or there are error messages, please see our section on "Working with R" on the website for this book at http://themacroscope.org/2.0/extra-help-with-r.

Now the whole suite of commands and parameters is available to you. A short demonstration script that uses the example data bundled with MALLET (since you already downloaded those data earlier in this chapter) can be found at the code section on http://themacroscope.org/2.0/code-r. (The full manual for the wrapper may be found at http://cran.r-project.org/web/packages/mallet/mallet.pdf; our example is based on Mimno's example.) Open it up. We will not provide every single line of code below, so we encourage you to work through the script you find online with this book in hand. We'll explain the important lines!

Let's look in more detail at how we build a topic model using this script.

```
documents <-
mallet.read.dir("mallet-2.0.7/sample-data/web/en/")
```

This line creates a variable called "documents," and it contains the path to the documents you wish to analyze. On a Windows machine, you would include the full path, i.e. "C:\\mallet-2.0.7\\sampled-data\\web\\". This is the default location for sample data when you unzipped Mallet; change the path if you changed the folder name. In that directory, each document is its own unique text file. Now we need to import those documents into MALLET. We do that by running this command:

```
mallet.instances <- mallet.import(documents$id,
```

---

[18]For an interesting use-case of this package, please see Ben Marwick's analysis of the *2013 Day of Archaeology* at https://github.com/benmarwick/dayofarchaeology. He published both the analysis and the scripts he has used to perform the analysis on GitHub itself, making it an interesting experiment in publishing data, digital methods, and discussion.

```
documents$text, "mallet-2.0.7/stoplists/en.txt", token.regexp
= "\\p{L}[\\p{L}\\p{P}]+\\p{L}")
```

It's complicated, but what's happening here is that your documents are being brought into R, as a new object called "mallet.instances". That is, a list with every document is listed by its id, with its associated text, where a stoplist has been used to filter out common stopwords, and a regular expression to keep all sequences of Unicode characters. It is worth asking yourself: is the default stoplist provided by MALLET appropriate for my text? Are there words that should be added or removed? You can create a stopword list in any text editor by opening the default one, adding or deleting as appropriate, and then saving with a new name and the .txt extension. The next step is to create an empty container for our topic model:

```
n.topics <- 30
topic.model <- MalletLDA(n.topics)
```

We created a variable called "n.topics." If you reran your analysis to explore a greater or lesser number of topics, you would only have to change this one line to the number you wished. Now we can load the container up with our documents:

```
topic.model$loadDocuments(mallet.instances)
```

At this point, you can begin to explore for patterns in the word use in your document, if you wish, by finding out what the vocabulary and word frequencies of the document are:

```
vocabulary <- topic.model$getVocabulary()
word.freqs <- mallet.word.freqs(topic.model)
```

If you now type

```
length(vocabulary)
```

...you will receive a number; this is the number of unique words in your document. You can inspect the top 100 words thus:

```
vocabulary[1:100]
```

As Mimno notes in the comments to his code, this information could be useful for you to customize your stoplist. Jockers also shows us how to explore some of the distribution of those words using the "head" command (which returns the first few rows of a data matrix or data frame):

```
head(word.freqs)
```

You will be presented with a table with words down the side and two columns: term.freq and doc.freq. This tells you the number of times the word appears in the corpus and the number of documents in which it appears.

The script now sets the optimization parameters for the topic model. In essence, you can tune the model.[19] This line sets the "hyperparameters":

```
topic.model$setAlphaOptimization(20, 50)
```

You can play with these to see what happens, or you can choose to leave this line alone and accept MALLET's defaults. The next two lines generate the topic model:

```
topic.model$train(200)
topic.model$maximize(10)
```

The first line tells MALLET how many rounds or iterations to process through. More can sometimes lead to "better" topics and clusters. Jockers reports that he finds that the quality increases with the number of iterations only so far, before beginning to plateau.[20] When you run these commands, output will scroll by as the algorithm iterates. At each iteration, it will also give you the probability that the topic is likely.

Now we want to examine the results of the topic model. These lines take the raw output and convert it to probabilities:

```
doc.topics <- mallet.doc.topics(topic.model, smoothed=T,
normalized=T)
topic.words <- mallet.topic.words(topic.model, smoothed=T,
normalized=T)
```

One last bit of transformation will give us a spreadsheet with topics down the side and documents across the top (compare this with the "native" output of MALLET from the command line).

```
topic.docs <- t(doc.topics)
```

---

[19]See Hanna Wallach, David Mimno and Andrew McCallum (2009) "Rethinking LDA: Why Priors Matter," in *Proceedings of Advances in Neural Information Processing Systems* (NIPS), **22**, 1973–1981.Vancouver, BC: Curran Associates. http:// papers.nips.cc/paper/3854-rethinking-lda-why-priors-matter.

[20]Matthew Jockers, *Text Analysis with R for Students of Literature* (New York: Springer: 2014), 147.

```
topic.docs <- topic.docs / rowSums(topic.docs)
write.csv(topic.docs, "topics-docs.csv" )
```

This script will not work "out of the box" for you the first time, because your files and our files might not necessarily be in the same location. To use it successfully for yourself, you will need to change certain lines to point to appropriate locations on your own machine (regardless of whether it is Windows, Mac, or Linux). Study the example carefully. Do you see which lines need to be changed to access your own data?

This is a good starting point for your future work with R! If you want to try it out on your own data, you can change the directory with documents on line 21. There are a couple of ways you might try to visualize these results, too, within R. Let's begin by creating some topic labels with this code:

```
# Get a vector containing short names for the topics

topics.labels <- rep("", n.topics)for (topic in 1:n.topics)
topics.labels[topic] <- paste(mallet.top.words(topic.model,
topic.words[topic,], num.top.words=5)$words, collapse=" ")

# have a look at keywords for each topic topics.labels

# write these to a file write.csv(topics.labels,
"topics-labels.csv")
```

After creating your topic model, we can now create a clustergram of our topics. The following code will work:

```
# create data.frame with columns as documents and rows as topics
topic_docs <- data.frame(topic.docs)
names(topic_docs) <- documents$id

## cluster based on shared words
plot(hclust(dist(topic.words)), labels=topics.labels)
```

These lines create a clustergram of your documents based on the similarity of word use within the topics! Imagine trying to perform such a visualization in MS Excel. R is an extremely powerful programming environment for analyzing the kinds of data that historians will encounter. For a fun example of using R to topic model and visualize patterns across texts, see Ben Marwick's "A Distant Reading of the Day of Archaeology" https://github.com/benmarwick/dayofarchaeology.

Numerous online tutorials for visualizing and working with data exist; we would suggest Matthew Jockers' *Text Analysis with R for Students of*

Literature (http://link.springer.com/book/10.1007/978-3-319-03164-4) as
your next point of call if you wish to explore R's potential further.

A Proviso Concerning Using Other People's Tools

Tools and platforms are changing all the time, so there's an awful lot of work
for developers to make sure they're always working. One tool that we quite
like is called *Paper Machines* (http://papermachines.org), and it holds a lot
of promise since it allows the user to data mine collections of materials kept
within the Zotero reference manager. It was built by Jo Guldi and Chris
Johnson-Roberson.[21] It is a plugin that you install within Zotero; once
enabled, a series of contextual commands, including topic modeling, become
available to you by right-clicking on a collection within your Zotero library.
At the current time of writing it can be quite fiddly to use, and much will
depend on how your system is configured. However, it's only in version 0.4,
meaning it's really not much more than a prototype. It will be something
to keep an eye on. At http://themacroscope.org/2.0/paper-machines you
can see the kinds of things that Paper Machines aspires to do.

We mention this here to highlight the speed with which the digital landscape of tools can change. When we initially wrote about Paper Machines,
we were able to topic model and visualize John Adams' diaries, scraping
the page itself using Zotero. When we revisited that workflow a few months
later, given changes that we had made to our own machines (updating
software, moving folders around and so on, and changes to the underlying HTML of the John Adams' diaries website), it — our workflow — no
longer worked! Working with digital tools can sometimes make it necessary
to not update your software! Rather, keep in mind which tools work with
what versions of other supporting pieces. Archive a copy of the tool that
works for you and your setup, and keep notes under what conditions the
software works. Open source software can be "forked" (copied) on GitHub
with a single click. This is a habit we should all get into (not only does it
give us the archived software, but it also provides a kind of citation network demonstrating the impact of that software over time). In digital work,
careful documentation of what works (and under what conditions) can be

---

[21]The code for this plugin is open source and may be found at https://github.com/
chrisjr/papermachines. The Paper Machines website is at http://papermachines.org.

crucial to ensuring the reproducibility of your research. Historians are not accustomed to thinking about reproducibility, but it will become an issue.

Conclusion

In this chapter, you have been introduced to a number of tools for fitting topic models to a body of text: ranging from one document, to an entire diary, to multiple documents. Different tools have contrasting algorithms that implement topic modeling in particular ways, leading to unique outputs. This is worth underlining! Indeed, this mathematical approach to human history does not produce the same specific pattern each time we run it but rather a distribution of probabilistic outcomes. This can be difficult for us to get our heads around, but we must resist the temptation to run a topic model and accept at face value its results as being "the" answer about our corpora of materials. Turns out historians still have a job! Phew.

The topic model generates hypotheses, new perspectives, and new questions: not simple answers, let alone some sort of mythical "truth." The act of visualization of the results too is as much art as it is science, introducing new layers of interpretation and engagement. On our companion website, we have written an essay that uses topic modeling to understand the historiographical discourses in the *Dictionary of Canadian Biography,* a multi-authored, multi-volume work that explores the lives of over 8,000 historical Canadians (http://themacroscope.org/2.0/8000-canadians). As you read that essay, consider for yourself the choices we have made in how we perform the topic model and in how we visualize the results. How justified are we in those choices? How could different tools change our perspective and hence our conclusions? Do the visualizations help our argument, or hinder it? When you encounter someone else's topic model, do not accept it at first glance. Rather, to understand the potentials and pitfalls, you must be aware of how the tools work and their limitations. Andrew Goldstone and Ted Underwood published an article called "The Quiet Transformations of Literary Studies: What Thirteen Thousand Scholars Could Tell Us," a topic modeling exercise on what scholars had written about literary history.[22] In a companion blog post to that piece, Goldstone details the construction and

---

[22] Andrew Goldstone and Ted Underwood (May 28, 2014), "The Quiet Transformations of Literary Studies: What Thirteen Thousand Scholars Could Tell Us," Preprint for New Literary History available at https://www.ideals.illinois.edu/handle/2142/49323.

implication of a "topic browser" that he built to support the conclusions of the journal article.[23] Goldstone writes,

> [J]ust as social scientists and natural scientists grit their teeth and learn to program and produce visualizations when they need to in order to support their analysis, so too must those of us in the humanities. Solutions off the shelf are not great at answering expert research questions. What should come off the shelf are components that the researcher knows how to put together.

In the next chapter, we pause for a moment to consider ways all of these data could be visualized. The rhetorical impact of an excellent visualization should not be understated. This discussion of visualization and the principles of good design leads us to one particular kind of visualization whose popularity seems to be growing daily: the social network diagram. Social network analysis and its visualization have been conflated a great deal; yet it is entirely possible to have one without the other. We will argue in the final two chapters that historians need to understand social network analysis as a way of representing and querying the social relationships between historical actors in the past. And only *then* should we think about how to represent the network. As you will see, a "network diagram" is often not the best choice!

---

[23] See Andrew Goldstone (29 April 2014), "The Quiet Transformations of Literary Studies," *AndrewGoldstone.com*, available online, http://andrewgoldstone.com/blog/2014/05/29/quiet/.

Chapter 5

Making Your Data Legible:
A Basic Introduction
to Visualizations

By this point in the book, you know how to gather data and we are beginning to explore various ways to visualize it. While historians often make use of graphs and charts, the training of a historian typically includes very little on the principles of information visualization. Here we provide guidance on the various issues at play when the historian turns to data visualization.

It should now be clear that reading history through a macroscope will involve visualization. Visualization is a method of deforming, compressing, or otherwise manipulating data in order to see them in new and enlightening ways. A good visualization can turn hours of careful study into a flash of insight or can convey a complex narrative in a single moment. Visualizations can also lie, confuse, or otherwise misrepresent if used poorly. What are the types of visualizations? Why might you choose one kind of visualization over another, and to what end? How can we use visualization techniques most effectively? We will also explore several visualizations which have been used to great rhetorical and analytical effect by historians.

Why Visualize?

A 13th century Korean edition of the Buddhist canon contains over 52 million characters across 166,000 pages. Lewis Lancaster describes a traditional analysis of this corpus as such:

> The previous approach to the study of this canon was the traditional analytical one of close reading of specific examples of texts followed by a search through a defined corpus for additional examples. When confronted with 166,000 pages, such activity had to be limited. As a result,

analysis was made without having a full picture of the use of target words throughout the entire collection of texts. That is to say, our scholarship was often determined and limited by externalities such as availability, access, and size of written material. In order to overcome these problems, scholars tended to seek for a reduced body of material that was deemed to be important by the weight of academic precedent.[1]

As technologies advanced, the old limitations were no longer present; Lancaster and his team worked to create a search interface (Fig. 5.1) that would allow historians to see the evolution and use of glyphs over time, effectively allowing them to explore the entire text all at once. No longer would historians need to selectively pick which areas of this text to scrutinize; they could quickly see where in the corpus their query was most-often used and go from there.

This approach to distant reading — that is, seeing where in a text the object of inquiry is densest — has since become so common as to no longer feel like a visualization. Amazon's Kindle has a search function called X-Ray which allows the reader to search for a series of words and see the frequency with which those words appear in a text over the course of its pages. In Google's web browser, Chrome, searching for a word on a webpage highlights the scroll bar on the right-hand side such that it is easy to see the distribution of that word use across the page (Fig. 5.2).

The use of visualizations to show the distribution of words or topics in a document is an effective way of getting a sense for the location and frequency of your query in a corpus, and it represents only one of the many uses of information visualization. Uses of information visualization generally fall into two categories: exploration and communication.

Exploration

When first obtaining or creating a dataset, visualizations can be a valuable aid in understanding exactly what data are available and how they interconnect. In fact, even before a dataset is complete, visualizations can be used to recognize errors in the data collection process. Imagine you are collecting metadata from a few hundred books in a library collection, making note of the publisher, date of publication, author names, and so on. A few

---

[1]Lewis Lancaster, "From Text to Image to Analysis: Visualization of Chinese Buddhist Canon" Abstract for *Digital Humanities DH 2010 King's College London 7th–10th July 2010,* http://dh2010.cch.kcl.ac.uk/academic-programme/abstracts/papers/html/ab-670.html.

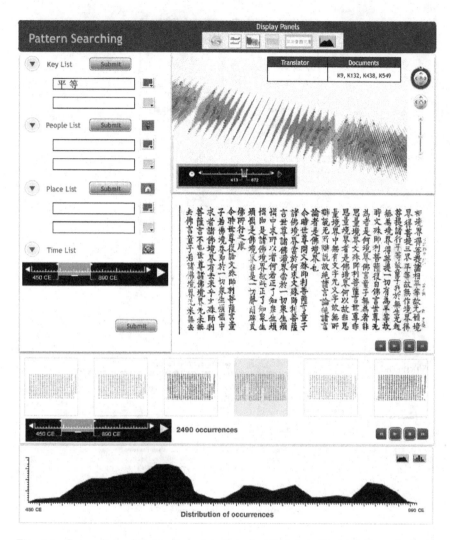

Fig. 5.1 Screenshot of Lancaster's interface for studying the evolution of glyphs over time.

simple visualizations, made easily in software like Microsoft Excel, can go a long way in pointing out errors. Notice how in the chart in Fig. 5.3, it can easily be noticed that whomever entered the data on book publication dates accidentally typed "1909" rather than "1990" for one of the books.

Similarly, visualizations can be used to get a quick understanding of the structure of data being entered, right in the spreadsheet. The visualization

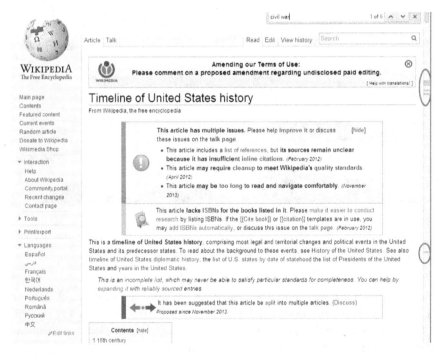

Fig. 5.2 Amazon's X-Ray search juxtaposed against Google Chrome's scroll-bar search term indicator. Screenshot courtesy Aslak Raanes.

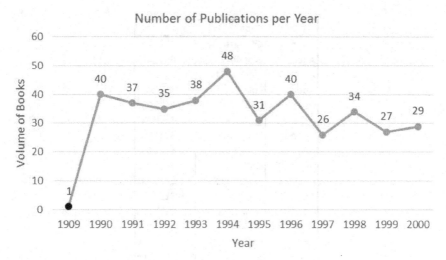

Fig. 5.3 An error in data entry becomes apparent quickly when data are represented as a chart.

in Fig. 5.4, of salaries at a university, makes it trivial to spot which department's faculty have the highest salaries and how those salaries are distributed. It utilizes basic functions in recent versions of Microsoft Excel.

More complex datasets can be explored with more advanced visualizations, and that exploration can be used for everything from getting a sense of the data at hand, to understanding the minute particulars of one data point in relation to another. The visualization in Fig. 5.5, ORBIS, allows the user to explore transportation networks in the Ancient Roman world. This particular display is showing the most likely route from Rome to Constantinople under a certain set of conditions, but the user is invited to tweak those conditions, or the starting and ending cities, to whatever best suits their own research questions.

Exploratory visualizations like this one form a key part of the research process when analyzing large datasets. They sit particularly well as an additional layer in the hermeneutic process of hypothesis formation. You may begin your research with a dataset and some preconceptions of what it means and what it implies, but without a well-formed thesis to be argued. The exploratory visualization allows you to notice trends or outliers that you may not have noticed otherwise, and those trends or outliers may be worth explaining or discussing in further detail. Careful historical research of those points might reveal even more interesting directions worth exploring, which can then be folded into future visualizations.

Name	Department	Salary
Anon 13	Chemistry	$248,045
Anon 7	Economics	$213,467
Anon 17	Economics	$172,500
Anon 6	Chemistry	$154,487
Anon 15	Chemistry	$145,723
Anon 4	Economics	$133,541
Anon 12	Chemistry	$128,953
Anon 16	English	$122,885
Anon 19	English	$117,203
Anon 14	Economics	$115,341
Anon 20	English	$110,136
Anon 21	Chemistry	$107,000
Anon 8	English	$105,038
Anon 18	English	$104,916
Anon 2	English	$74,206

Fig. 5.4   Even a spreadsheet can be considered a visualization.

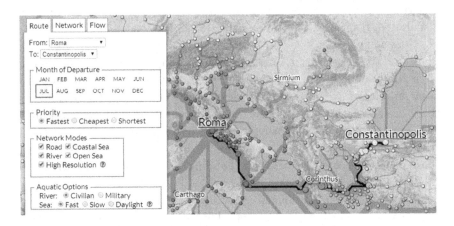

Fig. 5.5   Screenshot of a detail from ORBIS. Courtesy Elijah Meeks.

Communication

Once the research process is complete, visualizations still have an important role to play in translating complex data relationships into easily digestible units. The right visualization can replace pages of text with a single graph and still convey the same amount of information. The visualization created

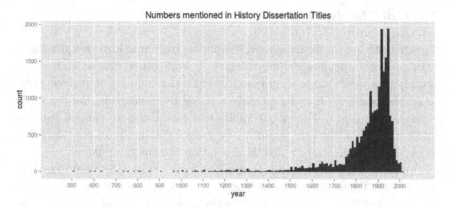

Fig. 5.6   The years mentioned in dissertation titles, after Schmidt, 2013. Courtesy Benjamin Schmidt.

by Ben Schmidt, reproduced in Fig. 5.6, for example, shows the frequency with which certain years are mentioned in the titles of history dissertations.[2] The visualization clearly shows that the great majority of dissertations cover the years after 1750, with spikes around the American Civil War and the World Wars. While the chart does describe the trends accurately, it does not convey the sheer magnitude of difference between earlier and later years as covered by dissertations, nor does it mention the sudden drop in dissertations covering periods after 1970.

Visualizations in publications are often, but not always, used to improve a reader's understanding of the content being described. It is also common for visualizations to be used to catch the eye of readers or peer reviewers, to make research more noticeable, memorable, or publishable. In a public world that values quantification so highly, visualizations may lend an air of legitimacy to a piece of research, which it may or may not deserve. We will not comment on the ethical implications of such visualizations, but we do note that such visualizations are increasingly common and seem to play a role in successfully analyzing data, proving your case for peer review, or helping make your work accessible to a general public. Whether the ends justify the means is a decision we leave to our readers.

---

[2]Ben Schmidt (May 9 2013), "What years do historians write about?" *Sapping Attention* http://sappingattention.blogspot.ca/2013/05/what-years-do-historians-write-about.html.

Types of Visualizations

Up until this point, we have used the phrase **information visualization** without explaining it or differentiating it from other related terms. We remedy that here: information visualization is the mapping of abstract data to graphic variables in order to make a visual representation. We use these representations to augment our abilities to read data; we cannot hope to intuit all relationships in our data by memory and careful consideration alone, and visualizations make those relationships more apparent.

An **information visualization** differs from a **scientific visualization** in the data it aims to represent, and in how that representation is instantiated. Scientific visualizations maintain a specific spatial reference system, whereas information visualizations do not. Visualizations of molecules, weather, motors, and brains are all scientific visualizations because they each already have a physical instantiation, and their visual form is preserved in the visualization. Bar charts, scatter plots, and network graphs, on the other hand, are all information visualizations because they lay out in space data that do not have inherent spatiality. An **infographic** is usually a combination of information and scientific visualizations embedded in a very explicit narrative and marked up with a good deal of text.

These types are fluid, and some visualizations fall between categories. Most information visualizations, for example, contain some text, and any visualization we create is imbued with the narrative and purpose we give it, whether or not we realize we have done so. A truly "objective" visualization, where the data speak for themselves, is impossible. Our decisions on how to encode our data and which data to present deeply influence the understanding readers take away from a visualization.

Visualizations also vary between static, dynamic, and interactive. Experts in the area have argued that the most powerful visualizations are static images with clear legends and a clear point, although that may be changing with increasingly powerful interactive displays that give users impressive amounts of control over the data. Some of the best modern examples come from the *New York Times* visualization team.[3] **Static visualizations** are those which do not move and cannot be manipulated; **dynamic visualizations** are short animations which show change, either over time or across some other variable; **interactive visualizations** allow the user to

---

[3]See the *New York Times*' data analysis and visualization blog, The Upshot. http://www.nytimes.com/upshot/.

manipulate the graphical variables themselves in real time. Often, because of change blindness, dynamic visualizations may be confusing and less informative than sequential static visualizations. Interactive visualizations have the potential to overload an audience, especially if the controls are varied and unintuitive. The key is striking a balance between clarity and flexibility.

There is more to visualization than bar charts and scatter plots. Scholars are constantly creating new variations and combinations of visualizations, and have been for hundreds of years. An exhaustive list of all the ways information has or can be visualized would be impossible, although we will attempt to explain many of the more common varieties. Our taxonomy is influenced by visualizing.org, a website dedicated to cataloguing interesting visualizations, but we take examples from many other sources as well.

Statistical charts and time series

Statistical charts are likely those that will be most familiar to any audience. When visualizing for communication purposes, it is important to keep in mind which types of visualizations your audience will find legible. Sometimes the most appropriate visualization for the job is the one that is most easily understood, rather than the one that most accurately portrays the data at hand. This is particularly true when representing many abstract variables at once: it is possible to create a visualization with color, size, angle, position, and shape all representing different aspects of the data, but it may become so complex as to be illegible.

Fig. 5.7 is a basic **bar chart** of the amount of non-fiction books held in a small collection, categorized by genre. One dimension of data is the genre, which is qualitative, and each is being compared along a second category, number of books, which is quantitative. Data with two dimensions, one qualitative and one quantitative, usually are best represented as bar charts such as this.

Sometimes you want to visualize data as part of a whole, rather than in absolute values. In these cases, with the same qualitative/quantitative split in data, most will immediately rely on **pie charts** such as the one in Fig. 5.8. This is often a poor choice: pie charts tend to be cluttered — especially as the number of categories increases — and people have difficulty interpreting the area of a pie slice.

The same data can be rendered as a **stacked bar chart** (Fig. 5.9), which produces a visualization with much less clutter. This chart also significantly decreases the cognitive load of the reader as well, as they merely need to

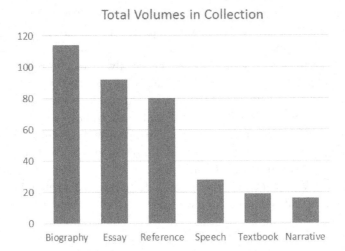

Fig. 5.7   A basic bar chart.

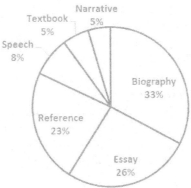

Fig. 5.8   A pie chart.

compare bar length rather than try to internally calculate the area of a slice of pie.

When there are two quantitative variables to be represented, rather than a quantitative and a qualitative, the visualization most often useful is the **line graph** or **scatterplot**. Volumes of books in a collection ordered by publication year, for example, can be expressed with the year on the

TOTAL VOLUMES IN COLLECTION

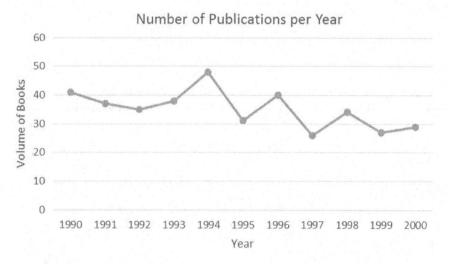

Biography, 33%	Essay, 26%	Reference, 23%	Speech, 8%	Textbook, 5%	Narrative, 5%

Fig. 5.9   A stacked bar chart.

Fig. 5.10   A line graph.

horizontal axis (*x*-axis) and the number of books on the vertical axis (*y*-axis). The line drawn between each (x, y) point represents our assumption that the data points are somehow related to each other, and an upward or downward trend is somehow meaningful (Fig. 5.10).

We could replace the individual lines between years with a trend line, one that shows the general upward or downward trend of the data points over time (Fig. 5.11). This reflects our assumption that not only are the year-to-year changes meaningful, but that there is some underlying factor that is causing the total number of volumes to shift upward or downward across the entire timespan. In this case, it seems that, on average, the number of books collected are decreasing as publication dates approach the present day, which can easily be explained by the lag in time it might take before the decision is made to purchase a book for the collection.

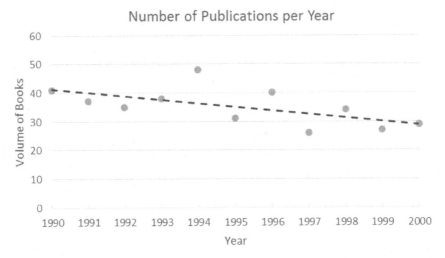

Fig. 5.11   The line in Fig. 5.10 is removed and replaced with a trendline on the points.

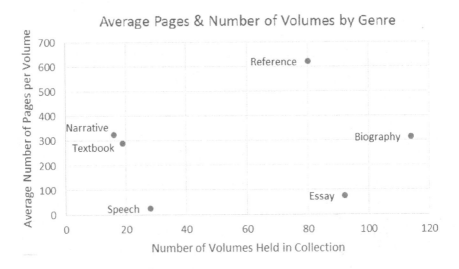

Fig. 5.12   A scatterplot.

Scatterplots have the added advantage of being amenable to additional dimensions of data. The scatterplot in Fig. 5.12 compares three dimensions of data: genre (qualitative), number of volumes of each genre in the collection (quantitative), and average number of pages per genre (quantitative). It shows us, for example, that the collection contains quite a few biographies,

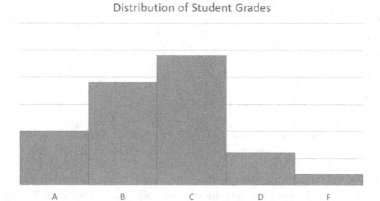

Distribution of Student Grades

Fig. 5.13   A histogram.

and biographies have much fewer pages on average than reference books; there are no discernible trends or correlations between any of the variables, and no new insights emerge from viewing the visualization.

The **histogram** is a visualization that is both particularly useful and extremely deceptive for the unfamiliar. It appears to be a vertical bar chart, but instead of the horizontal axis representing categorical data, a histogram's horizontal axis usually *also* represents quantitative data, subdivided in a particular way. Another way of saying this is that, in a bar chart, the categories can be rearranged without changing the meaning of the visualization, whereas in a histogram, there is a definite order to the categories of the bar. For example, Fig. 5.13 represents the histogram of grade distributions in a college class. It would not make sense for the letter grades to be in any order but the order presented below. Additionally, histograms always represent the distribution of certain values; that is, the height of the bar can never represent something like temperature or age, but instead represents the *frequency* with which some value appears. In Fig. 5.13, bar height represents the frequency with which students in a college course get certain grades.

The histogram (Fig. 5.13) shows that the distribution of students' grades does not follow a true bell curve. A bell curve would have shown there to be as many As as Fs in the class, whereas this curve shows a skew towards As. This is not surprising for anyone who has taught a course, but it is a useful visualization for representing such divergences from expected distributions.

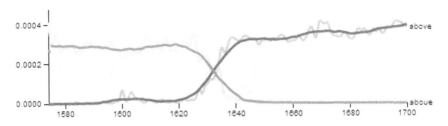

Fig. 5.14   The changing frequency of "aboue" and "above". Courtesy Anupam Basu.

Despite their seeming simplicity, these very basic statistical visualizations can be instigators for extremely useful analyses. The visualization in Fig. 5.14 shows the changing frequency of the use of "aboue" and "above" (spelling variations of the same word) in English printed text from 1580–1700. Sam Kaislaniemi noted in a blog post how surprising it is that the spelling variation seems to have changed so drastically in a period of two decades. This instigated further research, leading to an extended blog post and research into a number of other datasets from the same time period.

Maps

Basic maps should also be considered visualizations, often — but not always — visualizing latitudinal and longitudinal coordinates (maps, of course, pre-date coordinate systems). Even these seemingly straightforward representations are loaded with significant choices, as laying two-dimensional coordinates onto a 3D world means making complicated choices around what map projection to use. For example, the Mercator projection — a variant of which is used in the standard GIS map coordinate system WGS84, as well as the basic Web Mercator projection that underlies Google Maps (itself at the heart of many digital humanities projects) — makes shapes near the poles larger. This visualization decision means that Greenland might appear nearly as large as Africa, which is actually nearly 14 times bigger. As geospatial historian Jim Clifford noted to us when reading our open online version, "Cartography is as much an art as it is a science." While many of these choices are outside the scope of our book, they are significant.

As content is added to a map, it may gain a layer or layers of information visualization. One of the most common geographic visualizations is the **choropleth**, where bounded regions are colored and shaded to represent some statistical variable (Fig. 5.15). Common uses for choropleths include

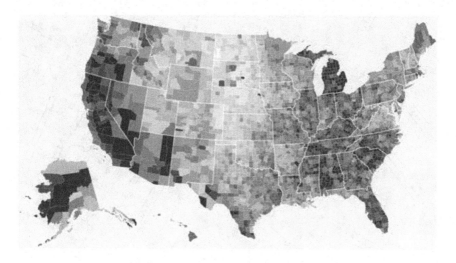

Fig. 5.15 A choropleth map.

representing population density or election results. The below visualization, created by Mike Bostock, colors counties by unemployment rate, with darker counties having higher unemployment. Choropleth maps should be used for ratios and rates rather than absolute values, otherwise larger areas may be disproportionately colored darker due merely to the fact that there is more room for people to live.

For some purposes, choropleths provide insufficient granularity for representing density. In the 1850s, a cholera outbreak in London left many concerned and puzzled over the origin of the epidemic. Dr. John Snow created a **dot density map** (Fig. 5.16) showing the location of cholera cases in the city. The visualization revealed that most cases were around a single water pump, suggesting the outbreak was due to a contaminated water supply.

For representing absolute values on maps, you should instead consider using a **proportional symbol map**. The map depicted in Fig. 5.17, created by Mike Bostock, shows the populations of some of the United States' largest cities. These visualizations are good for directly comparing absolute values to one another, when geographic region size is not particularly relevant. Keep in mind that often, even if you plan on representing geographic information, the best visualizations may not be on a map. In this case, unless you are trying to show that the higher density of populous areas is in the Eastern United States, you may be better served by a bar chart,

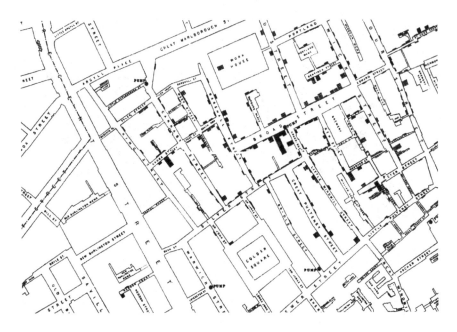

Fig. 5.16   John Snow's dot density map.

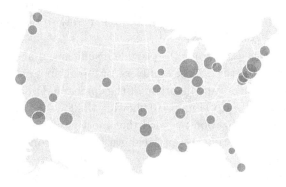

Fig. 5.17   A proportional symbol map showing the population of the largest cities in the United States.

with bar heights representative of population size. That is, the latitude and longitude of the cities are not particularly important in conveying the information we are trying to get across.

Data that continuously change throughout geographic space (e.g. temperature or elevation) require more complex visualizations. The most

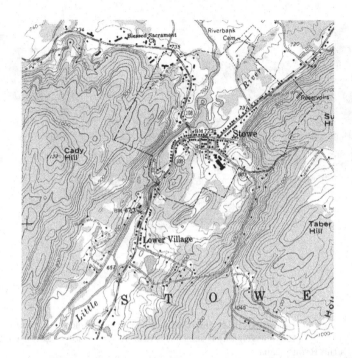

Fig. 5.18   Detail of a topographic map. Courtesy United States Geological Survey.

common in this case are known as **isopleth**, **isarithmic**, or **contour maps**, and they represent gradual change using adjacent, curving lines. Note that these visualizations work best for data that contain smooth transitions. Topographic maps (Fig. 5.18) use adjacent lines to show gradual changes in elevation. The closer together the lines, the more rapidly the elevation changes.

Geographic maps have one feature that sets them apart from most other visualizations: we know them surprisingly well. While few people can label every US state or European country on a map accurately, we know the shape of the world enough that we can take some liberties with geographic visualizations that we cannot take with others. **Cartograms** are maps that distort the basic spatial reference system of latitude and longitude in order to represent some statistical value. They work because we know what the reference is supposed to look like, so we can immediately intuit how cartogram results differ from the "base map" we are familiar with. The cartogram depicted in Fig. 5.19, created by M.E.J. Newman, distorts state sizes by their population and colors the states by how they voted in the

Fig. 5.19   Newman's cartogram of the 2008 US Presidential election results. Darker shade of gray (blue in color version) is the Democrats, lighter shade of gray (red in color version) is the Republicans.

2008 US presidential election.[4] It shows that, although a greater *area* of the United States may have voted Republican, those areas tended to be quite sparsely populated.

Maps are not necessarily always the most appropriate visualizations for the job, but when they are used well, they can be extremely informative.

In the humanities, map visualizations will often need to be of historical or imagined spaces. While there are many convenient pipelines to create custom data overlays of maps, creating new maps entirely can be a gruelling process with few easy tools to support it. It is never as simple as taking a picture of an old map and scanning it into the computer; the aspiring cartographer will need to painstakingly match points on an old scanned map to their modern latitude and longitude, or to create new map tiles entirely. The below visualizations are two examples of such efforts: the first (Fig. 5.20) is a reconstructed map of the ancient world, which includes

---

[4]M.E.J. Newman (2008), "Maps of the 2008 US Presidential Election Results," http://www-personal.umich.edu/~mejn/election/2008/. One may also download Newman's data to explore.

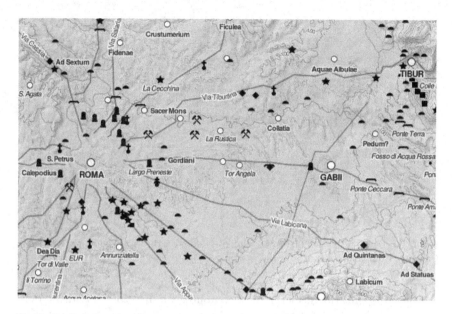

Fig. 5.20   Detail centered on Rome, digital map of the Roman Empire. Courtesy the Pelagios project.

aqueducts, defense walls, sites, and roads, by Johan Åhlfeldt with Pelagios,[5] and the second (Fig. 5.21) is a reconstructed map of Tolkien's Middle Earth by Emil Johansson.[6] Both are examples of extremely careful humanistic work that involved both additional data layers and changes to the base map.

Hierarchies and trees

Whereas the previous types of visualizations dealt with data that were some combination of categorical, quantitative, and geographic, some data are inherently relational and do not lend themselves to these sorts of visualizations. Hierarchical and nested data are a variety of network data, but they are a common enough variety that many visualizations have been designed with them in mind specifically. Examples of this type of data include family

---

[5] "Pelagios" is a project linking together open data on the internet as it pertains to ancient places. See http://pelagios.dme.ait.ac.at/maps/greco-roman/. This map is discussed in detail in Johan Åhlfeldt "A digital map of the Roman Empire" 19 September 2012 http:// pelagios-project.blogspot.ca/2012/09/a-digital-map-of-roman-empire.html.

[6] http://lotrproject.com/map/. For a discussion about this project, see http:// lotrproject.com/about/.

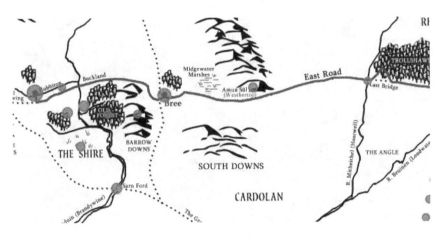

Fig. 5.21   Detail of the LOTRProject map of Middle Earth, with The Shire to the left. Courtesy Emil Johansson.

lineages, organizational hierarchies, computer subdirectories, and the evolutionary branching of species.

The most common forms of visualization for this type of data are **vertical** and **horizontal trees**. The horizontal tree in Fig. 5.22 shows the children and grandchildren of Josiah Wedgwood. These visualizations are extremely easy to read by most people and have been used for many varieties of hierarchical data. Trees have the advantage of being more legible than most other network visualizations but the disadvantage of being fairly restrictive in what they can visualize.

Another form of hierarchical visualization, called a **radial tree**, is often used to show ever-branching structures, as in an organization. The radial tree in Fig. 5.23, a 1924 organization chart in a volume on management statistics by W.H. Smith,[7] emphasizes how power in the organization is centralized in one primary authority. It is important to remember that stylistic choices can deeply influence the message taken from a visualization. Horizontal and radial trees can represent the same information, but the former emphasizes change over time, whereas the latter emphases the centrality of the highest rung on the hierarchy. Both are equally valid, but they send very different messages to the reader.

---

[7]W. H. Smith (1924), *Graphic Statistics in Management*, New York, NY: McGraw-Hill Book Company; this is reproduced on the Visual Complexity database at http://www.visualcomplexity.com/vc/project.cfm?id=10.

Fig. 5.22   Horizontal tree map showing the descendants of Josiah Wedgwood.

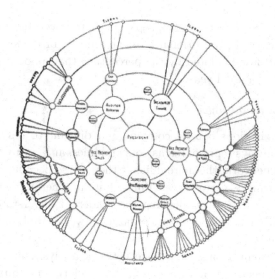

Fig. 5.23   Radial tree diagram showing the organization of a corporation.

One of the more recently popular hierarchical visualizations is the **treemap** designed by Ben Shneiderman. Treemaps use nested rectangles to display hierarchies, the areas of which represent some quantitative value. The rectangles are often colored to represent a third dimension of data, either categorical or quantitative. The visualization in Fig. 5.24 is of

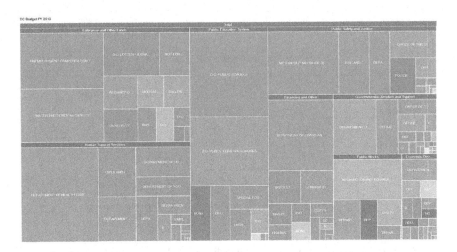

Fig. 5.24   Washington, DC's budget, 2013, as a treemap. Courtesy Justin Grimes.

Washington DC's budget in 2013, separated into governmental categories. Rectangles are sized proportionally to the amount of money received per category in 2013 and colored by the percentage that amount had changed since the previous fiscal year.

Networks and matrices

Network visualizations can be complex and difficult to read. Nodes and edges are not always represented as dots and lines, and even when they are, the larger the network, the more difficult they are to decipher. The reasons behind visualizing a network can differ, but in general, visualizations of small networks are best at allowing the reader to understand individual connections, whereas visualizations of large networks are best for revealing global structure.

Network visualizations, much like network analysis, may or may not add insight depending on the context. A good rule of thumb is to ask a network-literate friend reading the final product whether the network visualization helps them understand the data or the narrative any more than the prose alone. It often will not. We recommend not including a visualization of the data solely for the purpose of revealing the complexity of the data at hand, as it conveys little information and feeds into a negative stereotype of network science as an empty methodology. We will go into network visualizations in some depth in Chapter 6, and the reader may wish to skip ahead.

In fact, we recommend that, where possible, complex network visualizations should be avoided altogether. It is often easier and more meaningful for a historical narrative to simply provide a list of the most well-connected nodes, or for example, a scatterplot showing the relationship between connectivity and vocation. If the question at hand can be more simply answered with a traditional visualization that historians are already trained to read, it should be.

Small Multiples and Sparklines

Small multiples and sparklines are not exactly different types of visualization than those that have already been discussed, but they represent a unique way of presenting visualizations that can be extremely compelling and effective. They embody the idea that simple visualizations can be more powerful than complex ones, and that multiple individual visualizations can often be more easily understood than one incredibly dense visualization.

Small multiples are exactly what they sound like: the use of multiple small visualizations adjacent to one another for the purposes of comparison. They are used in lieu of animations or one single extremely complex visualization attempting to represent the entire dataset. Fig. 5.25, by Brian Abelson of OpenNews, is of cold- and warm-weather anomalies in the United States since 1964.[8] Cold-weather anomalies are in blue and warm-weather anomalies are in red. This visualization is used to show increasingly extreme warm weather due to global warming.

Sparklines, a term coined by Edward Tufte, are tiny line charts with no axis or legend. They can be used in the middle of a sentence, for example to show a changing stock price over the last week ($\frown\diagdown$), which will show us general upward or downward trends, or in small multiples to compare several values. Microsoft Excel has a built-in sparkline feature for just such a purpose. Fig. 5.26 is a screenshot from Excel, showing how sparklines can be used to compare the frequency of character appearances across different chapters of a novel.

The sparklines in Fig. 5.26 quickly show Carol as the main character and that two characters were introduced in Chapter 3, without the reader needing to look at the numbers in the rest of the spreadsheet.

---

[8]See Brian Abelson (April 22, 2014), "Finding Evidence of Climate Change in a Billion Rows of Data," *Source Open News*, see https://source.opennews.org/en-US/articles/finding-evidence-climate-change-billion-rows-data/for details.

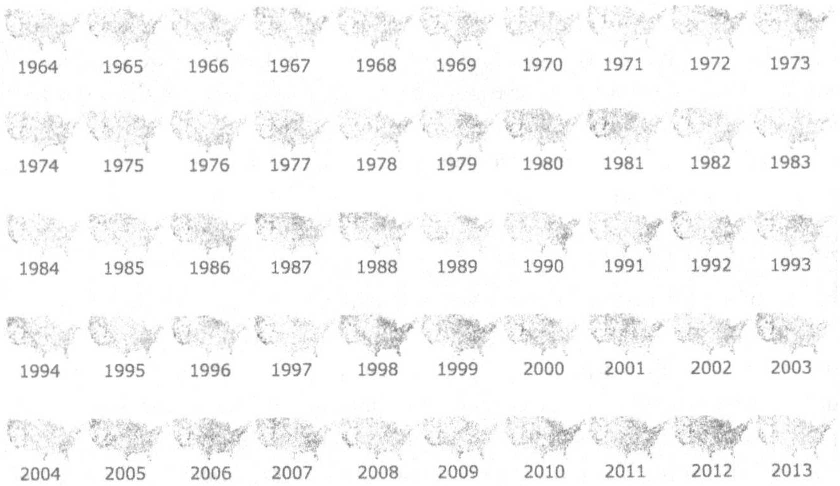

Fig. 5.25   Small multiples, a series of maps representing weather anomalies in the United States since 1964. Courtesy Brian Abelson.

		How often a character name is mentioned				
		Chapter 1	*Chapter 2*	*Chapter 3*	*Chapter 4*	*Chapter 5*
Alice		15	2	2	6	21
Bob		0	0	19	25	24
Carol		31	39	28	34	25
Dan		0	0	15	12	1
Eve		7	0	0	1	0

Fig. 5.26   Sparklines in MS Excel, depicting character appearances in a novel.

Choosing the right visualization

There is no right visualization. A visualization is a decision you make based on what you want your audience to learn. That said, there are a great many *wrong* visualizations. Using a scatterplot to show average rainfall by country is a wrong decision; using a bar chart is a better one. Ultimately, your choice of which type of visualization to use is determined by how many variables you are using, whether they are qualitative or quantitative, how you are trying to compare them, and how you would like to present them. Creating an effective visualization begins by choosing from one of the many appropriate types for the task at hand, and discarding inappropriate types as necessary. Once you have chosen the form your visualization will take, you must decide how you will create the visualization. What colors will you use? What symbols? Will there be a legend? The following sections cover these steps.

Visual Encoding

Once a visualization type has been chosen, the details may seem either self-evident or negligible. Does it really matter what color or shape the points are? In short, yes, it matters just as much as the choice of visualization that is being used. And, when you know how to effectively use various types of visual encodings, you can effectively design new forms of visualization that suit your needs perfectly. The art of visual encoding is in the ability to match data variables and graphic variables appropriately. Graphic variables include the color, shape, or position of objects in the visualization, whereas data variables include what is attempting to be visualized (e.g. temperature, height, age, country name, etc.)

Scales of measure

The most important aspect of choosing an appropriate graphic variable is to know the nature of your data variables. Although the form data might take will differ from project to project, it will likely conform to one of five varieties: nominal, relational, ordinal, interval, or ratio.

Nominal data, also called **categorical data**, is a completely qualitative measurement. It represents different categories or labels or classes. Countries, people's names, and different departments in a university are all nominal variables. They have no intrinsic order, and their only meaning is in how they differentiate from one another. We can put country names in alphabetical order, but that order does not say anything meaningful about their relationships to one another.

Relational data is data on how nominal data relate to one another. It is not necessarily quantitative, although it can be. Relational data requires some sort of nominal data to anchor it, and can include friendships between people, the existence of roads between cities, and the relationship between a musician and the instrument she plays. This type of data is usually, but not always, visualized in trees or networks. A quantitative aspect of relational data may be the length of a phone call between people or the distance between two cities.

Ordinal data is that which has inherent order, but no inherent degree of difference between what is being ordered. The first, second, and third place winners in a race are on an ordinal scale because we do not know how *much* faster first place was than second; only that one was faster than the other. Likert scales, commonly used in surveys (e.g. strongly disagree/disagree/neither agree nor disagree/agree/strongly agree), are an example of commonly-used ordinal data. Although order is meaningful for this variable, the fact that it lacks any inherent magnitude makes ordinal data a qualitative category.

Interval data is data that exists on a scale with meaningful quantitative magnitudes between values. It is like ordinal in that the order matters, and additionally, the difference between first and second place is the same as the distance between second and third place. Longitude, temperature in Celsius, and dates all exist on an interval scale.

Ratio data is data that, like interval data, has a meaningful order and a constant scale between ordered values, but additionally it has a meaningful zero value. Compare this to weight, age, or quantity; having no weight is physically meaningful and different both in quantity and kind to having some weight above zero.

Having a meaningful zero value allows us to use calculations with ratio data that we could not perform on interval data. For example, if one box weighs 50 lbs and another 100 lbs, we can say the second box weighs twice as much as the first. However, we cannot say a day that is 100°F is twice as hot as a day that is 50°F, and that is due to 0°F not being an inherently meaningful zero value.

The nature of each of these data types will dictate which graphic variables may be used to visually represent them. The following section discusses several possible graphic variables and how they relate to the various scales of measure.

Graphic variable types

Graphic variables are any of those visual elements that are used to systematically represent information in a visualization. They are building blocks. Length is a graphic variable; in bar charts, longer bars are used to represent larger values. Position is a graphic variable; in a scatterplot, a dot's vertical and horizontal placement are used to represent its x and y values, whatever they may be. Color is a graphic variable; in a choropleth map of United States voting results, red is often used to show states that voted Republican and blue for states that voted Democrat.

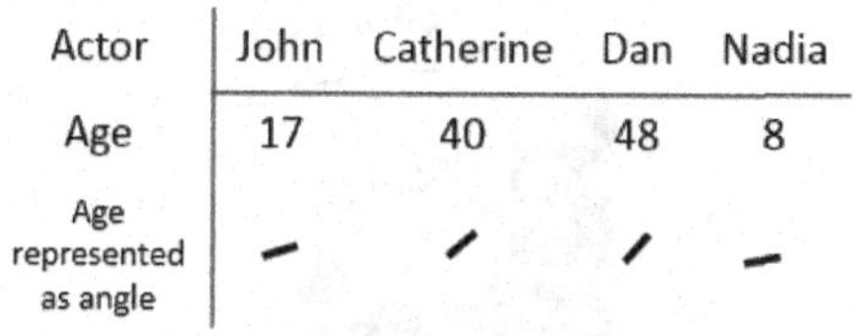

Actor	John	Catherine	Dan	Nadia
Age	17	40	48	8
Age represented as angle	―	╱	╱	―

Fig. 5.27   A misuse of angle to indicate age.

Unsurprisingly, some graphic variable types are better than others in representing different data types. Position in a 2D grid is great for representing quantitative data, whether it be interval or ratio. Area or length is particularly good for showing ratio data, as size also has a meaningful zero point. These have the added advantage of having a virtually unlimited number of discernible points, so they can be used just as easily for a dataset of two or two million. Compare this with angle. You can conceivably create a visualization that uses angle to represent quantitative values, as in Fig. 5.27. This is fine if you have very few, incredibly varied data points, but you will eventually reach a limit beyond which minute differences in angle are barely discernible. Some graphic variable types are fairly limited in the number of potential variations, whereas others have much wider range.

Most graphic variables that are good for fully quantitative data will work fine for ordinal data, although in those cases it is important to include a legend making sure the reader is aware that a constant change in a graphic variable is not indicative of any constant change in the underlying data. Changes in color intensity are particularly good for ordinal data, as we cannot easily tell the magnitude of difference between pairs of color intensity.

Color is a particularly tricky concept in information visualization. Three variables can be used to describe color: hue, value, and saturation (Fig. 5.28).

These three variables should be used to represent different variable types. Except in one circumstance, discussed below, hue should *only ever be used* to represent nominal, qualitative data. People are not well-equipped to understand the quantitative difference between e.g. red and green. In a bar chart showing the average salary of faculty from different departments, hue can be used to differentiate the departments. Saturation and value, on the other hand, can be used to represent quantitative data. On a map, saturation might represent population density; in a scatterplot, saturation of the individual data points might represent somebody's age or wealth.

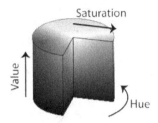

Fig. 5.28   Hue, value, and saturation.

The one time hue may be used to represent quantitative values is when you have binary diverging data. For example, a map may show increasingly saturated blues for states that lean more Democratic and increasingly saturated reds for states that lean more Republican. Besides this special case of two opposing colors, it is best to avoid using hue to represent quantitative data.

Shape is good for nominal data, although only if there are under half a dozen categories. You will see shape used on scatterplots when differentiating between a few categories of data, but shapes run out quickly after triangle, square, and circle. Patterns and textures can also be used to distinguish categorical data; these are especially useful if you need to distinguish between categories on something like a bar chart, but the visualization must be printed in black and white.

Relational data is among the most difficult to represent. Distance is the simplest graphic variable for representing relationships (closer objects are more closely related), but that variable can get cumbersome quickly for large datasets. Two other graphic variables to use are enclosure (surrounding items which are related by an enclosed line), or line connections (connecting related items directly via a solid line). Each has its strengths and weaknesses, and a lot of the art of information visualization comes in learning when to use which variable.

Cognitive and Social Aspects of Visualization

Luckily for us, there are a few gauges for choosing between visualization types and graphic variables that go beyond the merely esthetic. Social research has shown various ways in which people process what they see, and that research should guide our decisions in creating effective information visualizations.

About a tenth of all men and a hundredth of all women have some form of **color blindness**. There are many varieties of color blindness; some people see completely in monochrome, others have difficulty distinguishing between red and green, or between blue and green, or other combinations besides. To compensate, visualizations may encode the same data in multiple variables. Traffic lights present a perfect example of this; most of us are familiar with the red, yellow, and green color schemes, but for those people who cannot distinguish among these colors, top-to-bottom orientation sends the same signal. If you need to pick colors that are safely distinguishable by most audiences, a few online services can assist. One popular service is colorbrewer (http://colorbrewer2.org/), which allows you to create a color scheme that fits whatever set of parameters you may need.

In 2010, Randall Munroe conducted a massive online survey asking people to name the colors they were randomly presented.[9] The results showed that women disproportionately named colors more specifically than men, such that where a woman might have labeled a color as neon green, a man might have just named it green. This does not imply women can more easily differentiate between colors, as some occasionally suggest, although part of the survey results definitely do show the disproportionate amount of men who have some form of color blindness. Beyond sex and gender, culture also plays a role in the interpretation of colors in a visualization. In some cultures, death is signified by the color black; in others, it is signified by white. In most cultures, both heat and passion are signified by the color red; illness is often, but not always, signified by yellow. Your audience should influence your choice of color palette, as readers will always come to a visualization with preconceived notions of what your graphic variables imply.

Gestalt psychology is a century-old practice of understanding how people perceive patterns. It attempts to show how we perceive separate visual elements as whole units — how we organize what we see into discernible objects (Fig. 5.29). Among the principles of gestalt psychology are:

- **Proximity**. We perceive objects that are close together as being part of a single group.

---

[9] Monroe, Randall. 2010. "Color Survey Results" xkcd. http://blog.xkcd.com/2010/05/03/color-survey-results/.

Fig. 5.29   A gestalt box.

Fig. 5.30   Pre-attentive processing.

- **Similarity**. Objects that are visually similar (e.g. the same color) will be perceived as part of a single group.
- **Closure**. We tend to fill in the blanks when there is missing information; if we see a box of which two corners are absent, we will still see the box as a single unit, rather than two disjointed line segments.

These and other gestalt principles can be used to make informed decisions regarding graphic variables. Knowing what patterns tend to lead to perceptions of continuity or discontinuity is essential in making effective information visualizations.

At a more fine-grained level, when choosing between equally appropriate graphic variables, research on **preattentive processing** can steer us in the right direction. We preattentively process certain graphic variables, meaning we can spot differences in those variables in fewer than 10 milliseconds. Color is a preattentively processed graphic variable and thus, in Fig. 5.30, you will very quickly spot the dot that does not belong. That the processing is preattentive implies you do not need to actively search for the difference to find it.

Size, orientation, color, density, and many other variables are preattentively processed. The issue comes when you have to combine multiple graphic variables and, in most visualizations, that is precisely the task at hand. When combining graphic variables (e.g. shape and color),

Fig. 5.31   Spatially distinct groups, spatially distinct colors.

what was initially preattentively processed often loses its ease of discovery. Research into preattentive processing can then be used to show which combinations are still useful for quick information gathering. One such combination is spatial distance and color. In Fig. 5.31, you can quickly determine both the two spatially distinct groups and the spatially distinct colors.

Another important limitation of human perception to keep in mind is **change blindness**. When people are presented two pictures of the same scene, one after the other, and the second picture is missing some object that was in the first, it is surprisingly difficult to discern what has changed between the two images. The same holds true for animated/dynamic visualizations. We have difficulty holding in our minds the information from previous frames, and so while an animation seems a noble way of visualizing temporal change, it is rarely an effective one. Replacing an animation with small multiples, or some other static visualization, will improve the reader's ability to notice specific changes over time.

Making an Effective Visualization

If choosing the data to go into a visualization is the first step, picking a general form the second, and selecting appropriate visual encoding the third, the final step for putting together an effective information visualization is in following proper esthetic design principles. This step will help your visualization be both effective and memorable. We draw inspiration for this section from Edward Tufte's many books on the subject, and Angela Zoss's excellent online guide to Information Visualization.[10]

---

[10]Zoss, Angela. (2015). "Introduction to Data Visualization". Duke University Libraries, http://guides.library.duke.edu/content.php?pid=355157. The work of Edward Tufte is brought together at http://www.edwardtufte.com/tufte/.

One seemingly obvious principle that is often not followed is to make sure your visualization is **high resolution**. The smallest details and words on the visualization should be crisp, clear, and completely legible. In practice, this means saving your graphics in large resolutions or creating your visualizations as scalable vector graphics. Keep in mind that most projectors in classrooms still do not have as high a resolution as a piece of printed paper, so creating a printout for students or attendees of a lecture may be more effective than projecting your visualization on a screen.

Another important element of visualizations, often left out, are **legends** that describe each graphic variable in detail and explain how those graphic variables relate to the underlying data. Most visualization software do not automatically create legends, and so they become a neglected afterthought. A good legend means the difference between a pretty but undecipherable picture and an informative scholarly visualization. Adobe Photoshop and Illustrator, as well as the free Inkscape and Gimp, are all good tools for creating legends.

A good rule of thumb when designing visualizations is to reduce your data : ink ratio as much as possible. Maximize data, minimize ink. Extraneous lines, bounding boxes, and other design elements can distract from the data being presented. Fig. 5.32 shows a comparison between two identical charts, except for the amount of extraneous ink.

A related rule is to avoid **chartjunk** at all costs. Chartjunk are those artistic flourishes that newspapers and magazines stick in their data visualizations to make them more eye-catching: a man blowing over in a heavy storm next to a visualization of today's windy weather, or house crumbling down to represent the collapsing housing market. Chartjunk may catch the eye, but it is ultimately distracting from the data being presented and readers will require more time to digest the information being presented to them.

Stylized graphical effects can be just as distracting as chartjunk. "Blown out" pie charts where the pie slices are far apart from one another, 3D bar charts, and other stylistic quirks that Excel provides are poor window decoration and can actually decrease your audience's ability to read your visualization. In a 3D tilted pie chart, for example, it can be quite difficult to visually estimate the area of each pie slice. The tilt makes the pie slices in the back seem smaller than those in the front, and the 3D aspect confuses readers about whether they should be estimating area or volume.

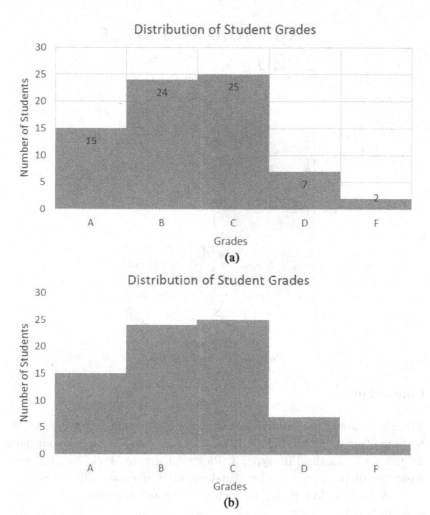

Fig. 5.32 The same chart, with and without extraneous lines and data labels.

While not relevant for every visualization, it is important to remember to label your axes and to make sure each axis is scaled appropriately. Particularly, the vertical axis of bar charts should begin at zero. Figure 5.33 is a perfect example of how to lie with data visualization by starting the axis far too high, making it seem as though a small difference in the data is actually a large difference.

Expenditures since 1980

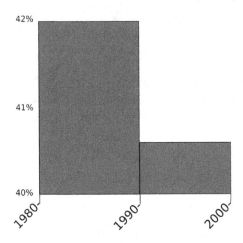

Fig. 5.33   A chart that lies.

Conclusion

There is an art to perfecting a visualization. No formula will tell you what to do in every situation, but by following these steps — 1. Pick your data, 2. Pick your visualization type, 3. Pick your graphic variables, 4. Follow basic design principles — the visualizations you create will be effective and informative. Combining this with the lessons elsewhere in this book regarding text, network, and other analyses should form the groundwork for producing effective digital history projects.

As with every lesson in this book, this chapter is only a starting point. There is a rich and growing literature on information visualization. Colin Ware's *Information Visualization* (2015) is a phenomenal textbook for beginning to think about visualization in terms of cognitive science and human perception.[11] Edward Tufte's oeuvre is useful for his insights into effective, efficient, and esthetically sensible approaches to visualizing data,

---

[11]Colin Ware (2015), *Information Visualization*, 3rd Edition: Perception for Design (Interactive Technologies), Boston: Morgan Kaufmann.

especially his books *The Visual Display of Quantitative Information* (1983) and *Envisioning Information* (1990).[12] Katy Börner's recent book *Visual Insights* (2014) provides a good point of entry into the practice of making visualizations yourself.[13] Elijah Meeks, one of the prime movers behind the Stanford ORBIS project, has written a handbook to creating visualizations using the d3.js framework. D3.js is beyond the remit of our book, but if you are looking to create "data driven documents" that can be integrated into interactive websites, *D3.js in Action* (2015) is well worth considering.[14]

Recently, visualization as an interpretive, historical, and humanistic practice has enjoyed some scrutiny and prominence. Daston and Galison's recent tome, *Objectivity* (2010), explores the history of objectivity as a concept in the sciences, paying special attention to the role of visualizations in constructing scientific objects.[15] Johanna Drucker's work focuses both on the creation of humanities-inflected visualizations and on the theory of visualizations as interpretive objects, especially in her recent book *Graphesis* (2014).[16] Of particular importance to digital historians is the visualization of missing and uncertain data: a hot topic at recent digital humanities conferences.

In recent years, one particular kind of visualization — the network diagram — has risen to prominence. Partly this is a function of the metaphors of the "Internet" and "World Wide Web" rising to such dominance, but it is also a function of a great deal of research into the statistical properties of networks. Allied with this research was the need to develop ways to present this research. Over the last decade, the technical difficulties of representing networks with more than a few hundred nodes have dropped as computing power and memory have ramped up; but crucially, the software used to measure and visualize networks has become more user friendly. The downside to this is that there have been many analyses and visualizations that have used the tools and metaphors of network analysis without any real appreciation of the dangers and limitations.

---

[12]Edward R. Tufte (1983), *The Visual Display of Quantitative Information*, Cheshire, Conn.: Graphics Press and Edward R. Tufte (1990), *Envisioning Information*, Cheshire, Conn.: Graphics Press.

[13]Katy Börner (2014), *Visual Insights*, Cambridge: MIT Press.

[14]Elijah Meeks (2015), *D3.js in Action*, Shelter Island, NY: Manning.

[15]Lorraine Daston and Peter Galison (2010), *Objectivity*, New York: Zone.

[16]Johanna Drucker (2014), *Graphesis: Visual Forms of Knowledge Production*, Cambridge: Harvard University Press.

The network, as a metaphor, is ubiquitous in historical research. The formal analysis and use of network methods will be an incredible boon to historians, adding nuance and precision to an already important metaphor. We turn to network analysis and visualization in our final two chapters, in the hopes that we can foster *better* network analyses and visualizations in the humanities.

Chapter 6

Network Analysis

Networks and network visualizations are becoming increasingly important in digital humanities and digital history research. There are, however, very few resources meant for historians and the particular challenges that network analysis poses for us. In this chapter, we cover the fundamentals of network analysis so that the approach can be used in your own research — and you will know how to critically read others' use of networks in theirs.

Formal networks are mathematical instantiations of the idea that entities and connections between them exist in consort. They embody the idea that connectivity is key in understanding how the world works, both at an individual and a global scale. Graph theory, social network analysis, network science, and related fields have a history dating back to the early 18th century, cropping up in bursts several times since then. We are currently enjoying one such resurgence, not incidentally co-developing along with the popularity of the Internet, a network backbone connecting much of the world to one system.

The idea that relationships are essential to understanding the world around us is, of course, ancient. The use of formal network methods for historical research, however, is much more recent, with only a few exceptions dating back beyond 30 years. Marten Düring has aggregated a thorough multilingual bibliography at http://historicalnetworkresearch.org. This chapter will go over a few examples of how historians have used networks, in what situations you might or might not want to use them, and the details of how networks work mathematically and technically.

In the 1960s, Eugene Garfield created the "historiography," a technique to visualize the history of scientific fields using a network of citations or historical narratives laid out temporally from top to bottom.[1] Garfield developed a method of creating historiographs algorithmically, and his contemporaries hoped the diagram would eventually be used frequently by historians. The idea was that historians could use these visuals to quickly get a grasp of the history of a discipline's research trajectories, either for research purposes or as a quick summary in a publication.

A citation analysis by White and McCann looking at an 18th century chemistry controversy took into account the hierarchical structure of scientific specialties.[2] The authors began with an assumption that, if two authors both contributed to a field, the less prominent author would always get cited alongside the more prominent author, while the more prominent author would frequently be cited alone. One scientist is linked to another if they tend to be subordinate to (only cited alongside of) that other author. The resulting networks, called entailograms, proved particularly useful in showing the solidification of a chemical "paradigm" over a period of 35 years. Lavoisier begins as a lesser figure in 1760 and eventually becomes the most prominent chemist by 1795; by that time, most chemists who were cited at all were cited alongside Lavoisier. Following the entailogram over time reveals conflict and eventual resolution.

Citation analysis, whose practitioners are also called bibliometricians or scientometricians, is a rapidly growing discipline. Despite the hopes of its founders and though many of its practitioners conduct historical research, historians rarely engage with the field.

Historical sociologists, anthropologists, economists, and other social scientists have been using formal network methods for some time and tend to exchange ideas with historians more readily. One such early sociological work, by Peter Harris, also employed citation analysis, but of a different sort. Harris analyzed citations among state supreme courts, looking at the interstate communication of precedent from 1870–1970.[3] By exploring who relied on whom for legal precedent over the century, Harris showed

---

[1] Eugene Garfield (1973), "Historiographs, Librarianship, and the History of Science," in *Toward a Theory of Librarianship: Papers in Honor of Jesse Hauk Shera*, Conrad H. Rawski (ed), Metuchon, NJ: Scarecrow Press, pp. 380–402.

[2] Douglas R. White and H. Gilman McCann (1988), "Cites and Fights: Material Entailment Analysis of the Eighteenth-Century Chemical Revolution," in *Social Structures: A Network Approach*, Barry Wellman and Stephen D. Berkowitz (eds), Cambridge, UK: Cambridge University Press, pp. 380–400.

[3] Peter Harris (1982), "Structural Change in the Communication of Precedent among State Supreme Courts, 1870–1970," *Social Networks*, **4**(3), 201–212.

that authority was originally centralized in a few Eastern courts but slowly became more diffuse across a wide swath of the United States. Network approaches can be particularly useful at disentangling the balance of power, either in a single period or over time. A network, however, is only as useful as its data are relevant or complete. We need to be extremely careful when analyzing networks not to read power relationships into data that may simply be imbalanced.

In a study on 19th century women's reform in New York, Rosenthal *et al.* revealed three distinct periods of reform activity through an analysis of organizational affiliations of 202 women reform leaders.[4] These 202 women were, together, members of over a thousand organizations, and the researchers linked two organizations together based on how many women belonged to them both. The result was a network of organizations connected by the overlap in their member lists and a clear view of the structure of women's rights movements of the period, including which organizations were the most central. The study concludes, importantly, by comparing network-driven results to historians' own hypotheses, comparing its strengths and weaknesses with theirs. For research on organizations, network analysis can provide insight on large-scale community structure that would normally take years of careful study to understand. As much as networks reveal communities, they also obscure more complex connections that exist outside of the immediate data being analyzed.

The study of correspondence and communication networks among historians dates back centuries, but its more formal analysis is much more recent. The *Annales* historian Robert Mandrou[5] and the historian of science Robert A. Hatch[6] both performed quantitative analyses of the Early Modern Republic of Letters, exploring the geographic and social diversity of scholars, but neither used formal network methods. In a formal network

---

[4]Naomi Rosenthal, Meryl Fingrutd, Michele Ethier, Roberta Karant, and David McDonald (1985), "Social Movements and Network Analysis: A Case Study of Nineteenth-Century Women's Reform in New York State," *American Journal of Sociology*, **90**(5), 1022–1054.

[5]Robert Mandrou (1978), *From Humanism to Science 1480-1700*, 2nd edn, Atlantic Highlands, NJ: Humanities Press.

[6]Robert Alan Hatch (1998), "Between Erudition & Science: The Archive & Correspondence Network of Ismaël Boulliau," in *Archives of the Scientific Revolution: The Formation and Exchange of Ideas in Seventeenth-Century Europe*, Michael Cyril William Hunter (ed), Woodbridge: Boydell & Brewer.

study of Cicero's correspondence, Alexander and Danowski[7] make the point that large-scale analyses allow the historian to question not whether something exists at all, but whether it exists frequently. In short, it allows the historian to abstract beyond individual instances to general trends. Their study looks in 280 letters written by Cicero; the network generated was not that of whom Cicero corresponded with, but of information generated from reading the letters themselves. Every time two people were mentioned as interacting with one another, a connection was made between them. Ultimately the authors derived 1,914 connections between 524 individuals. It was a representation of the social world as seen by Cicero. By categorizing all individuals into social roles, the authors were able to show that, contrary to earlier historians' claims (but more in line with later historians), knights and senators occupied similar social and structural roles in Cicero's time. This is an example of a paper that uses networks as quantitative support for a prevailing historical hypothesis regarding the structural position of a social group. Studies of this sort pave the way for more exploratory network analyses; if the analysis corroborates the consensus, then it is more likely to be trustworthy in situations where there is not yet a consensus.

In what is now a classic study (perhaps the only study in this set relatively well-known beyond its home discipline), Padgett and Ansell used networks deftly and subtly to build a historical hypothesis about how the Medici family rose to power in Florence.[8] The authors connected nearly 100 15th century Florentine elite families via nine types of relations, including family ties, economic partnerships, patronage relationships, and friendships. Their analyses reveals that, although the oligarch families were densely interconnected with one another, the Medici family — partially by design and partially through happy accident — managed to isolate the Florentine families from one another in order to act as the vital connective tissue between them. The Medici family harnessed the power of the economic, social, and political network to their advantage, creating structural holes and becoming the link between communities. Their place in the network made the family a swing vote in almost every situation, giving them a power that eventually gave rise to a 300 year dynasty.

[7]Michael C. Alexander and James A. Danowski (1990), "Analysis of an Ancient Network: Personal Communication and the Study of Social Structure in a Past Society," *Social Networks*, **12**(4), 313–335.

[8]John F. Padgett and Christopher K. Ansell (1993), "Robust Action and the Rise of the Medici, 1400–1434," *American Journal of Sociology*, **98**(6), 1259–1319.

Before Facebook and MySpace, the first network of people to come to mind would probably be kinship or genealogical networks with linkages between family members. Historiographic studies of these networks stem from early prosopographical (or collective biography) methods, but explorations using social network analysis are more recent. Looking at a large town in southwest Germany in the early 19th century, Lipp explored whether and how the addition of an electoral system affected the system of kinship networks that previously guided the structure of power in the community.[9] Surprisingly, in an area to become known for its democratic reforms, Lipp showed that a half century of elections had not reduced the power of kinship in the community — in fact, kinship power only became stronger. Lipp also used the network to reveal the prominent actors of local political factions and how they connected individuals together. In this case, networks were the subject of study rather than used as evidence, in an effort to see the effects of political change on power structures.

Trade networks are particularly popular among economists but have also had their share of historical studies. Using the records of nearly 5,000 voyages taken by traders of the East India Company between 1601 and 1833, Erikson and Bearman show how a globalized economy formed out of ship captains seeking profit out of the malfeasance of private trade.[10] Captains profited by using company resources to perform off-schedule trades in the East, inadvertently changing the market from a dyadic East–West route to an integrated and complex global system of trading. The authors used a network as evidence, in this case the 26,000 links between ports each time two were connected along a trading route. Over 200 years, as more ports became connected to one another, the East India Company lost control in a swath of local port-to-port connections. The authors show that the moments at which private trade was at its peak were also critical moments in the creation of more complex trade routes. While network analysis is particularly powerful in these many-century longitudinal studies, they also must be taken with a grain of salt. Without at least a second dataset of a different variety that is connected to the first, it is difficult to disentangle what effects were caused by the change in network structure, and what effects

---

[9]Carola Lipp (2005), "Kinship Networks, Local Government, and Elections in a Town in Southwest Germany, 1800–1850," *Journal of Family History*, **30**(4), 347–365.
[10]Emily Erikson and Peter Bearman (2006), "Malfeasance and the Foundations for Global Trade: The Structure of English Trade in the East Indies, 1601–1833," *American Journal of Sociology*, **112**(1), 195–230.

were merely external and changed both the network and the effect being measured. Global networks also tend to entangle geographic and relational distances, a fact which should not be glossed over when trying to understand the lived experiences of historical actors, which may diverge greatly from a network representation.

Folklorists have a long tradition of classifying folktales based on types, motifs, and various indices in order to make finding, relating, and situating those tales easier on the scholars balancing thousands upon thousands of tales. These schemes are often inadequate to represent the multidimensional nature of folktales, such as a tale that is classified as being about manor lords, but also happens to include ghosts and devils as well. Tangherlini and colleagues[11] came up with a solution by situating a collection of 19th century Danish folktales in a network that tied tales to subjects, authors, places, keywords, and the original classification schemes, resulting in a network connecting 3,000 entities together by 50,000 ties and made them easily browsable in an online interface. The interface made it significantly easier for folklorists to find the tales they were looking for. It also aided in serendipitous discovery, allowing scholars to browse many dimensions of relatedness when they were looking at particular tales or people or places.

Lineage studies with networks are not limited to those of kinship. Sigrist and Widmer[12] used 1,000 18th century botanists, tracing a network between masters and disciples, to show how botany both grew autonomous from medical training and more territorial in character over a period of 130 years. The authors culled their group of botanists from various dictionaries and catalogues of scientific biography, and found by connecting masters to disciples, they saw botanists from different countries had very different training practices, and the number of botanists who traveled abroad to study decreased over time. The study juxtaposes a history of change in training practices and scientific communities against traditional large scientific narratives as a succession of discoveries and theories.

As is clear, historical network analysis can be used in a variety of situations and for a variety of reasons. The entities being connected can be articles, people, social groups, political parties, archaeological artefacts, stories,

---

[11] James Abello, Peter Broadwell and Timothy R. Tangherlini (2012), "Computational Folkloristics," *Communications of the ACM*, **55**(7), 60.

[12] René Sigrist and Eric D. Widmer (2012), "Training Links and Transmission of Knowledge in 18th Century Botany: A Social Network Analysis," *Redes: Revista Hispana Para El Análisis de Redes Sociales*, **21**, 347–387.

and cities; citations, friendships, people, affiliations, locations, keywords, and ship's routes can connect them. The results of a network study can be used as an illustration, a research aid, evidence, a narrative, a classification scheme, and a tool for navigation or understanding.

The possibilities are many, but so too are the limitations. Networks can be dangerous allies; their visualizations, called graphs, tend to be overused and little understood. Ben Fry, a leading voice in information visualization, aptly writes:

> There is a tendency when using graphs to become smitten with one's own data. Even though a graph of a few hundred nodes quickly becomes unreadable, it is often satisfying for the creator because the resulting figure is elegant and complex and may be subjectively beautiful, and the notion that the creator's data is "complex" fits just fine with the creator's own interpretation of it. Graphs have a tendency of making a data set look sophisticated and important, without having solved the problem of enlightening the viewer.[13]

It is easy to become hypnotized by the complexity of a network, to succumb to the desire of connecting everything and, in so doing, learning nothing. The following chapter, beyond teaching the basics of what networks are and how to use them, will also cover some of the many situations where networks are completely inappropriate solutions to a problem. In the end, the best defense against over — or improperly — using a network is knowledge; if you know the ins and outs of networks, you can judge how best to use them in your research.

Network Analysis Fundamentals

As we showed in the previous section, networks are versatile tools for exploring our connected world. Unfortunately, the rhetorical utility of networks can occasionally overshadow their formal nature. It is not uncommon to read scholarly articles that invoke the vocabulary of networks without acknowledging any underlying formal definitions, rendering a metaphorically rich argument devoid of any real substance. While network analysis is frequently not the most appropriate method of analysis, when it *is* invoked appropriately, it should be treated with a healthy respect for the many years

---

[13]Ben Fry, *Visualizing Data: Exploring and Explaining Data with the Processing Environment* (Sebastopol, CA: O'Reilly Media, 2007).

of research that have gone into building its mathematical and conceptual framework.

The first part of this section introduces that framework, beginning first with basic vocabulary, progressing through mathematical means of measurement at both the small and large scale. Part two describes how to put the concepts in action, including what network data look like and how to manipulate or visualize them. Part three discusses when network analysis is appropriate and when it is not.

Basic Concepts and Network Varieties

Nodes, edges, and attributes

Networks, also called graphs, are the mathematical answer to the assumption that many things in this world worth studying are *interdependent*, and need to be treated as such. Despite their name, networks are *dichotomous*, in that they only give you two sorts of things to work with: entities and relationships. Entities are called **nodes** (Fig. 6.1) and the relationships between them are called **edges** (Fig. 6.2). Everything about a network pivots on these two building blocks.

Nodes can be all sorts of things, from ideas to people to bricks. Because networks have cropped up in many different disciplines over the years, all with their own vocabularies, you may see nodes referred to by many names including: *vertices*, *actors*, *agents*, or *points*. They can be used interchangeably.

Edges connect nodes (Fig. 6.2). They may represent the amount of words two books share, a friendship between two people, or a similar

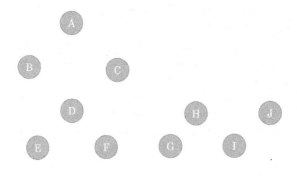

Fig. 6.1   Nodes.

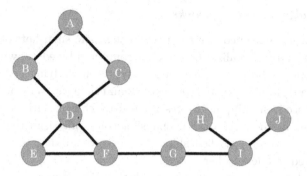

Fig. 6.2 Edges connecting nodes.

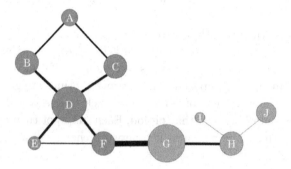

Fig. 6.3 Nodes and edges with attributes (depicted by the size of the node and the weight of the edge).

originating location connecting two museum objects. With very few exceptions, formal network representations allow for edges between two, and only two, nodes. If siblings Alice, Bob, and Carol share a kinship connection, three edges will exist (connecting Alice to Bob, Bob to Carol, and Alice to Carol), rather than one edge connecting all three. You may see edges referred to as *arcs*, *links*, *ties*, or *relations*.

Over the years, new methods have allowed researchers to use more than simple node and edge representations in analyses. Often, edges and nodes can take on any number of individual **attributes** (Fig. 6.3). In a network where nodes are cities and edges are the travel routes between them, each city can contain attributes like its population or primary spoken language, and each edge can have attributes like travel time or mode of transportation.

Static and dynamic networks

Many networks one encounters appear to be **static** snapshots of a moment in time: one large visualization of nodes connected by edges, whether it be about people or books or ideas. In reality, the underlying networks often represent a **dynamic** process that evolves and changes over time. Networks of ports based on shipping routes necessarily change with economic and weather conditions, and a static snapshot could only lead to a picture of dozens of ports with docked ships, and occasional ships at sea, but all unconnected to one another.

Network analysts generally deal with these issues in one of three ways:

1. Aggregate all of the data into one giant network representing the entire span of time, whether it is a day, a year, or a century. The network is static.
2. Slowly build the network over time, creating snapshots that include the present moment and all of the past. Each successive snapshot includes more and more data, and represents each moment of time as an aggregate of everything that led up to it. The network continues to grow over time.
3. Create a sliding window of time, e.g. a week or five years, and analyze successive snapshots over that period. Each snapshot then only contains data from that time window. The network changes drastically in form over time.

Each method has its benefits and drawbacks, and historians should think carefully about which would best suit their method of inquiry.

Isolates, dyads, and triads

The smallest unit of meaningful analysis in a network is a **dyad**, or a pair of nodes connected by an edge between them (Fig. 6.4). Without any dyads, there would be no network, only a series of disconnected **isolates**. Dyads are, unsurprisingly, generally discussed in terms of the nature of

Fig. 6.4   A dyad.

Fig. 6.5 A dyad engaged in a reciprocal relationship.

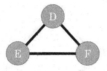

Fig. 6.6   A triad.

the relationship between two nodes. The dyad of two medieval manuscripts may be strong or weak depending on the similarity of their content, for example. Studies of dyads in large networks most often revolve around one of two concepts: **reciprocity**, whether a connection in one direction is reciprocated in the other direction, or **assortativity**, whether similar nodes tend to have edges between them.

A dyad of two Twitter users may be considered reciprocal if both parties follow one another, and an entire Twitter network may have a higher or lower **reciprocity** overall depending how many dyadic relationships tend to be reciprocal (Fig 6.5).

Assortativity, also called **homophily**, is the measure of how much like attracts like among dyads in a network. On the Web, for instance, websites (nodes) tend to link (via edges) to topically similar sites. When dyads connect assortatively, a network is considered **assortatively mixed**. Networks can also experience **disassortative mixing**, for example when people from isolated communities with strong family ties seek dissimilarity in sexual partners.

A **triad** is a group of three dyads, and another frequent unit of network analysis. The various possible configurations of three nodes are invoked surprisingly often in network analyses, even when looking at networks with millions of nodes, and is more versatile than one might expect (Fig 6.6).

For example, if brick type A and brick type B are often found at the same archaeological site, as are brick types A and C, how often are brick types B and C found at the same site (thus connecting the A–B–C triangle)? Asking that question of all the archaeological sites found in a several hundred mile

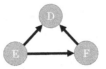

Fig. 6.7   A triad demonstrating transivity.

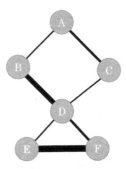

Fig. 6.8   A weighted network.

radius might yield the degree to which a trade economy was tightly knit. **Transitivity** is the concept that when A is connected to B and C, B and C will also be connected (Fig 6.7). Some networks, like those between friends, feature a high degree of transitivity; others do not.

In an evolving network of correspondents, if Alice writes to Bob, and Bob to Carol, we can ask what the likelihood is that Alice will eventually write to Carol (thus again closing the triangle). This tendency, called **triadic closure**, can help measure the importance of introductions and knowing the right people in a letter-writing community.

Weighted versus unweighted

One attribute sometimes associated with edges is **weight**. Weight is a numeric value quantifying the strength of a connection between two nodes. Most often, the higher the weight of the edge between them, the more similar or closely connected the two nodes; occasionally, though, edge weight can be used to quantify dissimilarity rather than similarity. Weight is usually connoted by line-thickness in visualizations.

Weighted networks, as they are called when they include weighted edges (Fig. 6.8), can take many forms. A network of people connected by

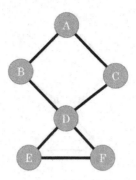

Fig. 6.9   An unweighted network.

whom they call on the phone can be weighted by the total number or length of phone calls. A network of scientific articles can be weighted by the total number of words each shares with the other. A network of activist organizations can be connected based on how many members they share. **Unweighted networks** can include the network of websites that link to each other, the US electrical grid, or a kinship network in a family tree (Fig. 6.9).

Most common algorithms used to measure things about networks (finding the most central or important nodes, calculating network density, etc.) don't play well with attributes of nodes or edges. Attributes like type or category or name are a very difficult fit into algorithmic formalisms. Edge weight is an exception to this rule. Many network measurement algorithms can take edge weight into account when performing their calculations. The calculation finding the most central person in a phone-call network should potentially change if two people occupy the same structural place in the network (keep in contact with the same people) but one makes calls vastly more frequently than the other.

Directed versus undirected

The second-most common attribute of edges is directedness. A **directed edge** is one that is part of an asymmetrical relationship, and an easy way of thinking about them is by imagining arrow tips on the edges (Fig 6.10).

Citation networks, for example, can make **directed networks**. A dozen papers written after 2005 can cite Mark Newman's famous 2004 article on

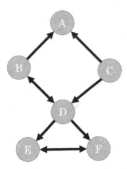

Fig. 6.10 A network with directed edges.

finding communities in networks,[14] but that does not imply that Newman's paper cites them back. Twitter follower and followee relationships form a similarly asymmetrical network; some follows are reciprocated, but others are not. Trade networks may sometimes be asymmetrical, with goods not always traveling in both directions.

Similarity networks are generally symmetrical and thus **undirected**; *Brave New World* is just as similar to *1984* as *1984* is to *Brave New World*. Facebook is also undirected, as in order for you to choose someone as a friend, they too must choose you as a friend. Highway networks are undirected, as they go in both directions, but local city road networks may be directed, as there can be a mix between one- and two-way streets.

Unlike with weighted networks, on which you can often safely use an algorithm made for unweighted networks and still get methodologically plausible results, you must be extra careful when analyzing directed networks. The directionality of an edge can have huge repercussions to a network's structure, and so algorithms made for undirected networks to find local communities or node importance might produce very unlikely results on a directed network. Be careful that you only use algorithms made specifically for directed networks when analyzing them.

Bipartite and k-partite

Basic networks, and most network algorithms, can only support one type of node per network. You can connect books that influence other books, or people who co-author together, but it has been (until now) a methodological

---

[14]M. E. J. Newman (2004), "Detecting Community Structure in Networks," *The European Physical Journal B — Condensed Matter and Complex Systems*, **38**(2), 321–330.

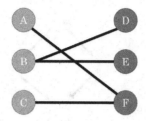

Fig. 6.11   A bipartite network.

faux pas to connect authors and books in the same network. You cannot connect apples and oranges. This is not an immediately obvious limitation, but because of the assumptions underlying most network analyses, adding multiple types of nodes in the same network can severely limit the use of the dataset. This is not a theoretical limitation, but a practical one; in general, network scientists have not yet created many algorithms to deal with these **multimodal networks**.

However, there are situations — especially when dealing with complex humanities datasets — when this multimodality can be useful. The most basic example is a **bipartite network**, also called a *bimodal* or *2-mode* network (Fig. 6.11). As the name implies, these networks support two types of nodes. For mathematical reasons to be described later, in bimodal networks, you must be careful to only allow edges *between* types and not allow edges *within* types. Taking the most recent example, this means you can draw edges from books to authors, but not between authors or between books.

Generalizing from there, some graphs can be **multimodal** or *k*-**partite**. An italic *k* is just a network scientist's way of saying your-favorite-number-goes-here. Like with bipartite networks, *k*-partite networks feature nodes of various types that can only link between — not among — each other. These networks might represent vastly complex trade networks, with nodes as books, authors, publishing houses, cities, and so forth. There are even fewer algorithms out there for dealing with *k*-partite networks than there are for bipartite ones, so although these varieties of networks are very useful for the initial planning and preparation of your data, you will need to reduce the complexity of the network before running any of the analyses included with most network software packages.

Directed or bipartite network transformations

The previous sections suggested that analyses on directed or bimodal networks require slightly more forethought and a more nuanced understanding

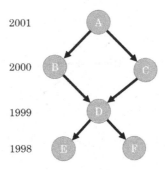

Fig. 6.12   A citation network as a directed network.

of the underlying algorithms. Although there are workflows for working with these more complicated network types, there are also methods of transforming them into simpler networks that are easier to work with, and in certain circumstances, more useful.

A citation network is an example of a directed network that, for various reasons, tends to be difficult to analyze (Fig. 6.12). For example, articles always cite earlier work (the directed arrows pointing toward the past). Because citations go to previous work rather than contemporary similar research, it winds up being difficult for algorithms to find communities of practice in the network.

Bibliometricians, people who study citations, have developed two reciprocal methods of transforming a directed, past-facing citation network into an undirected network of either current communities of practice or articles from the past that should be categorized together.

Bibliographic coupling networks are networks of scholarly articles that are connected if their bibliographies are similar. When two articles reference a common third work in their bibliographies, they get an edge drawn between them; if those two articles share ten references between them, the edge gets a stronger weight of ten. A bibliographic coupling network, then, connects articles that reference similar material and provides a snapshot of a community of practice that emerges from the decisions authors make about whom to cite. It does not change over time: articles do not change their bibliographies as time goes by.

This method is generalizable to any sort of directed network, not just citations. In practice, any time you have a directed network, you can connect two nodes if their edges point to the same third node.

Co-citation networks are the functional opposite of bibliographic coupling networks. In this case, two scholarly works are connected if they appear together in a bibliography, and the more times they are cited together, the stronger the edge between them. As opposed to bibliographic coupling networks, co-citation networks connect articles not by the choices their authors make, but by the choices future authors make about them. Also unlike bibliographic coupling networks, co-citation networks change over time: two articles may live long, separate lives before some author decides to cite them both in the same third article. In this way, co-citation networks are an evolving picture of various scholarly communities' disciplinary canons; not a view of the past as it saw itself, but a view of the past as the present decides to connect it together.

Co-citation networks are also generalizable well beyond the realm of scholarly articles; in a directed network, if two edges point from one node to two others, those two nodes get an undirected edge drawn between them. For example, in a family tree where directed edges point from parents to children, performing a co-citation analysis would produce an undirected network that connects siblings together.

Bipartite networks, those with two types of edges, can similarly be transformed into **unipartite networks**, with only one type of node, in a method quite similar to co-citation or bibliographic coupling. If you have a bipartite network of scholarly societies as one type of node, connected by edges to their members, the other type of node, you can collapse the network into a unipartite one by connecting people who are members of the same organization, or connecting societies if they share members. This collapse is useful, for example, if you want to explore which societies were more likely to influence each other via member transference and how information might have spread from one society to the next. The resulting collapsed network in this case includes only society nodes, and edges between them are stronger if the societies share more members, but the opposite network can also be generated (Fig. 6.13).

Multigraphs, hypergraphs, multiplex networks, and self-loops

The four concepts listed here are brought up mainly as ones to avoid if at all possible; common network software packages not only often do not support these features but may actually stop working or perform math incorrectly if they are included. The concepts all relate to more complex varieties of

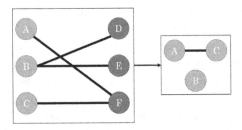

Fig. 6.13   Collapsing a bipartite network into a unipartite one (for instance, a network of members *and* scholarly societies to a network of scholarly societies *where members are the edges*).

edge relationships, and although they are legitimate ways of representing complex networks, they are not yet standard enough in network science to be explored by the historian first dipping her toes into network science.

Multigraphs are those networks that are permitted to have **parallel edges** between a pair of nodes. It means what it sounds like: duplicate edges between nodes, as in a trade network with a new edge every time some exchange is registered between the same two cities. While in theory these networks are just another reasonable representation of a series of networked events, in practice, software tends to break around them. A stopgap solution is to code a single edge with attributes to replace the parallel edges; for example, giving the trade network a weight attribute that increases as the number of exchanges go up. It is worth pointing out that in a directed network, as with Twitter follows, an edge directed from A to B (A follows B) is not considered parallel to an edge directed from B to A (B follows A). These are fine, and most software supports this use.

It is unfortunate that **hypergraphs** are rarely supported by either software packages or network data structures, as they can introduce a lot of nuance that is usually lost. Hypergraphs allow **hyperedges**, single edges that connect multiple nodes. Hypergraphs can be considered functionally equivalent to bipartite graphs; as with the society/membership example before, a group of people can be connected with one hyperedge if they all are members of the same society. In this case, the nodes are the people and the hyperedges are the societies. If you want to use hyperedges, you can create a bipartite network instead.

We saw **multiplex networks** in the previous section on the various ways network analysis has been used to study history, when discussing the Medici's relationships with other Florentine families. A multiplex network is one that allows multiple types of edges, similar to k-partite networks that allow multiple node types. Often multiplex networks also include parallel edges, when there can be many types of edges between the same two nodes. One example would be a national network of transportation between cities, where there can be air, sea, road, or train edges between any two cities, and often more than one of those options for each pair. As will become clear, the standard network data structures make coding networks like this difficult, but you can use the same shortcut you use for multigraphs: create only one edge between nodes, but give it multiple attributes to identify its various types. In the example above, an edge between New York City and Liverpool might have four different attributes, boat (true), road (false), train (false), plane (true), rather than four separate edges.

The last variety of odd edge covered here is the **self-loop**. More innocuous than the rest, a self-loop is simply an edge that goes from and to the same node. A structural network that aggregates people into single nodes representing their entire social class, and edges connecting them based on interactions between classes, would presumably have self-loops on every node because each social class has people that talk to each other. An email network, with nodes as people and edges as the volume of emails sent between them, would have self-loops for people who email themselves. Self-loops are supported by all software packages, but can sometimes subtly affect algorithms in ways that will change the results but not produce errors. For this reason, it is good to avoid self-loops if you can, unless you know specifically how they will affect the algorithms you plan on using to measure your network.

Explicit and natural versus implicit and derived

Although in practice the networks produced look and act the same, the various ways a network is created have repercussions on how it should be interpreted and analyzed. This introduction will not go beyond pointing out the difference, because interpretations can vary depending on particular use cases.

Historians will want to note when their networks are **explicit/physically instantiated** and when they are **implicit/derived**. An explicit network could be created from letters between correspondents or roads that physically exist between cities. A derived network might be that of the subjectively-defined similarity between museum artefacts or the bibliographic coupling network connecting articles together if they reference similar sources.

The difference between explicit and implicit networks is not a hard binary; it can be difficult or impossible to determine (or not a reasonable question) whether the network you are analyzing is one that has its roots in some physical, objective system of connections. It is still important to keep these in mind, as metrics that might imply historical agency in some cases (e.g. a community connected by letters they wrote) do not imply agency in others (e.g. a community connected by appearing in the same list of references).

Local Metrics — Close Reading/The Trees

One of the benefits of networks is their ability to offer several perspectives of analysis, both across scales and subsections. A node occupies a particular neighborhood, which in turn has its own neighbors, all of which fit together in the global network. This allows the historian to see not only how historical actors interact with their immediate relations, but how standard or unique those interactions are and how they affect or are influenced by the larger whole.

There are many formal ways to explore these interactions, and they are often classified according to their scale. Sometimes you want to look at your networks under a macroscope to clarify general patterns and structure, but other times you may want to focus in with your microscope to discover local variations or intricacies. For example, you may want to pinpoint the most well-connected political lobbyists or the most well-traveled trading routes. The advantage of applying network analysis to these questions is that local effects are always contextualized or driven by global interactions. The following section shows some basic metrics used to approach networks at the node, dyad, or triad level, the smallest of scales.

Paths — path length, shortest path, average path length

A **path** is a fairly intuitive concept: it is the series of edges between two nodes. The interpretation of a path changes from dataset to dataset, but its formal definition remains the same.

The ORBIS project, a map of the ancient Roman world, allows you to calculate paths between any two cities. In most cases, there are multiple routes between any two cities and those routes can vary in size. The number of roads one needs to traverse to get from Rome to Constantinople is the **path length**; a direct route would take you across 23 roads, but you could also take a wide detour through modern day Spain, requiring you to traverse across another 30 roads. The path between two nodes that requires the fewest steps possible is the **shortest path**.

Both historians and historical actors are often interested in optimizing their path according to some criteria, whether it is shortest distance, least expensive, or fastest travel time. These are often not the same. The shortest path between two cities, for example, may go through a treacherous mountain path. There may also be multiple shortest paths, such as two routes that diverge but require the same amount of steps.

You can get an idea of how well connected your network is by looking at *all* shortest paths between every possible pair of nodes and averaging them together. This **average path length** is a measurement of the connectedness of a network. In networks with a fairly high average path length, like ORBIS, one can expect that, if they picked a node at random, it would take them quite a few steps to get to where they need to go. Other networks have a fairly low average path length, like the network of movie stars who act in movies together. This low average path length is what allows the movie trivia "Six Degrees of Kevin Bacon" game to exist. It is played by picking an actor at random and naming actors they co-starred with until you reach Kevin Bacon. For example, the path length between Edward Norton and Kevin Bacon is three: Edward Norton starred in *Fight Club* with Brad Pitt; Brad Pitt starred in *Ocean's Eleven* with Julia Roberts; Julia Roberts starred in *Flatliners* with Kevin Bacon (Fig. 6.14).

It is important to adapt your interpretation of path length based on the dataset and historical question being asked. Paths between cities are fairly easy to interpret and can be useful for historians who want to infer, for example, the most likely route someone traveled. Historically, the distance between two cities is a meaningful measurement, one that enables trade and travel, and one that continues to be meaningful the farther away one travels. Paths between two family members on a genealogical network are a little different. Very close paths are inherently meaningful but unless the question being asked deals with genetics, inbreeding, or royalty, it is very

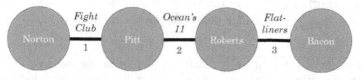

Fig. 6.14 Path length between Edward Norton and Kevin Bacon, via co-starring in movies.

difficult to distinguish the meaningful difference between a path length of five or 15. Average path lengths at a population level, however, once again become meaningful. For example, the average genealogical path length of Ashkenazi Jews is quite low, suggesting an insulated and often isolated population compared to other ethnic groups of similar size.[15]

Remember that average path length is a property of a network, whereas shortest path and path length are properties of a pair of nodes, described by a particular series of edges.

Centrality and prestige — degree, closeness, and betweenness

Historians are often interested in locating the most active or well-connected actors in a network, whether that means the early modern thinkers whose ideas were the most influential, or the cities that were most often traveled through due to their central position on trading routes. The metrics used to explore these topics are **centrality**, when the directionality of edges is not relevant to the question, or **prestige**, when directionality is relevant. There are many ways to measure both centrality and prestige, and how they are interpreted can change depending on the method and the data at hand. While these metrics can become mathematically complex, often the simplest solutions are the best ones.

Degree centrality is generally the first network metric taught; it is both simple and powerful, and it is an attribute that every node in a network has. A node's **degree** is, simply, how many edges it is connected to. This generally correlates with how many **neighbors** a node has, where a node's neighborhood is those other nodes connected directly to it by a single edge. In Fig. 6.15, each node is labeled by its degree.

In a network of Facebook friendships, the higher someone's node degree, the more friends they have. In a network of non-fiction books connected to one another by shared topics, an encyclopedia would have an extremely high degree because its topical diversity would connect it to most other books in the network. High degree centrality corresponds to well-connectedness, and what that implies differs depending on the network at hand.

---

[15]Shai Carmi, Ken Y. Hui, *et al.* (2014), "Sequencing an Ashkenazi reference panel supports population-targeted personal genomics and illuminates Jewish and European origins," *Nature Communications*, **5**, 4835. http://www.nature.com/ncomms/2014/140909/ncomms5835/full/ncomms5835.html.

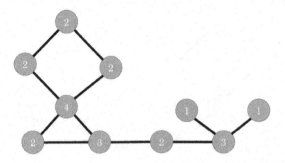

Fig. 6.15   Degree centrality.

In fairly small networks, up to a few hundred nodes, degree centrality will be a fairly good proxy for the importance of a node in relation to a network. If we have a network of 100 authors, connected to one another when they co-author a work, those with the highest degree are those who co-author with the most other people in the network. It reasonably follows, if the data collection was thorough, that these high degree authors are the ones responsible for connecting this network together; they are a force of cohesion in the network.

This use of degree centrality also works on larger networks but one must be more careful when interpreting importance. If we have a network of 10,000 co-authors, drawn from articles published in late-20th century physics, a few extremely high-degree nodes will crop up that are of little importance to network cohesiveness.

A few more recent works in high-energy physics have hundreds or thousands of authors on a single article.[16] Each of the authors on one of these articles would by definition have hundreds of co-authors, and thus they would all have an extremely high degree centrality. This would be the case even if none of the authors had co-authored works with people outside this one article, resulting in hundreds of authors with high degree centrality who may have very little importance to the cohesiveness of the overall network. A historian viewing the network as simply an ordered-list of the highest degree nodes would have difficulty discerning the truly central figures in the network, whereas even a brief glance at a network visualization would reveal the peripherality of the so-called high-degree nodes.

---

[16]See, for instance, Atlas Collaboration (2012), "Observation of a new particle in the search for the Standard Model Higgs boson with the ATLAS detector at the LHC", *Physics Letters B*, **716(1)**, 1–29 http://dx.doi.org/10.1016/j.physletb.2012.08.020.

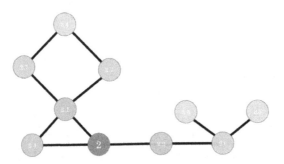

Fig. 6.16   Closeness centrality.

Network scientists have created more complex metrics to deal with these and other potentially confounding effects. Two such metrics are **between-ness centrality** and **closeness centrality**, both of which are attributes that can be calculated for each individual node, and both of which attempt to contextualize the local centrality measurement against the larger network.

A node's **closeness centrality** is a measure of how close it is to every other node in the network (Fig. 6.16). In the network of travel routes and cities of the ancient Roman Empire modeled by ORBIS, the city with the highest closeness centrality is the one that would be the fastest to travel to from any given city in the network. A city that has many direct routes to other cities, but is still at the periphery of the network (e.g. Emerita Augusta, present-day Mérida, Spain), would have a high degree centrality but still would not be ranked high on closeness centrality. Rome would likely have a high closeness centrality, as it is both directly connected to many cities and geographically central enough that it would take very few roads to get to any other city on the map.

There are multiple ways to calculate closeness centrality, but the simplest one is to take the average distance from a node to every other node on the network. In the Roman city example, if there are 100 cities in the network (including Rome), the closeness centrality is found by finding the shortest paths from Rome to all 99 other cities, adding their distances together, and dividing by 99. The resulting number is the average path length from Rome to any other city, and the lower it is, the closer Rome is to the rest of the world. This calculation can then be repeated for every other city in order to find which cities have the lowest closeness centrality. Note that, unlike most other centrality metrics, closeness is ranked by the lowest number rather than the highest.

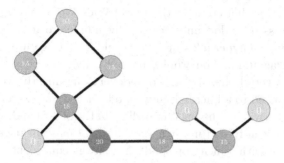

Fig. 6.17   Betweenness centrality.

Another centrality measurement that mitigates the issue of high-degree nodes on the periphery is **betweenness centrality** (Fig 6.17). In the Roman city network example, the city with the highest betweenness centrality is the one that a traveler is most likely to travel through when going from any one destination to any other. Formally, it is the node that sits on the shortest paths between all node-pairs in the network.

In the United States, the road system in the state of Indiana is such that, on almost any road trip from one corner of the state to another, the fastest route is one that goes through Indianapolis. The city is the hub of Indiana from which the highway spokes emanate; to get from Bloomington to Terra Haute, one must travel through Indianapolis; to get from Muncie to Columbus, one must travel through Indianapolis. As the city sits in the middle of the shortest paths between most pairs of cities in the state, it has the highest betweenness centrality.

Calculating betweenness and closeness centralities requires finding the shortest path between every pair of nodes in a network, which can be computationally time-consuming depending on the size of the network.

PageRank

PageRank is an algorithm developed by Google to improve search results. It gives high scores to popular pages. PageRank is a measurement of **prestige**, which means it measures the centrality of a node and takes edges leading to or from it into account. Its calculation is more mathematically complex than will be addressed in this book, however as long as you understand the concept behind it, you can accurately employ it in your historical research.

If you were a robot crawling the World Wide Web, following hyperlinks you come across at random and occasionally jumping to another site entirely even if there is no hyperlink to it, you would be acting out one method of calculating PageRank. You would, undoubtedly, find yourself ending up on some sites very frequently and others very infrequently. Wikipedia, for example, is linked to all across the web; odds are if you keep clicking links at random, you will end up on Wikipedia. On the other hand, you probably would not frequently end up at a *Lord of the Rings* fan page from 1997. The frequency with which you land on a site is equivalent to that site's PageRank; Wikipedia, BBC, and Amazon all have high PageRanks because the probability of ending up there by clicking links is quite high.

Another way of conceptualizing PageRank is by pretending each website has a certain amount of votes it can give to other sites and it signifies those votes by hyperlinking to the sites it votes for. The more votes a site has gotten, the more it is allowed to give. Also, every single site has to use *all* its votes, which means if BBC collects a lot of votes (a lot of sites link to it), but it itself only links to one other site (e.g. Wikipedia), all of the votes in BBC's possession go to that one site. Thus, even if BBC were the *only* site to link to Wikipedia, Wikipedia would still have a huge PageRank, because it collected all of BBC's votes.

This type of algorithm was originally developed for science citation networks, where an article replaces a website and a citation replaces a hyperlink. It is a surprisingly powerful algorithm for finding important nodes in directed networks of any sort. A historian calculating the PageRanks of letter-writers in early modern Europe would find they correspond quite well with the figures everyone remembers. PageRank can also be deceptive, however. A famous head of state and the recipient of letters from powerful people, for example, may have written the majority of her letters to a secretary. Even if this secretary played a fairly small role in early modern politics, her PageRank would have been quite high because she received the lion's share of her employer's votes.

Local clustering coefficient

The **local clustering coefficient** (LCC) measures the extent to which a node's neighbors are neighbors of one another. Every node has its own LCC; nodes with low LCCs connect separate communities and nodes with high LCCs do not (Fig. 6.18). Formally, the LCC of a node is calculated by dividing the number of edges between neighbors of that node divided

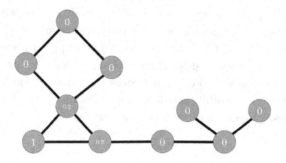

Fig. 6.18   Local clustering coefficient.

by the number of possible edges between its neighbors. In your friendship network, this manifests as the number of your friends who are friends with one another, divided by the total possible number of friendships between pairs of your friends.

This can be a useful measurement for many varieties of historical networks. In social or communication networks, a node with a high LCC may be in a brokerage position. As a short connection between otherwise disconnected people, this person can act as a conduit for information or can play a part in introducing communities together. In an electrical grid, a few high LCC nodes might be a sign of a weak network — if one high LLC node goes offline, sections of the grid may become disconnected. In a network of languages connected by their linguistic similarities, a high LLC node may be a language which two geographically distant languages contribute to, or adapt from.

Global Metrics — Distant Reading/The Forest

An aggregate of individual components is not a network. A network is what happens when the relationships between individual components come together and every entity therein becomes part of a coherent whole. Network analysis at the global level reveals subtle trends that may not be apparent when exploring individual nodes or edges, and oftentimes it can lead to shifts in the types of questions historians ask.

Global network measurements also betray one of the shortcomings of network analysis for historical research: homogeneity. Certain fundamental properties of how people and things self-organize tend to create networks that look remarkably similar when zoomed out. At this scale, it can be difficult to tell apart a network of Italian families from a network of genetic similarity in rats. A danger historians need to watch out for when reporting these measurements is that they often do not imply any sort of novelty about the network under study. These global metrics are most useful when measured *in comparison to* other networks; early modern and present day social networks both exhibit scale-free properties, but the useful information is in how those properties differ from one another.

Density

The most basic global network measurement is of its **density**. Every network's density ranges between zero and one, and is defined by the number of edges it has divided by the number of edges it potentially could have. The social network of a small 13th century village would have incredibly high density, as almost everyone would know almost everyone else. The density measurement for a network connecting American cities by interstate highways would be quite low, on the other hand, because the farther two cities are from one another, the less likely they are to have a highway traveling directly between them. Distance would be much less of a limiting factor if this were a network of commercial flights.

Historians can find a use for density in comparisons across networks. In trade networks of iron, cotton, and tobacco, for example, each traded good may travel to just as many outposts and cities, but the trading networks might have incredibly different densities. This might suggest differences in demand or of transportation expense across certain routes. An increasing density over time among a group of authors connected by co-authorships and citations would reveal the solidification of a community of scholars, or perhaps even a new discipline.

Generally speaking, the densest networks are also the least analytically fruitful. With every node connected to every other, the basic measurements like centrality or reciprocity have very little meaning. If you find yourself with an extremely dense network, it is usually a sign that the data need to be prepared differently or a different technique should be used.

Diameter

A network's **diameter** is a function of its shortest path lengths. Formally, it is a network's longest shortest path, or a measurement of how many edges one needs to traverse to travel between the two most disparate nodes on a network. Even networks with a short average path length may have a high diameter. In the movie trivia game "Six Degrees of Kevin Bacon," for example, an actor who played one minor role in an early 20th century silent film might be 15 steps away from a voice actor of a cartoon movie produced last year. This would be an example of a network with a short average path length but a large diameter. In fact, the diameter of a movie co-acting network is likely undefined because there are bound to be some actors that can never reach the rest of the network.

For the historian, it is unlikely that the diameter will be more useful than the average path length on most occasions. Most of our networks are incomplete; they are subsets of networks from the past that we have constructed or reconstructed, but which do not represent the entirety of what we wish to study. It may be that the data are lost or not completely digitized, or that we wish to constrain our problem to a smaller scale. Whatever the case, nodes at the periphery of a historical network often only appear so because that is where the data end. In those cases, a network's diameter is more a measurement of a historian's reasoning when creating a dataset than a useful metric for understanding the past. While this holds particularly true for a network's diameter, it is in general important to think through how the process of collecting data may affect any algorithm that is applied to it.

Reciprocity and transitivity

Reciprocity and transitivity are global network metrics that have implications for the way in which networks evolve. As they both measure actual edges against expected edges, they are related to, but more specific than, measurements of density.

In a directed network, **reciprocity** measures the extent to which dyads form reciprocal relationships. In a network with reciprocity of one, every directed edge is reciprocated. On Facebook, for example, you cannot list someone as a friend without them also listing you as a friend; thus, the Facebook friendship network has reciprocity of one. Reciprocity is equal to the number of reciprocal edges divided by the number of total edges in a network. Networks with no reciprocated edges have a reciprocity of zero. One example is a legal precedent citation network, as the edges must point toward previously decided cases and two cases cannot cite each other as precedents.

Social networks tend to become more reciprocal over time. On Twitter, as in life, one-way transactions generally become two-way relatively quickly. Unsurprisingly, in the early modern Republic of Letters, we see this as well. The probability that a person will correspond with another in the network increases if they have a history of previous contact. Reciprocity is then not only a measurement of a network but also a prediction of its future. The metric is an extremely valuable one in most circumstances. Historians might measure the reciprocity of military engagements among nations of opposing alliances, giving them insight into the balance of power in a war.

Transitivity is a global measurement of how frequently triads are completely connected. It is similar to reciprocity in that it divides actual connections by potential ones. If A connects to B, and B to C, a transitive edge is one that connects A and C. Transitivity is essentially the percent of connected dyads with transitive edges between them. Like with reciprocity, many evolving networks tend toward a higher transitivity, and the mechanism is fairly straightforward. In social networks, you often meet new people through pre-existing friends. Once you are connected to your friend's friend, you have created a closed triangle where all three nodes are connected to one another.

Networks with high transitivity often appear clumpy, with many small communities of densely connected individuals. A historian may wish to see the evolution of transitivity across a social network to find the relative importance of introductions in forming social bonds.

Degree distribution, preferential attachment, and scale-free networks

All the global network measurements covered so far produce a simple number that is easy to compare across networks. Not all useful measurements can collapse into one number, however, and one example is a network's **degree distribution** (Fig 6.19). Recall that a node's degree is defined by the number of edges connected to it. A network's degree distribution is an ordered list of the degrees of every node in that network, usually visually represented in a chart. It is used to determine how skewed node degree tends to be across a network.

It is easy to think that most networks would have a "normal" distribution of node degrees; that is, some nodes have a tiny amount of edges connected to them, some nodes have quite a few, but most sit squarely in the middle. This is generally not the case. Social networks, article citation

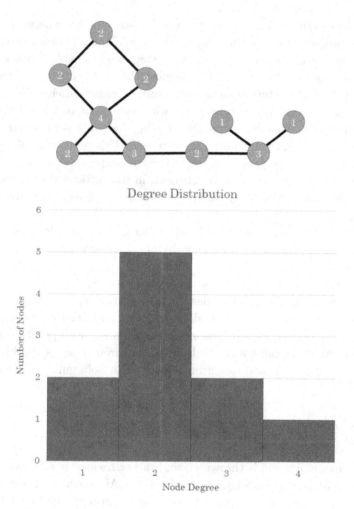

Fig. 6.19   Degree distribution of the network displayed above.

networks, airline travel networks, and many others feature a significantly more skewed degree distribution. A few hub nodes have huge numbers of edges, a handful more have a decent amount of edges but significantly fewer, and most nodes are connected by very few edges.

In network parlance, this long-tailed degree distribution is usually called **scale free** or **power law**, although the networks described as such often do not meet the formal mathematical definitions of those terms. Scale-free networks have a handful of major hubs that keep the rest of the nodes connected to one another. In transportation networks, these are the cities one has to go through to reach anywhere; in correspondence networks, these are the people without whom information would spread much more slowly.

A number of mechanisms have been suggested to explain this similarity across so many networks, but the most convincing historical argument revolves around **preferential attachment**, or rich-get-richer. In a friendship network, this means that those who have a lot of friends are at a higher risk of making even more friends; they have a larger circle that can, in turn, introduce them to even more people. This positive feedback loop continues until a few people dominate the landscape in terms of connectivity. This is also true of citation networks, in that articles that already are highly cited are more likely to be seen by other scholars and cited again in turn.

This fairly ubiquitous feature of networks can provide some insight for historians but not necessarily by its very existence. If a historical network exhibits a long-tail distribution, with very prominent hub nodes, the structure itself is not particularly noteworthy. What is worthwhile is figuring out which nodes made it to the top and why. Why do all roads lead to Rome? How did Mersenne and Hartlib develop such widespread correspondence networks in early modern Europe? The answers to these questions can cut to the heart of the circumstances of a historical period, and their formalization in networks can help guide us toward an answer.

Global clustering coefficient, average shortest path, and the small world

The term small world is thrown around rather frequently as a catchall for any network that seems surprisingly close-knit. Although this is not exactly wrong, the term has a formal definition, and mistaking the folk definition for the formal one can lead to misunderstandings or improper conclusions. A **small world** network is one in which the shortest path between any two random nodes grows proportionally to the logarithm of the number of nodes in the network. This means that, even if the network has many, many nodes, the **average shortest path** between them is quite small. These networks also have a high **global clustering coefficient**, which is the average LCC across all nodes.

In short, a small world network is one in which groups of nodes tend to cluster together into small communities, and the path between any two nodes is usually quite short. The "Kevin Bacon" network is one such small world, as are certain transportation and communication networks. It is not uncommon for small world networks to share many qualities with scale-free networks, and the two can overlap.

The further back in history one goes, the less the globe looks like a small world network. This is because travel and distance constraints prevented short connections between disparate areas. However, if one defines the network as only those connections within a sufficiently small region for the time period, small world properties tend to reappear.

Historians can draw a number of inferences from small world networks, including the time it might have taken for materials to circulate within and across communities and the relative importance of individual actors in shaping the past. The existence of these networks can also play a role in thinking through counterfactual history. Small world networks tend to be resilient against small contingent events upsetting the network structure, which means information, diseases, and so forth will tend to spread widely and quickly regardless of small historical perturbations.

Connecting the Global/Distant with the Local/Close

The true benefit of networks for historians lies not in the local (that is what we have always been good at), nor the global (we have some experience with that, too), but in the way it connects the two. Local features are embedded seamlessly into the whole unit, and global properties are very clearly made up of the aggregate of individual parts. This makes network analysis a promising methodology for connecting the historiographic traditions of microhistories and the Braudelian *longue durée*.

Hubs and bridges

Networks help us pinpoint those channels or individuals that are essential for connecting disparate communities. These can take the form of individual nodes, which are often called hubs, or an edge between a node pair, called a bridge. Each of these terms has multiple formal definitions, but the ideas are the same: a **hub** is a node without which the path between its neighbors would be much larger, and a **bridge** is an edge which connects two otherwise unconnected communities.

Hubs relate to many of the concepts already covered. Scale-free networks usually have a few very central hubs, which themselves tend to have high betweenness centralities. That is, they sit on the shortest path between many pairs of nodes. These nodes are vulnerable points in the network; without them, information takes longer to spread or travel takes quite a bit longer. A hub in a network of books connected by how similar their content is to one another would have a different meaning entirely: the most central node would likely be an encyclopedia, because it covers such a wide range of subjects. The meaning of these terms always changes based on the dataset at hand.

Bridges also relate to previous concepts. In small world networks, bridges are those edges that connect two dense but isolated clusters together, thus allowing the network to retain a surprisingly small average path length alongside such close-knit communities. The simplest historical example of a bridge is a bridge itself, connecting two landmasses across a body of water. If that bridge collapses, people would need to go well out of their way to get from one side to the other.

Hubs and bridges help connect the local with the global because they are individual metrics that are defined by how they interact with the rest of the network. On its own, a single marriage between two families might seem unremarkable, but if these are royal families marrying into some until-then disconnected foreign power, or two people marrying across faiths in a deeply religious community, one simple bridge takes on new meaning. Network analysis aids in finding these unusually connective entities en masse and with great speed, leaving the historian with more time to explore the meaning behind this connection.

Cliques, communities, and connected components

What are hubs or bridges connecting? There are a slew of terms that describe different organizational patterns of networks but the three most basic are cliques, communities, and connected components. A **clique** is a section of a network that is maximally dense; that is, every node is connected to every other node. Individual nodes in cliques may be connected to nodes outside of the clique. In a network of authors citing other authors, a clique is a subset of authors who all cite one another. An individual author may cite others outside of the clique as well but those external authors are not part of the clique unless they cite and are cited by every other member. All closed triads are by definition cliques, and more cliques lead to a higher clustering coefficient. By definition, any group of connected nodes, each with an LCC of one, will form a clique because, for each, every neighbor is a neighbor to every other.

Sometimes cliques are too strict to be useful when looking for groups of nodes in networks. There may be a network of corporations that are connected to one another if they share people on the board of directors. Not every corporation shares directors with the same other companies, but it is still clear that the same group of people are connecting these companies together, even if they do not strictly form a clique. These well-connected groups of nodes, though not maximally connected, form a **community**. There are many different ways to define a community, and communities may or may not be overlapping. One popular definition of a community is a group of nodes that have more internal edges between them than external edges connecting to other communities. It is a metric of relative density.

Like most network concepts, a community is not well defined. Multiple algorithms produce different results and group the network in different ways. Some algorithms group edges, some group nodes; others produce hierarchically nested communities, or communities that overlap. The most frequently used community detection method, called modularity, places every node in a network into a community based on how well-connected its neighbors are. Modularity is successful when there's a high ratio of edges connecting nodes *within* any given community compared to edges linking out to other communities. The best community detection approach is the one that works best for your network and your question; there is no right or wrong, only more or less relevant. A good "sanity check" is to see if the algorithm you're using puts the people or entities you know *should* be grouped together in the same community and leaves out the ones that do not belong. If it works on the parts of the data you know, you can be more certain it works on the parts of the data you do not.

The most inclusive term for a group of nodes is a connected component. A **connected component** is simply a group of nodes that can possibly reach one another via a path of any number of edges. Undirected networks are occasionally classified by the number of connected components they contain; that is, the number of different groups of nodes which are completely disconnected from one another.

Although this class of node-group seems so large as to be effectively meaningless, connected components can be very useful to understand, for example, who could possibly have heard a particular rumor. They define the scope of a connected world. The one caveat for historical networks is that we often lack the full story, and nodes that appear disconnected might be otherwise if more evidence presented itself. This is why, in historical network analysis, it is often better to rely on the edges and nodes that do exist than those that do not. Measurements of connectivity should be seen as lower bounds: your network is *at least as connected as* this measurement shows; the shortest path *is at most this long*.

The strength of weak ties and structural holes

The premise of this section is that networks reveal the interplay between global properties and local activities, and this discussion on weak ties and structural holes is a prime example of just such a benefit. Many networks form as small worlds. They are densely packed communities with many links between communities, which allows any community to reach another in only a few steps.

This is the view from the macroscope; under the microscope, the focus shifts. Two cliques, adjacent to one another, happen to have a single edge connecting them together. This single edge, connecting two otherwise insular and disconnected clusters, is called a **weak tie**, as the connection between these two communities could break easily. A downed power-line, for example, could disconnect two sections of an electrical grid, or a single estranged cousin may break the connection between two sides of a family. Careful readers will have noted that the definition of a weak tie is curiously similar to that of a bridge. This dichotomy, the weakness of a connection alongside the importance of a bridge, has profound effects on network dynamics.

In social networks, weak ties may be old college friends whom you barely keep in touch with; in early trade networks, a weak tie may be that single treacherous trade route between two disconnected worlds, offering great reward at great peril. In practice, weak ties tend to be weak not only because their breaking can fragment the network but also because the connections themselves tend to be tenuous. On weighted networks, these edges generally have a very low weight. This is the case because of the way networks tend to evolve. If you have a particularly close friend from another community, you are more likely to introduce him to your other close friends, at which point the connection between the two communities immediately multiplies. The tie is no longer weak.

These weak ties, however, are extremely important.[17] We will once again use the example of social networks, however this property holds across many

---

[17] The canonical study is Mark Granovetter (1973), "The Strength of Weak Ties," *The American Journal of Sociology*, **78**(6), 1360–1380.

other varieties as well. When an individual is looking for something, for example a new job, it is unlikely she will look to her closest friends for advice. She and her best friends know the same people, they have access to the same resources and information, they are interested in the same sort of things, and as such are particularly poor sources for news. Instead, she will reach out to her cousin whom she knows works for an organization that is hiring, or an old teacher, or someone else with whom she has a weak connection. Empirically, network studies have shown connections to outside communities tend to be the most fruitful.

The strength of weak ties has been hypothesized as a driving force behind the flourishing of science in 17th century Europe.[18] Political exile, religious diaspora, and the habit of young scholars to travel extensively, combined with a relatively inexpensive and fast postal system, created an environment where every local community had weak ties extending widely across political, religious, and intellectual boundaries. This put each community, and every individual, at higher risk for encountering just the right serendipitous idea or bit of data they needed to set them on their way. Weak ties are what make the small community part of the global network.

The study of weak ties is the study of the connections between separated communities, but the beneficial effects of spanning communities also accrue in nodes. Someone or something sitting at the intersection of two or more otherwise disconnected communities is said to occupy a **structural hole**[19] in the network, and that position accrues certain advantages on both the node and the network. As weak ties correspond to bridges, structural holes are the negative space that become filled by hubs (in sociology, sometimes known as **brokers**). People who fill structural holes in corporations have empirically been shown to find more career success. In the first section of this chapter, the Medici family was said to have strategically created structural holes in the network of Florentine families. From this position, the Medici were the only family who could reap the benefits of every community in the network; they were able to play the communities against one another, and they could act as network gatekeepers whenever they saw fit. In early modern Europe, individuals like Henry Oldenburg, the Secretary of the Royal Society, sat at the center of many networks and were able to funnel

---

[18]Davis Lux and Harold Cook (1998), "Closed circles or open networks? Communicating at a distance during the scientific revolution," *History of Science*, **36**, 179–211.

[19]Ronald S. Burt (2004), "Structural Holes and Good Ideas," *American Journal of Sociology*, **110**, 349–399, doi:10.1086/421787.

the right information to those who needed it and keep it from those who should not have had access.

Networks and Time

Network science is a young science; the study of temporal networks, though extensive, is still in its infancy. As important a subject as the evolution of networks over time is for historiography, its undeveloped state in the literature will make this section necessarily brief.

There is no consensus on how temporal networks should be represented. It is clear, for example, that the network of trade between cities in and around the Roman Empire changed drastically over time, however we cannot say with certainty when particular routes were in use or when they were not. Even if we could peer directly into the past, it is not easy to define the point at which a route's use changed from sporadic to regular.

Even in modern networks with full data availability and clear-cut events, it is not clear how to model network change. The network of phone calls in the United States creates an ever-changing network, where each phone call is an additional edge. You cannot take a snapshot of a single moment, however, and say it represents the call network of the United States, because what about all the people who call each other at different points throughout the day?

One solution is to aggregate phone data into **time slices**, or chunks of time at a particular resolution (hour, day, month, year) for which all phone data are combined. In this approach, each time slice is a snapshot of the network, and the study of how that snapshot changes at each slice is the study of the evolving network. This approach is the most common, but because small perturbations can lead to drastic reconfigurations of networks, it is sometimes difficult to compare time slices against one another.

The other obvious solution, modeling every bit of network data at every moment, may make for a more pleasantly continuous network but is notoriously difficult to represent in a meaningful way. It is also difficult to write algorithms that map to our current conceptual framework of network analysis under these dynamic approaches.

We hope that a renewed interest among historians in network analysis, and a willingness to collaborate with network scientists, will pave the way for more nuanced and meaningful approaches to understanding the evolution of networks over time.

Further Reading and Conclusion

There are many resources available to those interested in delving further into network analysis. *Networks, Crowds, and Markets* by Easley and Kleinberg[20] is an approachable introduction and most similar to what this section would look like if it had been expanded into its own book. It is particularly noteworthy for its ability to connect abstract network concepts with real, modern social phenomena. Wasserman and Faust's *Social Network Analysis*[21] is a canonical textbook that focuses on smaller scale network analysis, and the associated issues of data collection and preparation. It is more mathematical than the former, and recommended for the historian who wants to go from understanding network analysis to applying it, especially on small-to-medium scale datasets. Newman's *Networks: An Introduction*[22] is *the* network textbook for modern, large-scale network analysis of any sort, from metabolic networks to social. It is highly formal and mathematical, and is recommended for those who want to seriously engage with their network science colleagues, and who want to help develop new algorithms, tools, and methods for historical network analysis.

Textbooks also exist for the various network analysis software packages available, which encompass both concepts and tool use. For those already familiar with UCINET, or who are particularly interested in matrix manipulations, *Analyzing Social Networks* by Borgatti, Everett, and Johnson[23] is the book to read. Those wishing to do network analysis in Excel using NodeXL should find *Analyzing Social Media Networks with NodeXL* by Hansen, Shneiderman, and Smith.[24] Pajek, one of the most feature-rich network analysis programs, can be learned from *Exploratory Social Network Analysis with Pajek* by De Nooy, Mrvar, and Batagelj.[25] The Network

---

[20]David Easley and Jon M. Kleinberg (2010), *Networks, Crowds, and Markets: Reasoning About a Highly Connected World*, Cambridge, UK: Cambridge University Press.

[21]Stanley Wasserman and Katherine Faust (2010), *Social Network Analysis: Methods and Applications*, 1st edn, Cambridge, UK: Cambridge University Press.

[22]Mark E. J. Newman (2010), *Networks: An Introduction*, 1st edn, New York, NY: Oxford University Press.

[23]Stephen Borgatti, Martin G. Everett and Jeffrey C. Johnson (2013), *Analyzing Social Networks*, 1st edn, Thousand Oaks, CA; London: SAGE Publications Ltd.

[24]Derek Hansen, Ben Shneiderman and Marc A. Smith (2010), *Analyzing Social Media Networks with NodeXL: Insights from a Connected World*, 1st edn, Burlington, MA: Morgan Kaufmann.

[25]Wouter de Nooy, Andrej Mrvar and Vladimir Batagelj (2005), *Exploratory Social Network Analysis with Pajek*, Cambridge, UK: Cambridge University Press.

Workbench (NWB) and the Sci^2 Tool both have extensive user manuals linked from their homepages.[26] Unfortunately, the software we recommend for historians beginning in network analysis, Gephi, does not yet have an extensive centralized learning guide.[27]

---

[26]Information for NWB can be found at http://nwb.cns.iu.edu/Docs/NWBTool-Manual.pdf; Sci^2 http://sci2.wiki.cns.iu.edu/.

[27]That said, Clement Levallois has a suite of excellent tutorials at http://clementlevallois.net/gephi.html.

Chapter 7

Networks in Practice

This section shows how to take the conceptual framework of network analysis and apply it in practice. A historical network analysis will often require a similar series of steps:

1. *Deciding on a dataset,*
2. *Encoding, collecting, or cleaning the data,*
3. *Importing the data into a network analysis package,*
4. *Analyzing the data,*
5. *Visualizing the data,*
6. *Interpreting the results,*
7. *Drawing conclusions.*

The framework is not universal, and the process usually requires a lot of repetition and some steps may be omitted or added depending on circumstance. Steps four and five, while covered in a small section in this book, are extremely open-ended, and historians who wish to learn more are encouraged to delve into the tool of their choice using the Further Reading section of this chapter. The steps we take the most time explaining usually take the least time in practice; less than 5% of the time spent on a project will be time spent analyzing and visualizing data. Most time will be spent on collecting, cleaning, and interpreting.

Picking a Dataset

How can you know whether the data you have will be amenable for network analysis? The answer depends on the project, of course, but unfortunately it is often difficult to tell at the outset of a project which data will be most useful, if any, for a network analysis. Many network analyses lead to dead ends, and the more experience you have, the earlier you will begin to notice when a network analysis might not be going anywhere. It is worth remembering though that a dead end is not a bad result; you will have learned something important about your information!

There are two veins of network analysis that need to be considered as you draw your materials together: will you be using networks for exploration or to prove a hypothesis about the past? Each has its own assumptions about data that carry ramifications for your interpretations. **Exploratory** network analysis is based around the idea that the network is important, but in as-yet unknown ways. **Hypothesis-driven** network analysis requires a preconceived idea about the world that the network analysis will either reinforce or discredit. For historical network analysis these two camps are often blurred,[1] but for the purposes of data creation, the distinction is useful.

Exploratory network analysis is by far the more difficult for creating data. If you do not yet have a strong concept of what may be of interest in a network, you will often be at the mercy of what data are most readily available. A good many network-oriented digital history projects begin this way; a historian is made aware of a pre-existing network dataset, which already comes with a set of pre-defined categories, and they explore that dataset in order to find whatever interesting information may arise from it. This is not a flawed approach, but it can be an extremely limiting one. The creation of these datasets is rarely driven by an interest in historical networks, and the categories available may only be able to explore a limited set of questions.

Hypothesis-driven network analysis, although perhaps more foreign to historians from its formal perspective, will reduce the likelihood of an analysis reaching a dead end. The first step is to **operationalize** a historiographic claim.[2] The claim might be that popularity among early electric blues musicians was deeply influenced by their connections to other musicians rather than to record labels. The claim helps constrain the potential dataset in time and scope, and lends itself to the collection of certain data. First you would need to pick nodes and edges: given our operationalization, this will be musicians and record labels connected by recordings and

[1] Fred Gibbs and Trevor Owens (2013), "The Hermeneutics of Data and Historical Writing," in K. Nawrotzki and J. Dougherty (eds), *Writing History in the Digital Age*, Ann Arbor, MI: University of Michigan Press, Webbook edition available at http://dx.doi.org/10.3998/dh.12230987.0001.001.

[2] Franco Moretti (December 2013), "Operationalizing: or, the function of measurement in modern literary theory," *Stanford Literary Lab Pamphlet* 6, http://litlab.stanford.edu/LiteraryLabPamphlet6.pdf.

contracts and collaborations. You must operationalize popularity; perhaps this can be done through the sale of records or the frequency with which certain songs were played on the radio. You can operationalize the strength of connections as well, perhaps as a function of the number of times two musicians recorded together or recorded with a particular label. Because it might be difficult to tell whether a connection to a musician or a label is more important, it would be useful to include the time of events in the data gathered. With all these data, you could then check whether those connected with certain people or labels tended to become more popular, using path lengths, or whether certain musicians were instrumental in introducing new musicians to record labels, by looking at triadic closure. Going into an analysis with a preformed hypothesis or question will make both the data gathering and analysis step much easier.

Software

It is important to decide on a software package to use before embarking on a network study because it can dictate which data you plan on collecting and how you plan on collecting them. Thankfully, you are not locked in to any particular software choice; file formats are convertible to one another, although the process can occasionally be occult, and sometimes an analysis requires the use of more than one tool. (Don't neglect the utility of your text editor, too, for generating and creating network files! See the file format section, below.)

UCINET

UCINET can be used to perform quite sophisticated analyses. Nevertheless, we do not recommend UCINET for most historians; it is not free software, is Windows-only, and has a steep learning curve.[3] However, for those who are already familiar with matrix mathematics, UCINET can be more intuitive than the other options. It has a lot of advanced features and has a wide user base among social network analysts. (Mac users can run Windows software using a variety of tools; one we use is http://winebottler.kronenberg.org/.) We do not recommend UCINET for creating visualizations. UCINET is available at https://sites.google.com/site/ucinetsoftware/home.

---

[3] An excellent guide to network analysis via UCINET is Robert Hanneman and Mark Riddle (2005), *Introduction to Social Network Methods*, Riverside, CA: University of California, Riverside. Online textbook, http://faculty.ucr.edu/~hanneman/nettext/.

Pajek

Pajek is a free program for network analysis with more features and algorithms than any other non-command-line tool. We do not recommend it for those starting out with network analysis, as it can be difficult to learn and is not intuitive. But it can perform sophisticated analyses, so those in need of algorithms they can find in no other tool might find Pajek suits their needs. Pajek is also Windows-only, has a wider user base, and newer versions can scale to fairly large networks. We do not recommend Pajek for creating visualizations. However, the Pajek format (which uses the .NET file extension) is an industry standard and most tools can read or create it. Pajek is available at http://pajek.imfm.si/doku.php.

Network Workbench and Sci²

The NWB and the Sci² Tool (both developed in collaboration with one of the authors of this handbook) are similar free tools for the manipulation of data, the analysis of networks, and the creation of visualizations. The first focuses on network analysis, and the second focuses on scientometrics (citation analysis and other similar goals). These tools have more features than the others with regards to data pre-processing, especially in the creation of networks out of both unstructured and structured data, but fewer specifically analytic tools than UCINET or Pajek. They are particularly useful for converting between file formats, they run on all platforms, and are slightly easier to use than Pajek and UCINET, though not as easy to use as NodeXL or Gephi. NWB is available at http://nwb.cns.iu.edu/. Sci² is available at https://sci2.cns.iu.edu/user/index.php (you will need to complete a free registration process to download it).

NodeXL

NodeXL is a free plugin for Microsoft Excel and is again unfortunately only available on the Windows platform. We recommend NodeXL for historians who are familiar with Excel and are just beginning to explore network analysis. The plugin is not as feature-rich as any of the others in this list, but it does make entering and editing data extremely easy and works very well for small datasets. NodeXL also provides some unique visualizations and the ability to import data from other packages; it does not scale well to networks of more than a few thousand nodes and edges. NodeXL can also be used to mine social media connections (Twitter user lists or hashtags, YouTube, Facebook). NodeXL can be downloaded at http://nodexl.codeplex.com/.

Gephi

Gephi is quickly becoming the tool of choice for network analysts who do not need the full suite of algorithms offered by Pajek or UCINET. Although it does not have the data entry or pre-processing features of NWB, Sci^2, or NodeXL, it is relatively easy to use (eclipsed in this only by NodeXL), it is usable on all platforms, it can analyze fairly large networks, and it creates beautiful visualizations. The development community is also extremely active, with improvements being added constantly. **We recommend Gephi for the majority of historians undertaking serious network analysis research.** Gephi is available at http://gephi.github.io.

Networks online: D3.js, gexf-js, and sigma.js

When it comes to network visualizations, an element of interactivity is at the top of most researchers' wish lists. Until recently, the only truly great options for online, interactive network visualizations came out of the Stanford Visualization Group under Jeffrey Heer, including the work of Mike Bostock. This team was responsible for a number of widely used visualization infrastructures, including the **prefuse** toolkit, a Java-based framework for creating visualizations; **flare**, an ActionScript (Adobe Flash) library for creating visualizations; and **protovis**, a JavaScript library for creating visualizations. The team's most recent venture, **D3.js**, is a highly flexible JavaScript-based framework for developing novel visualizations and is currently the industry standard for interactive, online visualizations. Mike Bostock is now a graphics editor at the *New York Times*, and the Stanford Visualization Group has moved to the University of Washington and is now known as the Interactive Data Lab.

D3.js is a complex language, and it can be difficult for beginners — even those familiar with coding — to use effectively.[4] A number of libraries have been created as a layer around D3.js that attempt to ease the process of creating visualizations, including **vega** and **NVD3**. All of these libraries require some knowledge of coding, however a little effort in learning them

---

[4]A very good introduction and tutorial to D3.js is by Elijah Meeks (2014), *D3.js in Action*, Shelter Island, NY: Manning Publications. As of this writing, the book is being live-written, with Meeks adapting content to take into account readers' feedback. http://www.manning.com/meeks/.

can be rewarded by highly customized interactive networks online. For those who do not want to code a visualization themselves, there are a few options for creating interactive online visualizations using Gephi. **Seadragon web export**, **Sigmajs Exporter**, and **Gexf-JS Web Viewer** are all plugins available through the Gephi marketplace for creating such visualizations (in Gephi, you can add new plugins by clicking on "tools" then "plugins").

Data in Abstract

Network data match network theory: their basic components are nodes and edges. There are three ways these are generally represented: as matrices, as adjacency lists, and as node and edge lists. Each have their own strengths and weaknesses, and they will be discussed below.

The same example network will be used in all three descriptions: a network of exchange between four fictional cities. The data types will be used to show how network data can have varying degrees of detail.

Matrices

Although not in most historians' toolboxes, the **matrix** is an extremely useful representation for small networks and it happens to double as a simple network visualization. The below is a network of trade between four fictional cities: Netland, Connectia, Graphville, and Nodopolis. A "0" is placed when there is no trade route between cities, and a "1" if there is.

	Netland	Connectia	Graphville	Nodopolis
Netland		1	0	1
Connectia			1	1
Graphville				0
Nodopolis				

From this matrix, we can infer that Connectia trades with Netland, Graphville, and Nodopolis; and Nodopolis trades with Netland. Notice only the **upper triangle** of the matrix is filled in; the **diagonal** (shaded) is left unfilled because it is not meaningful for cities to trade with themselves, and the **lower triangle** is left unfilled because, in a symmetrical undirected network, any information in that corner would be redundant and identical. We already know that Netland trades with Connectia so we do not need to repeat ourselves. The network is unweighted because all we know is whether trade exists between two cities (represented by 0 or 1), we do not know the amount of trade.

	Netland	Connectia	Graphville	Nodopolis
Netland		$10mil	0	$4mil
Connectia			$2mil	$4mil
Graphville				0
Nodopolis				

This matrix is identical to the previous, but it now represents a weighted network. It shows $10 million in trade between Connectia and Netland, $2 million between Connectia and Graphville, $4 million between Connectia and Nodopolis, and $4 million between Netland and Nodopolis. This representation could be extended even further.

		Target			
		Netland	Connectia	Graphville	Nodopolis
Source	Netland		$6mil	0	$1mil
	Connectia	$4mil		$1mil	$3mil
	Graphville	0	$1mil		0
	Nodopolis	$3mil	$1mil	0	

The matrix now represents a directed, weighted network of trade between cities. The directionality means the trade relationships between cities can be represented asymmetrically, thus broken up into their constituent parts. Directional networks require filling both the upper and lower triangle of the matrix. **Source** and **Target** are the network terms of choice for the nodes that do the sending and those that do the receiving, respectively. In the above matrix, Netland (the source) sends $6 million to Connectia (the target) and $1 million to Nodopolis (the target). Netland (the target) receives $4 million from Connectia (the source) and $3 million from Nodopolis (the source).

If we wanted to extend this representation even further, we could create multiple parallel matrices. Parallel matrices could represent time slices, so each matrix represents trade between cities in a subsequent year. Alternatively, parallel matrices could represent different varieties of trade, e.g. people, money, and goods. This is one method to encode a multiplex network.

Matrices were, at one point, the standard way to represent networks. They are fairly easy to read, do not take up much space, and a lot of the network analysis algorithms are designed using matrix mathematics. As networks have become larger, however, it is becoming more common to represent them in adjacency lists or node and edge lists. The matrix is still readable by most network software, and some programs are optimized for use with matrices, particularly UCINET and, to a lesser extent, NodeXL.

Adjacency Lists

The **adjacency list** is a simple replacement for the matrix and a bit easier when it comes to data entry. Like a matrix, it can be used to represent many varieties of networks.

Netland	Connectia
Netland	Nodopolis
Connectia	Graphville
Connectia	Nodopolis

This adjacency list represents the same network as the first matrix. It is undirected and unweighted. Adding weights is as easy as adding an additional column of data.

		Weight
Netland	Connectia	$10mil
Netland ·	Nodopolis	$4mil
Connectia	Graphville	$2mil
Connectia	Nodopolis	$4mil

Adjacency lists can have any number of additional columns for every additional edge trait. For example, if this were a multiplex network encoding different *varieties* of trade, there might be two additional columns: one for goods, another for people. Each additional column could be filled with numerical values. Alternatively, columns could be used to encode the type of tie. In a family business network, a column for "type of relationship" could be filled in as "trade," "marriage," or "both."

Adjacency lists can also be used to represent directed, asymmetric networks, as below (treating columns as "source" and "target" to indicate directionality).

Source	Target	Weight
Netland	Connectia	$6mil
Netland	Nodopolis	$1mil
Connectia	Graphville	$1mil
Connectia	Nodopolis	$3mil
Connectia	Netland	$4mil
Graphville	Connectia	$1mil
Nodopolis	Netland	$3mil
Nodopolis	Connectia	$1mil

This is identical to the final matrix. In network visualizations, directedness is represented as an arrow going from the source to the target, which implies the directionality of an edge.

Node and Edge Lists

We recommend this data structure for historians embarking on a network analysis. It is widely used, easy to enter data manually, and allows additional information to be appended to nodes, rather than just to edges. The one down side of **Node and Edge Lists** is that they require more initial work, as they involve the creation of two separate tables: one for nodes and one for edges.

Nodes	
ID	Label
1	Graphville
2	Nodopolis
3	Connectia
4	Netland

Edges	
4	3
4	2
3	1
3	2

This node and edge list is equivalent to the first adjacency list and the first matrix. Notice particularly that nodes are now given unique IDs that are separate from their labels; this becomes useful if, for example, there are multiple cities with the same name. The two tables below show how to add weights and directionality, as well as additional attributes to individual nodes.

Nodes			
ID	Label	Population	Country
1	Graphville	700,000	USA
2	Nodopolis	250,000	Canada
3	Connectia	1,000,000	Canada
4	Netland	300,000	USA

Edges		
Source	Target	Weight
4	3	$6mil
4	2	$1mil
3	1	$1mil
3	2	$3mil
3	4	$4mil
1	3	$1mil
2	4	$3mil
2	3	$1mil

Although node and edge lists require more initial setup, they pay off in the end for their ease of data entry and flexibility. Unfortunately, not all software interprets these data structures in the exact same way, so it will be necessary to convert the gathered data into a format that the program can actually read.

File Formats

There are many file formats for networks, and most are instantiations of the three main data structures covered in the previous section. Below we describe them in some detail, using the four fictional cities as examples.

UCINET

UCINET's data format is fairly simple plain text but also fairly difficult to edit by hand. The most common format used by UCINET is the "full matrix," which incorporates a list of node labels that are defined before the matrix is written out. The matrix is assumed to have the same nodes in the same order on the horizontal and the vertical, as below.

```
dl N = 4
format = fullmatrix
labels:
netland, connectia, graphland, nodopolis
data:
0 1 0 1
0 0 1 1
0 0 0 0
0 0 0 0
```

Take a moment and notice how this is the same data structure as the first matrix example in the previous section (the Netland/Connectia trading system), although the exact specifications of the file format are unique to UCINET. The first line declares the number of nodes (4), the second declares the format, the third and fourth declare the labels, and subsequent lines describe the edges. While this is just a simple text file, we give it the file extension .dl, thus citynetwork.dl.

Pajek, NWB, & Sci²

The standard file formats for Pajek and NWB/Sci² are similar to one another, as they are both node and edge lists encoded in a single plain text file. In the Pajek file format (NET), we call nodes **vertices**, directed edges **arcs**, and undirected edges **edges**.

```
*Vertices 4
1 "Graphville"
2 "Nodopolis"
3 "Connectia"
4 "Netland"
*Edges
4 3
4 2
3 1
3 2
```

If the edges were directed, the subsection would be *Arcs* instead of *Edges*. Weight can be added to each edge by simply adding a number equivalent to the edge weight at the end of the line featuring that edge.

The NWB/Sci[2] file format (*.NWB) is quite similar, although it requires more declarations of network types and variables. It also requires a declaration of each variable type (int = integer, string = string of text, etc.). An example of an NWB file that has both additional node and edge information would look like this.

```
*Nodes    4
id*int    label*string    population*float    country*string
1    "Graphville"    700000    "USA"
2    "Nodopolis"    250000    "Canada"
3    "Connectia"    1000000    "Canada"
4    "Netland"    300000    "USA"
*DirectedEdges 8
source*int    target*int    weight*float
4    3    6000000
4    2    1000000
3    1    1000000
3    2    3000000
3    4    4000000
1    3    1000000
2    4    3000000
2    3    1000000
```

These file formats are very sensitive to small errors, so it is usually best not to edit them directly. That's why we have network programs!

GEXF

Gephi's XML-based file format, GEXF, is saved in plain text with a .gexf extension. It is fairly verbose but allows quite a bit of detail of a network to be saved.

```
<?xml version="1.0" encoding="UTF-8"?>
<gexf xmlns="http://www.gexf.net/1.2draft" version="1.2">
    <graph mode="static" defaultedgetype="undirected">
        <nodes>
            <node id="0" label="Graphville" />
```

```
            <node id="1" label="Nodopolis" />
            <node id="2" label="Connectia" />
            <node id="3" label="Netland" />
        </nodes>
        <edges>
            <edge id="0" source="3" target="2" />
            <edge id="0" source="3" target="1" />
            <edge id="0" source="2" target="0" />
            <edge id="0" source="2" target="1" />
        </edges>
    </graph>
</gexf>
```

These files are easy to read, but — again — should not be edited directly unless you really know what you're doing.

NodeXL

NodeXL files are not saved in plain text; instead, they are saved in the default Microsoft Excel format. Entering data directly into this format is the easiest of all the others, as it simply requires opening up the file in Excel and editing or adding as necessary, within the familiar spreadsheet environment.

Network Visualizations

Matrix diagrams tend to be used more by computational social scientists than traditional social network analysts. They are the exact, colorized versions of the matrix data structure discussed earlier in this chapter and are good for showing community patterns in medium-to-large networks. They do not suffer from the same clutter as force-directed visualizations, but they also do not lend themselves to be read at the scale of individual actors.

Figure 7.1 is a matrix visualization of character interactions in Victor Hugo's *Les Misérables*. We made this visualization using Excel to reinforce the fact that matrix visualizations are merely data structures that have been colored and zoomed out. Each column is a character in the book, as is each row, and the list of character names is in the same order horizontally and vertically. A cell is shaded red if the character from that row interacted with the character from that column; it is shaded white if they did not.

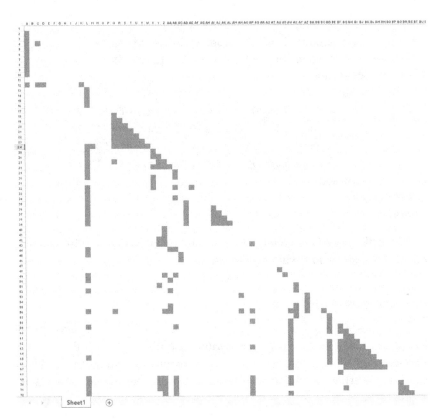

Fig. 7.1   A matrix visualization of *Les Misérables*. Microsoft Excel screenshot used with permission from Microsoft.

Note that only one of the matrix's triangles is filled, because the network is symmetric.

We performed community detection on the network and ordered the characters based on whether they were in a community together. That is why some areas are thick with red cells and others are not; each triangular red cluster represents a community of characters that interact with one another. The vertical columns that feature many red cells are main characters that interact with many other characters in the book. The filled-in column near the left-hand side, for example, is the character interactions of Jean Valjean.

Matrix diagrams can be extended to cover asymmetric networks by using both the matrix's upper and lower triangles. Additional information can be encoded in the intensity of a color (signifying edge weight) or the hue of the shaded cell (indicating different categories of edges).

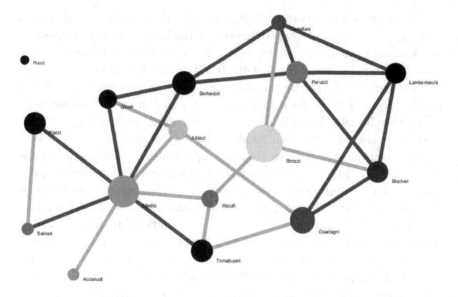

Fig. 7.2   A force-directed layout of inter-familial connections in Renaissance Florence.

Force-directed layouts are the visualizations most people think of when they think of network analyses. An example is in Fig. 7.2.

This visualization, created using the Sci^2 Tool, represents a subset of Ansell and Padgett's data concerning the network of connections amongst Renaissance Florentine families.[5] Force-directed layouts like this one attempt to reduce the number of edges that cross one another while simultaneously bringing more directly-connected nodes closer together. They do this by modeling the network as though it were a physics problem, as though each edge were a spring and each node a unit connecting various springs together. The computer simulates this system, letting the springs bounce around until each one is as little stretched as it possibly can be. At the same time, the nodes repel each other, like magnets of the same polarity, so the nodes do not appear too close together. Eventually, the nodes settle into a fairly legible graph like Fig. 7.2. This algorithm is an example of how force-directed layouts work, but they do not all use springs and magnets, and often they are a great deal more complex than how we have described them.

---

[5] John Padgett and Christopher Ansell (1993), "Robust Action and the Rise of the Medici, 1400–1434," *American Journal of Sociology*, **98**(6), 1259–1319.

There are a few important takeaways from this algorithm. The first is that the layout is generally **stochastic**, or random; there is an element of randomness that will orient the nodes and edges slightly differently every time it is run. The second is that the traditional spatial dimensions (vertical and horizontal) that are so often meaningful in visualizations have no meaning here. There is no x- or y-axis, and spatial distance from one node to another is not inherently meaningful. For example, had Fig. 7.2 been laid out again, the Acciaiuoli family could just as easily have been closer to the Pazzi than the Salviati family, as opposed to in this case where the reverse is true. To properly read a force-directed network visualization, you need to retrain your visual understanding such that you are aware that it is edges, not spatial distance, which mark nodes as closer or farther away.

This style of visualization becomes more difficult to read as a network grows. Larger instantiations have famously been called "spaghetti-and-meatball visualizations" or "giant hairballs," and it can be impossible to discern any particular details. Still, in some cases, these very large-scale force-directed networks can be useful in discerning patterns at-a-glance.

Other visualizations

Matrix and force-directed visualizations are the two most common network visualizations but they are by no means the only options. A quick search for chord diagrams, radial layouts, arc layouts, hive plots, circle packs, and others will reveal a growing universe of network visualizations. Picking which is appropriate in what situation can be more of an art than a science. Whatever layout you choose: does it help you understand the historical problem? Does it help make the argument more clear?

When Not To Use Networks

Network analysis can be a powerful method for engaging with a historical dataset but it is often not the most appropriate. Any historical database may be represented as a network with enough contriving but few should be. One could take the Atlantic trade network, including cities, ships, relevant governments and corporations, and connect them all together in a giant multipartite network. It would be extremely difficult to derive any meaning from this network, especially using traditional network analysis methodologies. The LCC, for example, would be meaningless, as it would be impossible for the neighbors of any one node to be neighbors with one another.

Network scientists have developed algorithms for multimodal networks, but they are often created for fairly specific purposes, and one should be very careful before applying them to a different dataset and using that analysis to explore a historiographical question.

Networks, as they are commonly encoded, also suffer from a profound lack of nuance. It is all well to say that, because Henry Oldenburg corresponded with both Gottfried Leibniz and John Milton, he was the short connection between the two men. However, the encoded network holds no information of whether Oldenburg actually transferred information between the two or whether that connection was at all meaningful. In a flight network, Las Vegas and Atlanta might both have very high betweenness centrality because people from many other cities fly to or from those airports, and yet one is much more of a hub than the other. This is because, largely, people tend to fly directly back and forth from Las Vegas, rather than through it, whereas people tend to fly through Atlanta from one city to another. This is the type of information that network analysis, as it is currently used, is not well equipped to handle. Whether this shortcoming affects a historical inquiry depends primarily on the inquiry itself.

When deciding whether to use networks to explore a historiographical question, the first question should be: to what extent is connectivity specifically important to this research project? The next should be: can any of the network analyses my collaborators or I know how to employ be specifically useful in the research project? If either answer is negative, another approach is probably warranted.

Networks in Action

Once you choose network analysis as a method, you must decide the series of steps to take to turn a historical question into an operational process. There are many ways to reach this goal. No proper path exists; the set of tools and order of steps taken are determined by the task at hand.

For example, let's imagine that you want to find important art dealers in the mid-20th century. You might sit down with the transaction books of private collectors and museums, and enter every art transaction (by hand!) into NodeXL, listing the buyer and seller. If you are on Windows, NodeXL is the obvious choice here because it is the easiest software for entering data by hand. Say that you find a few thousand entities buying or selling art, between whom over 10,000 art pieces changed hands. Knowing this network is a bit large for NodeXL, you export it in GRAPHML to format and load it into Gephi in order to explore the network. Once in Gephi, you visualize the network in a force-directed layout, noticing immediately some central players in the art world: a few famous dealers, some museums, and so forth. To further refine your search for art dealers worth researching in more depth, you run the appropriate algorithms and look for those with high centrality and low clustering coefficient. These, you reason, must be central figures between whom art flowed to otherwise disconnected communities. You highlight these nodes in red and publish them as an SVG file, to send to your publisher, so the illustration in your book clearly shows how these dealers spanned multiple communities. This would be a good network analysis, and you would detail and discuss these steps so that someone else could re-run your analyses to confirm, refute, or extend.

Other situations would require different steps and different software. Perhaps what you are interested in are the *holes* in the network, the patterning of non-connections. In such a case, you would probably use UCINET. It is beyond the scope of this book to produce tutorials for every potential situation and series of software packages dealing with network analysis. Instead, let us take a simple dataset and work through the process of loading it into the most likely piece of software you might use (Gephi) and see what we might find. We shall do some exploration. The *Further Reading* section at the end of the previous chapter will help the reader move beyond these basics.

Recall that in Chapter 3, you used Notepad++, regular expressions, and OpenRefine to create a comma-separated value file (CSV) of the diplomatic correspondence of the Republic of Texas. The final version of the file you created has a row for each letter listed in the volume, and in each row the name of the sender and the recipient. The file looks like this:

```
source,target
Sam Houston,J. Pinckney Henderson
James Webb,Alc6e La Branche
David G. Burnet,Richard G. Dunlap
...
```

This file is an edge list, as discussed in the previous section on network data types. If you no longer have the file, you can find it online at http://themacroscope.org/2.0/datafiles/texas-correspondence-OpenRefine.csv. Keep this file handy, as you will need to load it after you have installed Gephi. Install Gephi by going to http://gephi.github.io, downloading the appropriate install file for your operating system, and running it on your computer.

Installing Gephi on OS X Mavericks[6]

Mac users might have some trouble installing Gephi. We have found that, on Mac OS X Mavericks, Gephi does not load properly after installation. This is a Java-related issue, so you'll need to install an earlier version of Java than the one provided. To fix this, control click (or right-click) on the Gephi package, and select "show package contents." Click on "contents → resources → gephi → etc." Control-click (or right-click) on "gephi.conf" and open with your text editor. Find the line reading:

```
#jdkhome="/path/to/jdk"
```

and paste the following underneath:

```
jdkhome="/System/Library/Java/JavaVirtualMachines/1.6.0.jdk/Contents/Home"
```

Save that file. Then, go to http://support.apple.com/kb/DL1572 and install the older version of Java (Java 6). Once that is installed, Gephi should run normally.

Run Gephi once it is installed. You will be presented with a welcome window prompting you to open a recent file, create a new project, or load a sample file. Click "New Project" and then click the "Data Laboratory" tab on the horizontal bar at the top of the Gephi window (Fig. 7.3).

You will be presented with a blank screen as you have not yet populated Gephi with the correspondence data. To do so, click "Import Spreadsheet"

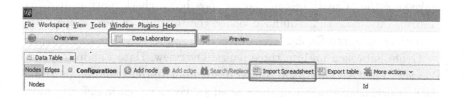

Fig. 7.3   Accessing the Data Laboratory in Gephi.

---

[6]The Yosemite operating system was released as this text was being finalized. Clement Levallois maintains an excellent web resource of Gephi guides and help files at http://clementlevallois.net/gephi.html including a very detailed guide to installing and running Gephi under Yosemite (as well as Windows 8).

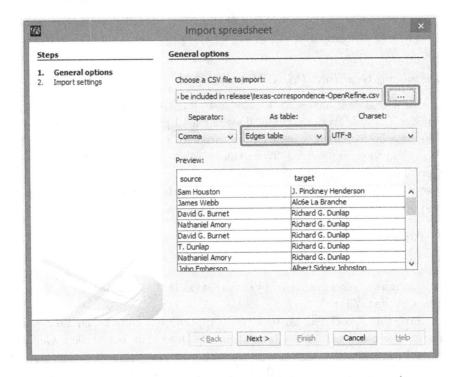

Fig. 7.4   The import spreadsheet dialogue box.

and select the file texas-correspondence-OpenRefine.csv by clicking on the button with the ellipsis (...) and navigating to the file (Fig. 7.4). Make sure that you are importing the file as an "Edges table." Click "Next" and make sure the "Create missing nodes" box has a check mark in it. Click "Finish," and note that you have loaded the Republic of Texas diplomatic correspondence into Gephi.

Gephi is broken up into three panes: Overview, Data Laboratory, and Preview. The Overview pane is used to manipulate the visual properties of the network: change colors of nodes or edges, lay them out in different ways, and so forth. The Overview pane is also where you can apply algorithms to the network, like those you learned about in the previous chapter. The Data Laboratory is for adding, manipulating, and removing data. Once your network is as you want it to be, use the Preview pane to do some final tweaks on the look and feel of the network and to export an image for publication.

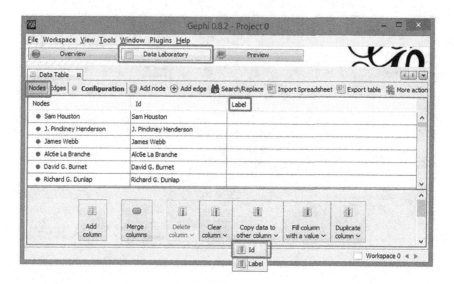

Fig. 7.5   Copying data from one column to another.

There is one tweak that needs to done in the Data Table before the dataset is fully ready to be explored in Gephi. Click on the "Nodes" tab in the Data Table and notice that, of the three columns, "Label" (the furthermost field on the right) is blank in every row. This will be a problem when viewing the network visualization, as those labels are essential for the network to be meaningful.

In the "Nodes" tab, click "Copy data to other column" at the bottom, select "ID", and press "Ok" (Fig. 7.5). Upon doing so, the "Label" column will be filled with the appropriate labels for each correspondent. While you're still in the Data Laboratory, look in the "Edges" tab and notice there is a "Weight" column. Gephi automatically counted every time a letter was sent from correspondent A to correspondent B and summed up all the occurrences, resulting in the "Weight." This means that J. Pinckney Henderson sent three letters to James Webb, because Henderson is in the "Source" column, Webb in the "Target,", and the "Weight" is three.

Clicking on the Overview pane will take you to a visual representation of the network you just imported. In the middle of the screen, you will see your network in the "Graph" tab. The "Context" tab, at the top right, will show that you imported 234 nodes and 394 edges. At first, all the nodes will be randomly strewn across the screen and make little visual sense (Fig. 7.6). Fix this by selecting a layout in the "Layout" tab — the best

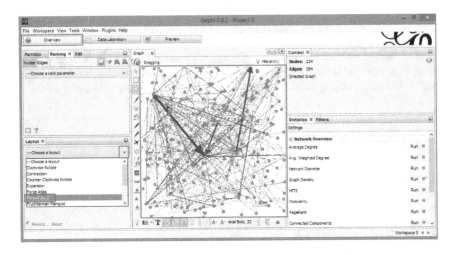

Fig. 7.6 Fixing the layout view.

one for beginners is "Force Atlas 2." Press the "Run" button and watch the nodes and edges reorganize on the screen into something slightly more manageable. After the layout runs for a few minutes, re-press the button (now labeled "Stop") to settle the nodes in their place.

You just ran a force-directed layout, as described earlier in this chapter. Each dot is a correspondent in the network, and lines between dots represent letters sent between individuals. Thicker lines represent more letters, and arrows represent the direction the letters were sent, such that there may be up to two lines connecting any two correspondents (one for each direction).

About two-dozen smaller components of the network will appear to shoot off into the distance, unconnected from the large, connected component in the middle. For the purpose of this exercise, we are not interested in those disconnected components, so the next step will be to filter them out of the network. The first step is to calculate which components of the network are connected to which others; do this by clicking "Run" next to the text that says "Connected Components" in the "Statistics" tab on the right-hand side (Fig. 7.7). Once there, select "UnDirected" and press "OK." Press "Close" when the report pops up indicating that the algorithm has finished running.

Now that this is done, Gephi knows which is the giant connected component (see Chapter 5 for details) and has labeled that component "0". To filter out everything but the giant component, click on the "Filters" tab on the right-hand side and browse to "Component ID *Integer (Node)*" in the

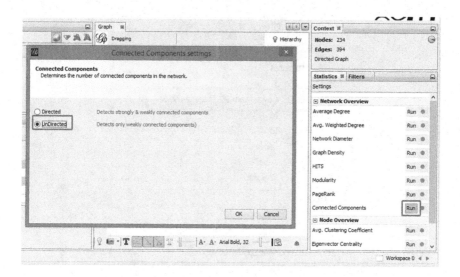

Fig. 7.7   Calculating connected components.

folder directory (you'll find it under "Attributes," then "Equal"). Double-click "Component ID *Integer (Node)*" and click the "Filter" button at the bottom (Fig. 7.8). Doing this removes the disconnected bundles of nodes.

So far, you have gone through the many steps it takes to finally analyze the data. The data-gathering step (1) in this case was pretty easy, as it simply involved downloading a text file from the Internet Archive. The data-cleaning step (2) was a bit more complex, as it involved data mining in Notepad++ using regular expressions and some smoothing in OpenRefine. Data preparation (3) involved loading your CSV into Gephi, adding labels to nodes, and filtering out unwanted data. Two steps are left: analysis (4) and visualization (5). In most history projects, the first three steps take the longest by many orders of magnitude, and each step is often revisited as your thoughts on the project evolve.

There are many possible algorithms you could use for the analysis step, but in this case you will use the PageRank of each node in the network. This measurement calculates the prestige of a correspondent according to how often others write to him or her. The process is circular, such that correspondents with high prestige will confer their prestige on those *they* write to, who in turn pass their prestige along to their own correspondents. The algorithm is described at length in Chapter 5, but for the moment let us take its results to equate with a correspondent's importance in the Republic of Texas letter network.

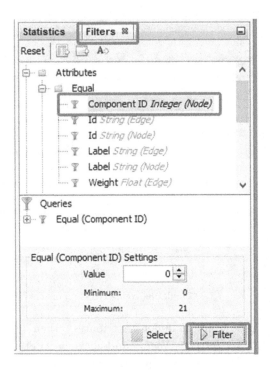

Fig. 7.8   Filtering components.

Calculate the PageRank by clicking on the "Run" button next to "PageRank" in the "Statistics" tab. You will be presented with a prompt asking for a few parameters; make sure "Directed" network is selected and that the algorithm is taking edge weight into account (by selecting "Use edge weight"). Leave all other parameters at their default. Press "OK" (Fig. 7.9).

Once PageRank is calculated, if you click back into the "Data Laboratory" and select the "Nodes" list in the Data Table, you can see that a new "PageRank" column has been added, with values for every node. The higher the PageRank, the more central a correspondent is in the network. Going back to the Overview pane, you can visualize this centrality by changing the size of each correspondent's node based on its PageRank. Do this in the "Ranking" tab on the left side of the Overview pane.

Make sure "Nodes" is selected, press the icon of a little red diamond, and select PageRank from the drop-down menu. In the parameter options just below, enter the "Min size" as 1 and the "Max size" as 10. Press "Apply,"

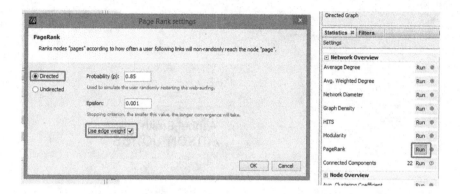

Fig. 7.9 Calculating PageRank.

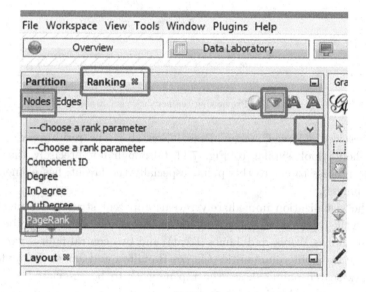

Fig. 7.10 Resizing nodes by PageRank.

and watch the nodes resize based on their PageRank (Fig. 7.10). To be on the safe side and decrease clutter, re-run the "Force Atlas 2" layout as described above, making sure to keep the "Prevent Overlap" box checked.

At this point, the network is processed enough to visualize in the Preview pane, to finally begin making sense of the data. In Preview, on the left-hand side, select "Show Labels," "Proportional Size," "Rescale Weight,"

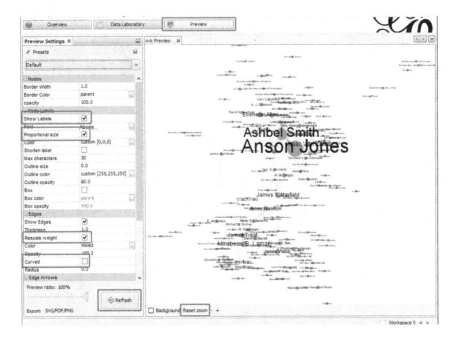

Fig. 7.11   Previewing the network visualization.

and deselect "Curved" edges. Press "Refresh." The resulting visualization should look similar to Fig. 7.11 (although not precisely the same — the process to get to this point, especially the layout, has elements of randomness).

The visualization immediately reveals apparent structure: central figures on the top (Ashbel Smith and Anson Jones) and bottom (Mirabeau B. Lamar, James Webb, and James Treat), and two central figures who connect the two split communities (James Hamilton and James S. Mayfield). A quick search online shows the top network to be associated with the last president of the Republic of Texas, Anson Jones; whereas the bottom network largely revolves around the second president, Mirabeau Lamar. Experts on this period in history could use this analysis to understand the structure of communities building to the annexation of Texas or they could ask meta-questions about the nature of the data themselves. For example, why is Sam Houston, the first and third president of the Republic of Texas, barely visible in this network?

A more nuanced historical view would take into account the temporal, evolving nature of the correspondence network. Gephi can support the analysis and visualization of evolving networks.[7] Such networks are extremely complex, both in terms of creating them and in terms of analysis. However they are the obvious next step for historians interested in applying network analysis to their own research.

Going Further: Dynamic Networks in Gephi

Network analysis is great when we are dealing with a static network. Most metric algorithms are built to work with networks that capture one moment in time (where moment can be defined as everything from a single day, to a week, to a month, to a span of years). Sometimes, it will make sense to consider a pattern of interactions (a network) that took place over a long period of time *as a single network*. For instance, in archaeological network analysis, given the nature of the material, a single network can encompass 200 years' worth of interactions.[8] But other times it would make more sense to see the shape of a network as an evolving, dynamic set of relationships, as in correspondence networks.

One could create a series of networks in time-slices — the exchange of letters between individuals in 1836 as one network; all those in 1837 as another; and so on. This can be a good approach (depending on your question), but it is subject to *edge effects*: the decision on where to draw the boundary changes the shape of the network. Fortunately, Gephi can deal with dynamic data and with edges that exist for varying durations, and can calculate some metrics on the fly (revisualizing on the fly as well).

But what does "duration" mean for a network? In a correspondence network, perhaps "duration" means "the time the letter is uppermost in one's mind." Perhaps it means "the time until I write a response," thus closing the relationship (and which implies that a correspondence network can have both directed and undirected edges). In Graham's 2006 network of land-owning relationships deduced from the archaeology and epigraphy of Roman stamped bricks, "duration" was considered to be open-ended

---

[7]For tutorials on how to use some of these features, see Clement Levallois' at http://www.clementlevallois.net/gephi/tuto/gephi_tutorial_dynamics.pdf and https://marketplace.gephi.org/plugin/excel-csv-converter-to-network/.

[8]Graham (2006) *Ex Figlinis: The Network Dynamics of the Tiber Valley Brick Industry in the Hinterland of Rome* BAR International Series 1486. Oxford: John and Erica Hedges Ltd does this with relationships of landholding around Rome in the first three centuries. See also Graham (2014) "On Connecting Stamps: Network Analysis and Epigraphy," *Nouvelles d'archéologie*, **135**, 39–44.

(in broad strokes, the stamps represent a kind of rental agreement and so, unless we find a parcel of land suddenly being leased under a different name, we can assume the relationship continues). The decisions that the historian makes while assembling, cleaning, and representing her data become the objects that the computer manipulates, so these issues are theoretically significant!

At the time of writing, Gephi is being prepared for an update that will alter the way the program imagines "duration" and "time" in networks. For more information about dynamic networks in Gephi, please see our companion website at http://themacroscope.org.

A Common Sin: Analyzing Two Mode Networks with One Mode Statistics

We often see network analyses where the nodes of the network actually make up more than one kind of thing. A network of small businesses connected to the churches that their workers attend, in small town North America in the 1960s, would be a two-mode network. Visualizing such a network can be a useful heuristic, a good initial exploration of one's data. Clumps and clusters might become apparent, and the role of, say, the Presbyterian church versus the Baptist, as a bridge for a variety of otherwise unconnected businesses might jump out.

However, any network metric calculated in Gephi on such a network would be specious since Gephi's default metrics are all founded on the assumptions of one-mode graphs. That is, the algorithm would work, but since the data *is founded on a different set of assumptions than the algorithm expects*, the resulting numbers are essentially meaningless. The solution then, if one wishes to build an argument based on the properties of these network data, is to transform it from a two-mode graph (where the nodes are two kinds of things, businesses and churches) into two one-mode graphs (where the nodes are one kind of thing, businesses to businesses, connected by virtue of church memberships; churches to churches by virtue of churchgoers' employers).

We can do this transformation automatically within Gephi using a plugin. There are a number of plugins for Gephi, most of which may be found at the "Gephi Marketplace" online or via the Tools → Plugins menu item within Gephi. To convert a two-mode network to two one-mode networks, look for the "multimode networks transformations" plugin. Install this plugin, and a new panel will open in Gephi, adjacent to the statistics panel. To convert your materials,

1. Make sure your initial CSV file with your data has a column called "type." Fill that column with "undirected." (You can add a new column within Gephi's data laboratory, or do it using a spreadsheet program instead.) The plugin assumes undirected data and therefore doesn't work correctly with directed graphs.
2. Then, once your CSV file is imported, create a new column on the nodes table; call it "node-type" — here you specify what the thing is. Fill it up accordingly. For instance, you might have as node types "worker" and "church".
3. Save your network; this next step will irrevocably change your data. Click "load attributes" on the multimode transformations panel. Under attribute type, select your column you created for step 2. Then, for left matrix, select worker — church; for right matrix, select church — worker.
4. Select "remove edges" and "remove nodes."
5. Hit "run."
6. Save your new one-mode network with a new name. Your new network here will be a network of workers connected to other workers by virtue of shared membership in a particular church.
7. To generate a network where the nodes are churches tied by shared workers, close Gephi, reload your original two-mode network, and in step 3, invert your matrix selections.

While a two-mode network can help us intuit interesting patterns within the data, for actual analysis, we need to transform it so that we have apples to apples, oranges to oranges.

Conclusion

A network visualization, or a network analysis, can be a powerful part of the historian's macroscope. It has taken us two chapters to discuss what networks are, what they can represent, and how they can be represented. We have shown how to load network data into one of the more popular network visualization and analysis programmes, Gephi. Many kinds of data can be represented as a network, and network methods can be combined with all of the techniques discussed in Chapters 3 and 4.

But should you? If you have detected a note of caution these last two chapters, you are not imagining things. We have been to enough conferences and read enough papers to know that there is, at present, an overabundance of enthusiasm for networks. Sometimes they have been used without due regard for their limitations. Sometimes, they are invoked as a metaphor but their *formal use* has been dismissed as leading to "spaghetti diagrams." That would be to throw the baby out with the bathwater. We believe that network approaches, properly and cautiously used, have much to offer the historian dealing with biggish data. These last two chapters have given you the tools and theoretical apparatus to use them wisely, to good effect, where they can do the most to support your historical understanding.

Conclusion

The historian was stuck. She had read Graham, Milligan, and Weingart, she had run several topic models and found interesting patterns. They helped focus her close reading on a series of passages, and by jumping back and forth between the micro and the macro, she felt she had a compelling story to tell. But how to tell it? How to publish her results? She turned to Digital Humanities Questions and Answers. Within a few days, she had received several suggestions, some of which she was familiar with, some of which she had to look up, from Twitter Bootstrap, to d3.js, to Omeka, and examples like "Mining the Dispatch" (http://dsl.richmond.edu/dispatch/). She settled on a strategy that combined both knowledge mobilization (as her funder, the Social Sciences and Humanities Research Council of Canada calls it: public outreach), data-as-publishing, and the surfacing of work via a post-peer review model.

Her data that she had collected and created (all of her spreadsheets, her topic modeling scripts, her network files), she deposited with Figshare.com. This gave her citable "digital object identifiers," or DOIs, so that others could find, cite, and build upon her research (providing metrics as well for the number of times others viewed, shared, or cited her data). It also allowed her to cite her specific data outputs in her own work. Then, using a combination of Twitter Bootstrap (a series of HTML, CSS, and other files to create the shell of a working website), she began to visualize her data using a variety of interactive diagrams, framing them with suggestions for patterns others might look for and what these patterns might mean. She created publicly editable Google documents to allow others to leave their own interpretations. She registered the site with Digital Humanities Now and tweeted its existence to the week's current editors. Soon, the site became "Editor's Choice," and a longer version of her preliminary discussion was selected for inclusion in the Journal of Digital Humanities. As the research funding drew to a close, she wrote the entirety up into a single paper, a kind of "archival" version of what the research discovered.

Meanwhile, graduate students and other researchers began incorporating her data into their own research, creating new facets on the original Old Bailey Online data...

Some of the terms in that above passage may be opaque to you today but they are all part of the community that you may be joining. When we work with big data, and digital tools more generally, we produce a lot of data *on our own* that we should share, we should visualize, and that we should interpret. Sharing spreadsheets is trivial, but *showing* people the patterns therein is not. In this volume, we've suggested some ways of visualizing those patterns, especially where the visualization itself is part of the analysis.

Visualization is also about *communication*. The first academic journals were about communicating the results of scholarship not to just other scholars, but to an interested public. With digital tools, we feel that historians (and humanists, more generally) have the opportunity to turn their practice inside out, to make the communication of their scholarship a central part of the scholarship by placing it on the web. Our big data tools are at their strongest when they are used in such a way that others can try them out too, to explore our conclusions *based on our own data* so that other stories can be told: perhaps even conflicting stories! This is a new kind of history — a kind of public humanities — where our readers might become participants in crafting the history. But it requires the skills of the builder, of the hacker, of the communicator. There are many guides to visualization out there,[1] but none written so far with historians in mind.[2] If you should use this volume in your teaching, you might wish to consider how it might be extended to include this aspect. Leave a comment on our companion website, or perhaps even build your own website!

We hope, strangely enough, that not every person who picked up this book will be a digital historian. But we hope that you now know that it exists: what algorithms are out there to help you in your research if you

---

[1] http://www.jiscinfonet.ac.uk/infokits/data-visualisation/ is a good introductory discussion of issues and trends that the scholar should be aware of. http://selection. datavisualization.ch/ is a compendium of many current tools being used (most of which are free or open source).

[2] However, Matthew Jockers (2014), *Text Analysis with R for Students of Literature*, Cham, Switzerland: Springer International and Elijah Meeks (2014), *D3.js in Action*, Shelter Island, NY: Manning Publications are good places to start.

want, or to help your graduate students, or to help your colleagues. We can use our computers for more than just word processing, and in fact, we want to again stress that even "old-fashioned" historians are actually part of this.

For, as we discussed in the first section of this book, the historian's workflow has already been impacted by digital methods. In December 2012, the academic consulting organization ITHAKA S+R released their comprehensive overview of historical research methods, "Supporting the Changing Research Practices of Historians." Jennifer Rutner and Roger Schonfeld point out how the "use of digitized finding aids, digitized collections, and digital cameras have altered the way that historians interact with primary sources."[3] As they note, historians find their sources using Google, they take pictures of archival collections, and some blog. The widespread incorporation of digital collections has had a profound impact on the historians craft. While most sources remain undigitized and the adoption of digital history on a large scale has been slow, our methods are changing.

As we have shown throughout this book, however, new technologies need to be used critically. We often use technology without reflection, without understanding how it *actually* works. The black box of Google has its utility, but so does a harnessing of new techniques and an understanding of how they work. An understanding of topic modeling, of keyword searching, of how networks can be employed, enriches not only your digital workflow but also the technologically-augmented conventional research approaches. It enables you to be a better critic, a better consumer of digital data, a better user.

For once you begin to think digitally, you can begin to question or study in greater detail the various tools that you use. Keyword searches in newspaper databases, to use an example fleshed out earlier in this book, require an understanding of firstly how keywords work and the issues around tokenization. And then, too, they require an understanding of how the words were made searchable in the first place: were the databases created through the nearly-perfect double-blind transcription (where two typists independently transcribe a source, and discrepancies are explored) or through the powerful but fallible OCR processes? An understanding of this approach

---

[3] Jennifer Rutner and Roger C. Schonfeld (December 10, 2012), *Supporting the Changing Research Practices of Historians*, Ithaka S+R, http://www.sr.ithaka.org/sites/default/files/reports/supporting-the-changing-research-practices-of-historians.pdf.

helps us evaluate scholarship, augment our own approaches, and break down barriers between "digital history" and the rest of the discipline.

In our introductory chapter, we stressed that digital methods do not *replace* conventional methodologies but rather augment and deserve to be incorporated into them. The multiplicity and variety of historical sources will continue to require hands-on adventures, and digital history does not replace the critical work done by oral historians, scholars of material culture, or simply those who do not have the budget necessary to sustain widespread digitization.

All of the techniques in our book can be fruitfully applied to more "standard" questions. Oral history transcripts can be fruitfully mined for recurrent places or organizations, suggesting further avenues. Names can be connected into networks, suggesting a further biographical study, for example. Topic modeling or computational clustering of research notes might suggest chapter structures. And basic visualizations, from the simplest Wordle word cloud to a more complicated network diagram, can enliven conventional publications or presentations with a splash of color and spatial reasoning.

There is one big historical omission in this book, but for good reason. We have not discussed maps and mapping to any great extent in this volume. Historical GIS (HGIS), archaeological GIS, spatial analysis: these are all subjects with their own histories, bodies of knowledge, best practices, and most importantly, introductory volumes. You might find that you wish to begin mapping the data that your text analysis has uncovered. While GIS can be quite daunting, researchers are working on tools that are meant less for environmental management (which is where GIS began) and more for historians and humanists.

For example, the Palladio platform (http://palladio.designhumanities. org) from the Center for Spatial and Textual Analysis allows for some quite complicated visualizations of flows over a map. Damian Shiels uses Palladio to explore the impact of the American Civil War in Ireland, while students in Caleb McDaniel's Digital History seminar in 2014 at Rice University used Palladio to visualize patterns in fugitive slave ads.[4] The beauty of Palladio is

---

[4] Damian Shiels (31 May 2014), "Visualising the Impact of the American Civil War in Ireland with Palladio" *Irish in the American Civil War*, available online at http://irishamericancivilwar.com/2014/05/31/visualising-the-impact-of-the-american-civil-war-in-ireland-with-palladio/. See also Clare Jensen, Kaitlyn Sisk and Aaron Braunstein "Using Palladio to Visualize Ads," *Digital History Methods*, available online at http://ricedh.github.io/01-palladio.html. A round-up of other uses of Palladio is presented by

that it can accept CSV or tab-separated values as inputs. Then, by following the intuitive prompts, quite complex visualizations can be made very easily (including point-to-point mapping, as in the movement of letters). The speed and ease that Palladio allows encourages experimentation, unlike most GIS or mapping tools, which require a heavy learning curve before one can get to the point of playing with data to see what patterns might be present. If, however, you do discover patterns that you would like to investigate in more detail, it might then be worthwhile to learn one or more of the more common GIS platforms, like QGIS. You have already encountered *The Programming Historian*; you should visit Jim Clifford's website *Geospatial Historian*, which is similarly an open-access textbook on HGIS methods.[5] For a series of case studies of what HGIS can offer, please see Bonnell and Fortin's edited volume *Historical GIS Research in Canada*.[6]

After Using Your Macroscope: Assessing Digital Scholarship

What if you do go all-in on these methods and approaches that we have been advocating? How do you convince others — from sceptical professors to, if you are already an academic, your colleagues — that your work is valid scholarship? How do you show the scholarship involved in creating a finely-tuned topic model to a colleague who is more familiar with writing papers based on standard paper-based sources? There will be a temptation to try to frame what you have done in terms of page counts, or monographs, or journal articles: but an interactive data-driven argument via a website is not like an undergraduate thesis or journal article at all. We need a new language to frame these new materials.

The problem with assessing what "counts" as scholarship is one that we have not addressed in this volume, but if you stayed with us this far, it deserves some consideration. The problem is that the goalposts are always going to be shifting. What was fairly technically demanding becomes easier

---

Mark Braude (30 June 2014), "Check out the latest version of the Palladio dataviz platform from Humanities + Design @ Stanford," *HASTAC*, http://www.hastac.org/news/check-out-latest-version-palladio-dataviz-platform-humanities-design-stanford.

[5] Jim Clifford, Josh MacFadyen and Daniel Macfarlane, *The Geospatial Historian: Open HGIS Lessons and Resources*, available online at http://geospatialhistorian.wordpress.com/.

[6] Jennifer Bonnell and Marcel Fortin (eds) (2014), *Historical GIS Research in Canada*, Calgary: University of Calgary Press.

with time, and so the focus shifts from "can we do x" to "what are the implications of x for y," or as Bethany Nowviskie put it, a similar moment to that shift from 18th century "Lunaticks" who laid the groundwork for 19th century science and industrialization.[7] Another problem is that, in digital work, the lone scholar is very much the outlier. It often takes a team — and who gets to be first author does not necessarily reflect the way the work was divvied up or undertaken. We should resist trying to shoehorn digital work into boxes meant for a different medium. Nowviskie writes,

> The danger here [... is that confronting this work] will instigate a search for print equivalencies — aiming to map every project that is presented ... to some other completed, unary and generally privately-created object (like an article, an edition, or a monograph). That mapping would be hard enough in cases where it is actually appropriate.

Nowviskie argues that, to make the case, we have to argue that digital work represents embodied, transformative processes. It's not about what becomes known but how we come to know them. That then is the problem for assessing digital work: how does this work change the process? That suggests a hierarchy too, of importance. Merely putting things online, while important, is not necessarily transformative *unless that kind of material has never been digitized before.* Then the conversation also becomes about how that work was done, the decisions made, and the relationship between the digital object and the physical one. We have a student working on a project, for instance, to put together an online exhibition related to Black History in Canada. This is important, but the exhibition itself is not transformative. The real scholarship, the real transformation, will happen when she starts exploring those materials through text analysis, putting a macroscopic lens on the whole corpus of materials that she has collected.

Digital Work is Public Work

The other important point about process is that digital work often has a public, outward looking face. Platforms like blogs allow for public engagement with our work — so digital work is a kind of public humanities. The

---

[7]Bethany Nowviskie (8 Jan 2012), "Two and a half cheers for the lunaticks," *Nowviskie.org*, available online at http://nowviskie.org/2012/lunaticks/.

structure of the Internet, of how its algorithms find and construct knowledge and serve that up to us via Google, is such that work that is valuable and of interest creates a bigger noise in a positive feedback loop. The best digital work is done in public. "Public" should not be a dirty word along the lines of "popular." The Internet looks different to each person who goes online (and our algorithms make sure that each person sees a personalized Internet, because that's how one makes money online), so hits on a blog post are not random meaningless clicks but rather an engagement with a broader community.

As far as academic blogging goes, that broader community is other academics and students. Print journals and peer-reviewed articles are just one way of engaging with our chosen communities. With post-publication models of peer review like *Digital Humanities Now* and the *Journal of Digital Humanities* (models that are making inroads in other humanities disciplines), we should treat these on an equal footing with the more familiar models. We would like to see amongst historians a perspective that regards digital work, or work in media other than print, on an equal footing with the more familiar forms. That is, as things that do not have equivalencies to those we traditionally expect and thus must be taken on their own terms. We would go so far as to argue that post-publication peer review is a greater indicator of significance and value than a regular, two blind reviewers into print model.

Project Management and Project Outputs

Sean Takats, of George Mason University, wrote about his experience of arguing for the scholarly merit of his work (as part of the tenure and promotion process). In particular, he made an argument for his major software development projects, which develop tools for historical research, as scholarship. He writes of project management,

> ... that it's actually the cornerstone of all successful research. It's project management that transforms a dissertation prospectus into a thesis, and it's certainly project management that shepherds a monograph from proposal to published book. Fellow humanists, I have some news for you: you're all project managers, even if you only direct a staff of one.[8]

---

[8]Sean Takats (7 February 2013), "A Digital Humanities Tenure Case, Part 2: letters and committees," *The Quintessence of Ham*, http://quintessenceofham.org/2013/02/07/a-digital-humanities-tenure-case-part-2-letters-and-committees/.

Digital work creates all sorts of outputs that are of use at many different stages to other researchers. These outputs should be considered as valuable publications in their own right. All of these can be made available online in digital archives built for the purpose of long-term storage. The number of times such outputs are downloaded or discussed online can often be measured; these measures should also be taken into account as a kind of citation.

Experimentation and Risk Taking

Finally, we believe that work that is experimental, that discusses what didn't work, should be recognized and celebrated. Digital history can be work that takes risks. But when those risks are documented, where the trials and errors are carefully collected and reflected upon, the results (white papers, publications, websites) are also scholarship. As Todd Presner writes, "To treat scholarship that takes on risk and the challenge of experimentation as an activity of secondary (or no) value for promotion and advancement, can only serve to reduce innovation, reward mediocrity, and retard the development of research."[9]

So What are the Hallmarks of Good Digital Research?

- It is work that is transformative;
- It is where multi-authored work is valued as much as the single-author opus;
- It is work that is outward facing and is recognized by others through linking, reposting, sharing (and other so-called "altmetrics"; see http://impactstory.org/ for one novel attempt to pull these all together);
- It imagines data as publication (see for instance http://opencontext.org/ in the archaeological world);
- It imagines code as publication;
- It experiments and takes risks and is open to discussion of what does and what does not work;
- It is where software development and project management are recognized as research;

---

[9]Todd Presner (2012), "How to Evaluate Digital Scholarship," *Journal of Digital Humanities*, **1**(4), http://journalofdigitalhumanities.org/1-4/how-to-evaluate-digital-scholarship-by-todd-presner/.

- And it is any work that lays the foundation for others to build higher and see further — the humble "how to."

This is by no means the definitive guide on digital work in history, nor do our recommendations here represent gospel or consensus. However, in the spirit of this book, we hope they provide a hook, a way in for the newcomer to digital work, for that larger conversation underway in (and beyond) our discipline.

We invite you to continue this conversation. Link to this book's website. Find the (inevitable) bugs in the code. Engage in the digital history conversation. A macroscope allows a broad overview of trends in our historical materials — and it invites many pairs of eyes to the eyepiece.

Index

Printed in the United States
By Bookmasters